T0382751

For those of us who live with a daily awareness of the possibility of collapse – in one of its myriad socio-environmental guises – this book offers a series of hopeful meditations on whether collapse is really so imminent and frightening or so unitary and permanent.

Dr. Brendon M. H. Larson, Professor and Associate Dean – Undergraduate Studies, School of Environment, Resources and Sustainability (SERS), University of Waterloo, Canada

"The end is a collaborative project" – with this motto the volume plunges into the cultural archives of the "collapse" imaginaries through which humanity has expressed its preoccupation with a stable and predictive world. The contributions creatively explore the fascination with loss and resurrection in environmental fiction and fact. In the context of climate change, they offer a much-welcomed reflection on how narratives of new beginnings mediate the traces of environments already given up.

Dr. Sabine Höhler, Associate Professor of Science and Technology Studies, KTH Royal Institute of Technology, School of Architecture and the Built Environment, Stockholm, Sweden

The Discourses of Environmental Collapse

In recent years, "environmental collapse" has become an important way of framing and imagining environmental change and destruction, referencing issues such as climate change, species extinction, and deteriorating ecosystems. Given collapse's pervasiveness across disciplines and spheres, this edited volume articulates environmental collapse as a discursive phenomenon worthy of sustained critical attention. Building upon contemporary conversations in the fields of archaeology and the natural sciences, this volume coalesces, explores, and critically evaluates the diverse array of literatures and imaginaries that constitute the discourse of environmental collapse. The volume is divided into three sections – *Doc Collapse*, *Pop Collapse*, and *Craft Collapse* – that explore representations of environmental collapse from the vantage point of diverse fields of inquiry.

Bringing together a broad range of topics and authors, this volume will be of great interest to scholars of environmental communication, environmental humanities, and environmental studies.

Alison E. Vogelaar is an associate professor of communication and media studies at Franklin University Switzerland, and co-editor of *Changing Representations of Nature and the City: The 1960s-1970s and Their Legacies* (with Gabriel Lee, Routledge, 2018).

Brack W. Hale is an associate professor of biology and environmental science at Franklin University Switzerland, where he is co-director of the Center for Sustainability Initiatives.

Alexandra Peat is an associate professor of literature at Franklin University Switzerland, and author of *Travel and Modernist Literature: Sacred and Ethical Journeys* (Routledge, 2011).

Routledge Studies in Environmental Communication and Media

For more information about this series, please visit: www.routledge.com

The Discourses of Environmental Collapse

Imagining the End

Edited by Alison E. Vogelaar,
Brack W. Hale and Alexandra Peat

Routledge
Taylor & Francis Group

LONDON AND NEW YORK

First published 2018
by Routledge

2 Park Square, Milton Park, Abingdon, Oxfordshire OX14 4RN
52 Vanderbilt Avenue, New York, NY 10017

Routledge is an imprint of the Taylor & Francis Group, an informa business

First issued in paperback 2020

Copyright © 2018 selection and editorial matter, Alison E. Vogelaar, Brack W. Hale and Alexandra Peat; individual chapters, the contributors

The right of Alison E. Vogelaar, Brack W. Hale and Alexandra Peat to be identified as the authors of the editorial material, and of the authors for their individual chapters, has been asserted in accordance with sections 77 and 78 of the Copyright, Designs and Patents Act 1988.

All rights reserved. No part of this book may be reprinted or reproduced or utilised in any form or by any electronic, mechanical, or other means, now known or hereafter invented, including photocopying and recording, or in any information storage or retrieval system, without permission in writing from the publishers.

Notice:
Product or corporate names may be trademarks or registered trademarks, and are used only for identification and explanation without intent to infringe.

British Library Cataloguing-in-Publication Data
A catalogue record for this book is available from the British Library

Library of Congress Cataloging-in-Publication Data
A catalog record for this book has been requested

ISBN: 978-1-138-21714-0 (hbk)
ISBN: 978-0-367-50764-0 (pbk)

Typeset in Sabon
by Apex CoVantage, LLC

Contents

Figures

Author biographies

Michael Egan is a contemporary historian, whose work revolves around the histories of catastrophe, environment, and the future. He is an associate professor and university teaching fellow in the Department of History at McMaster University in Hamilton, Ontario, and the author of *Barry Commoner and the Science of Survival: The Remaking of American Environmentalism* (MIT Press, 2007).

Jen England is an assistant professor of English at Hamline University in Saint Paul, Minnesota, where she teaches a range of courses in professional writing and rhetoric. Her research interests include environmental/sustainability rhetorics, community writing, technofeminism, and game studies. She's currently developing an interactive space on campus for students, faculty, and staff to conduct research and build community around games.

Ann Gardiner is lecturer of comparative literature and writing at Franklin University Switzerland. She received her PhD in comparative literature from New York University. Her current research and teaching interests explore the human-environment relationship, also from a historical perspective, and how texts of many kinds shape that relationship. She teaches courses in ethical approaches to the environment and ecocritical approaches to literature and film. Her newest research explores visual/graphic representations of the Anthropocene.

Matthew Griffiths is a critic and poet whose recent work includes the monograph *The New Poetics of Climate Change: Modernist Aesthetics for a Warming World* (Bloomsbury, 2017) and the collection *Natural Economy* (Red Squirrel, 2016).

Brack W. Hale is an associate professor of biology and environmental science at Franklin University Switzerland, where he has worked since 2006; he is also the co-director of the Center for Sustainability Initiatives at Franklin. His research interests have revolved around how humans interact with and impact the natural world. As a result, he has published numerous articles in the fields of biofuels, ecology and management of riparian areas, invasive species, natural areas conservation, sustainable travel and tourism, and waste management.

I.J. MacRae is an associate professor in the English and Social & Environmental Justice programs at Wilfrid Laurier University in Brantford, Ontario. He has worked as a documentary filmmaker for Canadian Geographic Presents, as a treeplanter in northern British Columbia, and received a master's in environmental studies from York University, witnessing variants of ecological collapse (and regeneration) from near and far.

Guy D. Middleton is a visiting fellow in the School of History, Classics and Archaeology at Newcastle University, UK. He has a longstanding interest in the archaeology of collapse and is also interested in the multiple discourses of collapse, in particular the environmental and popular, and how these intersect with our understanding of past (and future) collapses. His works on the subject include *Understanding Collapse: Ancient History and Modern Myths* (Cambridge University Press, 2017) and *The Collapse of Palatial Society in Late Bronze Age Greece and the Postpalatial Period* (Archaeopress, 2010).

Joanna Nurmis holds a PhD in journalism studies from the University of Maryland and currently works as a freelance content producer for the Stanford Woods Institute for the Environment. She previously obtained a master's degree in international relations. Her scholarly work focuses on the practice and meaning of photojournalism in international affairs, including specifically the representation of war and climate change.

Alexandra Peat is an associate professor of literature at Franklin University Switzerland where she teaches courses on modern and contemporary literature. She is the author of *Travel and Modernist Literature: Sacred and Ethical Journeys* (Routledge, 2011) and a co-author of *Modernism: Keywords* (Cuddy-Keane, Hammond, and Peat, Wiley-Blackwell, 2014), and she has also published on global modernism, practices of collaboration, and dystopia. She is currently working on a project on modernist Empire Exhibitions at the end of Empire.

Jesse D. Peterson is a PhD candidate at the Division of History of Science, Technology and Environment at KTH Royal Institute of Technology, Stockholm. He has an MSc in environmental humanities (U of U, 2013) and an MFA in creative writing (UNLV, 2010). He is part of ENHANCE, the KTH Environmental Humanities Laboratory, and helped found the literary arts journal *saltfront*. His research interests include exploring socio-natures of waste, ecology, and culture as well as practicing methods of creative scholarship. More of his writing can be found in Geohumanities, Terrain.org, and Provo Canyon Review.

Alison E. Vogelaar is an associate professor of communication and media studies at Franklin University Switzerland, where she teaches courses that variously explore the relationship between media, communication, and power. Her research interests include environmental and ecological discourses, advocacy and activism, maker and craft culture, and educational travel. She has recently co-edited with Gabriel Gee another environmentally themed volume, *Changing Representations of Nature and the City: The 1960s–1970s and their Legacies* (Routledge, 2018).

Acknowledgements

As an interdisciplinary and collaborative enterprise, this book has benefited from many productive discussions with, and helpful feedback from, a wide network of colleagues and interlocutors.

We would like to begin by thanking our colleagues in Environmental Humanities Switzerland whose 2015 workshop, "Environmental Justice, 'Collapse,' and Question of Evidence," hosted by Franklin University Switzerland, sparked our interest in the topic of collapse. The core ideas for this volume grew out of a paper presented at the 2015 Conference on Communication and Environment at the University of Colorado, and we are thankful for the generous feedback given there. We are very grateful to the whole team at Routledge – Annabelle Harris, Matthew Shobbrook, and Margaret Farrelly – for their faith in the project and their support at every stage. We thank the two reviewers of the original proposal whose generous feedback and comments undoubtedly helped us strengthen this book. We would also like to thank each of our contributing authors for being such thoughtful and responsive colleagues; we have learned so much from your contributions.

We would like to recognize Franklin University Switzerland for being the kind of place where an ecologist, literary scholar, and rhetorician could come together and find such provocative intersections among our work. We thank our dean, Sara Steinert Borella, for her support. And we are particularly appreciative of our students who, in classes and conversations, have brought light to this dark topic. We also thank Madeline Ames for her capable editorial assistance.

Last but certainly not least, we are grateful to our colleagues, friends, and families who have helped and supported us as we worked on this project: Claire Battershill, Ann-Marie Einhaus, and Sabine Höhler for their comments and advice at various stages of the project; Heather Turnbach and Fintan Hoey for moral support (and chocolate!); Ford Shanahan, Elle, and Neve for their encouragement; and Stevie, Freddie, Mollie, and Chess for being affectionate distractions.

Introducing the end

Alison E. Vogelaar, Alexandra Peat, and Brack Hale

[To] make sense of our lives from where we are, as it were, stranded in the middle, we need fictions of beginnings and fictions of ends, fictions which unite beginning and end and endow the interval between them with meaning.
(Frank Kermode, *The Sense of an Ending*, 1967, p. 190)

The work is going well. But it looks like the end of the world.
(Letter from F. Sherwood Rowland to his wife on discovering chlorofluorocarbons' ability to destroy the ozone layer)[1]

This collection is a meditation on discourses of collapse. It explores how under various existential, environmental, and epistemological pressures we have constructed our current moment of crisis as an age of collapse. Given the mounting evidence of environmental crises, such as climate change and its manifold effects (e.g., rising sea levels and migration, drought and starvation, soil erosion and unemployment), it comes as no surprise that concerns about whether we can sustain life in our communities and on our planet have become formulated as questions of collapse. In its broadest sense, collapse refers to "a range of processes and events that at their core have rapid or dramatic political and social change" (Middleton 2012, p. 267). The language of *environmental* collapse first emerged in the 1960s in the thrust of the environmental movement and was reinvigorated by the publication of biologist Jared Diamond's 2005 popular science book, *Collapse: How Societies Choose to Fail or Succeed*, which re-thinks the "collapse" of ancient and advanced civilizations, such as the Mayans, Easter Island, and ancient Egypt in the context of environmental degradation. As Frank Kermode, the great theorist of endings, reminds us, discourses of the end are not, however, unique to our own historical and cultural moment; indeed, contemporary manifestations of collapse are deeply indebted to prior iterations, from apocalypse to dystopia. Nonetheless, contemporary attempts to grapple with and articulate collapse are intensifying, amplifying, and extending. Whereas discourses of the end have traditionally been the purview of fiction, myth, and religion, this time, the end is a collaborative project involving all spheres of intellectual and cultural production, and our current prophets of the end (whether they be politicians, scientists, or philosophers) are more vociferous than ever. What is more, the end has gone not just global but planetary: to live in the so-called Anthropocene (Crutzen and Stoermer 2000) is to think in geological time, recognizing that human activity now constitutes a major geologic force; and also reminding us that Earth precedes, and will likely proceed without, humans.[2]

How, then, to begin a book about the discourses of the end? This question has tugged at us over the course of editing this volume, as we have constantly re-oriented ourselves to alternative beginnings. Which event? Which artifact? Which perspective to begin with? Any beginning, we worried, would shape the book and anticipate a particular ending. What is more, beginnings orient us in time: they set a timeframe into motion, and they also operate as timestamps. We came to understand that our preoccupation with beginnings was not simply structural; it was indeed innately connected to very subject matter of this volume. Despite the cultural preoccupation with imagining a tidy, if terrifying, linear trajectory, collapse betokens a crisis without clear beginning or end. It might then behoove us to imagine collapse in a different way, for even if our world is coming to an end, how we get there and what that will look like remains uncertain. By anticipating an end, collapse orients us to the future in ways that may be problematic for the present: to think that there is no future risks embracing either hedonism or apathy; on the other hand, to focus too much on the future risks eliding or not acting in the present. Equating certainty with despair, the writer and activist Rebecca Solnit cautions against bleak prophecies of the future. In the space between anticipating or forgetting the future lies uncertainty, which is, for Solnit, grounds for hope and action (2010).

We are aware that climate deniers have co-opted scientific uncertainty for political ends. There is, however, an important distinction between evoking uncertainty as grounds for stalling and inaction and using uncertainty as a way of thinking that encourages active engagement in creating a desirable future. Embracing uncertainty in this latter sense, we choose not to privilege a stable, singular beginning, offering instead three ways to begin our conversation about collapse. These do not constitute the only possible beginnings for this volume; they are in the end arbitrary, albeit significant. They nonetheless allow us to acknowledge the multiplicity of collapse, without privileging one single approach or example; to encompass the interdisciplinarity of collapse thinking; and finally to demonstrate the sheer pervasiveness of collapse as a mode of thinking turned "way of life" (Buell 2014).

In what follows we trace three parallel beginnings: an enviro-political event, a media phenomenon, and an artist's manufactured ruins. We propose these beginnings not as still points from which to make an entrance or frames with which to capture collapse but rather as streams that carry us along multiple discursive routes. Just as jet streams are shape shifters (insomuch as they shift in response to atmospheric forces), discursive streams have no clear beginning or end; they meander, break apart, join forces, and change direction in response to social and environmental forces. These streams are ephemeral and nonetheless elemental. Jet streams offer a fitting metaphor, particularly because as natural phenomena altered by human activity, they are themselves entangled in collapse. In positing our beginnings as discursive streams, then, we are not seeking an outside point from which to examine and look back objectively at our current moment of crisis, but rather seek to move between and put into conversation multiple perspectives and approaches that are part of a larger phenomenon.

Stream one: the enviro-political event

On June 1, 2017, Donald Trump, after much public speculation, pulled the United States out of the 2015 Paris Agreement on Climate Change Mitigation. Openly skeptical about the dangers of climate change, he had been publicly mulling this move for months. His withdrawal was read by many as a collapse of international governmental collaboration vis-a-vis the environment that signaled an increasingly unavoidable ecological collapse. More than 40 years earlier, the Club of Rome's study, *The Limits to Growth*, warned of global collapse caused by environmental pollution, uncontrolled human population growth, and overconsumption of the Earth's resources (Meadows et al. 1972). This list of concerns has continued to grow and is now dominated by the risks associated with global climate change. As the *LTG*'s first forecasts demonstrate, collapse has shifted from a question of *if* to *when*. In this context, Trump's actions were met with near global condemnation and yet, ironically have also strengthened the resolve of the remaining members of the Paris Agreement and reinforced existing subnational activism in the United States and elsewhere.

While Trump's abandonment of the Paris climate accord seemed, at the time, a key moment for this book to begin with, nearly every day since has brought a new event that seemed just as symbolic and poignant. Hurricane Harvey hit Houston, followed quickly by two category 5 hurricanes, Irma and Maria, which devastated much of the Caribbean; floods swept across South Asia, and forest fires devastated Portugal, Spain, and Western North America. This catalogue of devastation goes on, mounting evidence that collapse is perhaps neither if nor when, but *now*.

In this new context of seemingly constant crises, scientists, civil servants, and transnational bodies face the challenge of documenting collapse in ways that are both accessible and compelling. Since 1990, the Intergovernmental Panel on Climate Change (IPCC) has repeatedly forecast catastrophic climate change (their most recent assessment report was published in 2014). Conservative estimates of global ecological footprints (Ehrlich and Ehrlich 2013) show that our consumption of the world's resources continues to exceed the planet's ability to supply them (Hoekstra and Wiedmann 2014). A 2009 study in *Science* (Rockström et al.), updated in 2015 (Steffen et al.), found that three of nine "planetary boundaries" (namely, rate of biodiversity loss, climate change, and human interference in the nitrogen cycle) have already exceeded safe levels. Building upon this extensive data, and in an effort to develop a more rigorous framework for studying collapse, ecologists Graeme Cumming and Garry Peterson (2017) developed a set of four criteria to understand collapses past and future.[3] Their results highlight that collapse can be understood not just as a single, global catastrophic event, but also as smaller-scale events at local and regional levels. The catalogue of environmental devastation we cited previously demonstrates just this: while certainly understandable in the context of global trends, these events are experienced as local and regional collapses.

This proliferation of mediated evidence and documentation indicates a diligent, even desperate, effort to warn of and ward off collapse. And yet the very fact that this evidence continues to reproduce without provoking sufficient change at the appropriate levels suggests that we may require alternative approaches, which may even entail moving beyond "collapse" as a singular, overarching event and narrative.

There has been a tendency to represent collapse as a singular, game-changing event that ruptures the natural rhythms of the everyday. In her work on narrative, Rachel Bowlby notes how narrative structure often depends upon this contrast between "the one-off event and the ever so slightly moving everyday" (Bowlby 2016). As collapse discourse becomes pervasive, the difference between the everyday and the event is breaking down; in the frenetic pace of contemporary news cycles, the mundane has been eaten by the event. As our energy is increasingly spent "dealing with environmental crisis both semiotically and materially," environmental critic Frederick Buell notes that "global social-environmental crisis is no longer seen as an (apocalyptic) end ahead, but has become a way of life" (p. 264). Trying to keep up with the flurry of events and evidence can either overwhelm or induce apathy. We pay witness to catastrophes that destroy lives and communities, but on a global scale, they more often than not leave no mark, as they are overtaken by other events and fade into the deep web. While Buell contends this constant "depiction of risk and crisis suggests no revelation, produces no awakening," he nonetheless asserts that "normalization . . . does not mean banalization" (p. 265, p. 266); it may on the contrary inspire "imaginative possibilities" for creating stories and worlds that are both "profounder and more snarled" (p. 288).

Stream two: ghosts of extinction

On March 26, 2017, evolutionary biologist and author Richard Dawkins tweeted: "Can it be true? Has Thylacinus been seen alive? And in mainland Australia not Tasmania? I so want it to be true." His public exaltation over recent sightings of the purportedly extinct Tasmanian tiger (thylacine) in northern Queensland signals a cultural preoccupation with species extinction

Figure 0.1 The last thylacine?

as we head toward the "sixth extinction," a term popularized by environmental journalist Elizabeth Kolbert (2014). The thylacine, thought to have disappeared from mainland Australia at least 2000 years ago, survived in Tasmania until the last wild thylacine was shot by a farmer in 1930. The last known living thylacine died in captivity at Hobart Zoo in 1936. It was officially classified as extinct 50 years later, despite numerous reports of sightings both before and after this official designation, with a particularly enthusiastic spate in 2016/2017, no doubt propelled by Adelaide resident Neil Waters and his Thylacine Awareness Group.

What does the possible survival of this creature stir in us? "Why do we care," asks Ursula Heise, "about non-human species at risk" (2016, p. 2)? These are cultural questions of "what we value and what stories we tell, and only secondarily issues of science" (Heise 2016, p. 5). Dawkins's wistful "I so want it to be true" both captures the guilt underlying our growing awareness of human-induced species extinction and expresses the hope of survival against the odds. The possible re-emergence of the Tasmanian tiger might invite us to read this as a story of resilience. Resilience thinking, a disciplinary reaction to collapse thinking, proposes that systems are prone to adaptation and survival (McAnany and Yoffee 2009). This is not to suggest that resilience is a rejection or a negation of collapse but rather that it "includes collapse as part of a normal cyclical pattern" (Middleton 2017, p. 42). Cumming and Petersen remind us that "collapse and resilience are two sides of the same coin; collapse occurs when resilience is lost, and resilient systems are less likely to collapse" (2). As with collapse theory, the original iteration of resilience (Holling 1973) centered on systems as the unit of analysis, but we scale it down to the level of the species. If the Tasmanian tiger does indeed still live, it inspires hope that species may be more resilient to human interference than previously thought, and, more importantly, it gives us a chance to do better. If the Tasmanian tiger still lives, maybe this time we won't drive her to extinction.

But, we fear, the collective desire for her to live is also the desire to be the one to (re)discover her, both desires rooted in those human impulses toward discovery, knowledge, and control that got us in this mess in the first place. The yearning to know other creatures has at times nudged up against the will to control them. Tasmanian tigers are attractive precisely because they are elusive and unusual; moreover, as apex predators, their "perceived majesty and fierceness" gives them "the cultural standing" to become "tragic or elegiac figures" (Heise, p. 35). But what are the seekers of the Tasmanian tiger going to do if they ever get hold of one these elusive, quasi-mythic creatures? Will science re-classify her as extant and let her disappear again into the wild, or will the desire to understand her elusiveness and explain her apparent disappearance lead her once more to Hobart Zoo? Neil Waters disarmingly articulates the human impulse for discovery, knowledge, and control when he states, "the sad part is, we haven't found a dead one lying on the side of the road. Then we'd have some proof" (Hunt 2017).

The thylacine is just one example of popular culture's obsession with loss and the related urge to capture that which has been or might soon be lost. Being in the "sixth extinction" means that there are countless examples of species driven to extinction, often in silence. We might also note Joel Sartore's "Photo Ark," a National Geographic project that travels the world's zoos and animal parks to capture endangered animals in photographic form before they slip into extinction. These "stories about species that have already gone extinct or may soon disappear frequently rely on the politically mobilizing power of mourning and melancholy" (Heise 2016, p. 35). The Tasmanian tiger tweets, Facebook groups, and video reels all participate in a simultaneous performance of mourning and act of resurrection. These ghosts in the machine haunt us, function as evidence, and digitally resurrect the thylacine, who is then perhaps given a space to be mourned publicly. As Jeremy Hance asks:

> how do we grieve for extinct species when there are no set rituals, no extinction funerals, no catharsis for the pain caused by a loss that in many ways is simply beyond human comprehension? We have been obliterating species for over ten thousand years – beginning with the megafauna of the Pleistocene like woolly rhinos, short-faced bears and giant sloths – yet we have no way of mourning them.
>
> (2016)

Creating forms of and spaces for mourning lost creatures like the Tasmanian tiger in popular discourse, and indeed the pages of this book, allows for emotional release but is also a creative and political act.

Stream three: the artist who plays with ruins

It's a dreich day in August. A muddy farm track in Scotland's Pentland Hills winds past fields full of sheep and cows, arriving at the isolated garden of artist and avant-gardener Ian Hamilton Finlay who, with his wife Sue Finlay, cultivated the grounds of their country cottage into a sometimes playful and always provocative graveyard of manufactured ruins.[4] This garden full of false ruins pays ironic homage to civilizational collapses, constructing fragmented memorials to centuries of Western wars (from the ancient Greeks to Napoleon to the Falklands) and turning these into art. Little Sparta's name is an obvious allusion to the history of Western civilization, but it is also a tongue-in-cheek reference to nearby Edinburgh, the so-called Athens of the North, thus setting the constructed ruins of Finlay's garden up as a subversive rival to the historic monuments of the stately Scottish capital.

Entering Little Sparta through a wooden gate with the words "the fluted land" carved across the top beam, the visitor is free to wander through a series of what Finlay called "specific landscapes," including the small garden in front of his cottage, a Roman garden, a woodland garden, an English Parkland, and the "Temple Pool" garden, which encompasses a small manmade lake. Scattered around the landscapes are over 270 artworks, each a tribute to the passage of time and the role of art as remembrance (see Figure 0.2). Nature is not merely backdrop for Finlay's artistic production. His nod to the architectural language of "flutes" (the grooves that run along a column

Figure 0.2 "Buried Capital" at Little Sparta
Source: By courtesy of the Estate of Ian Hamilton Finlay

or a pilaster) playfully undermines the division between art and nature. If land can be "fluted," then, for Finlay, nature is itself both sculptable matter and that which sculpts human matters. Finlay's fragmented ruins are simultaneously juxtaposed and set in aesthetic harmony with a natural scene that has likewise been carefully tended and curated. A series of fragmented stone plaques lies on a grassy slope, each plaque inscribed with words that spell a warning from the Jacobin Saint-Just that "the present order is the disorder of the future"; a half-submerged ionic column disturbs the natural stillness of the pool; and then there are gravestones, scattered through the woods, paying faded tribute to real and imaginary losses. Nature and art thus co-create meaning, even if that meaning is nonsensical (why are Greek ruins littering Scotland's Pentland Hills?). Finlay mixes and merges organic and inorganic matter, such as twigs and carved wood, pebbles and smooth stone. The artist added to, edited, and transformed the garden throughout his life, and the aesthetic effects of the garden are, moreover, designed with an eye to the whimsy of the Scottish weather, the changes of the seasons, and the passage of time.

In inviting us to walk through his garden of ruins, Finlay offers an experience of collapse that is distinct from two-dimensional charts, models, and graphs that are meant to be studied from an objective distance. In her work on Finlay, the poet and literary critic Susan Stewart posits Finlay's monuments as imagined ruins, future ruins, or proleptic ruins (2017). Monuments, Stewart notes, are gestures to the future, and they speak to a human desire for preservation and permanence. We might think, for example, of Victor Burgin's characterization of monuments as "inert" (2008, p. 323) or Michel Foucault's discussion of archaeology as a discipline devoted to "silent monuments, inert traces, objects without context, and things left by the past" (1982, p. 7). Yet Finlay's fragmentary and ironically situated monuments are expressive, both because they are so often carved with playful words and phrases in multiple languages, and because they partake in a conversation about the very nature of memorialization. These crafted civilizational leftovers invite questions about what we choose to preserve and what we leave behind, and at the same time, they point to the accidental and fragmentary nature of history and memory. Little Sparta thus enacts a process of memorialization even as it draws attention to the inevitability of decay and destruction, and the randomness of what survives.

Finlay's garden of ruins sets up a conversation about collapse that highlights the relationship between monuments and memory, the interconnection between manmade and nature, and the ethical role of art as a response to crisis. It thus presages recent discussions, especially in art, that propose the Anthropocene as an opportunity "to re-imagine the human through biology and geology," an opportunity that, moreover, complicates the supposed apolitical nature of art and nature (Davis and Turpin 2015, p. 6). In their introduction to *Art in the Anthropocene*, Heather Davis and Etienne Turpin recall Henri Cartier-Bresson's disgust in the 1930s that "the world is going to pieces and people like [Ansel] Adams and [Edward] Weston are photographing rocks!" (p. 3). Like the rock artists that preceded him, Finlay's garden of rocks situates the viewer in geological time, helping us to think about how collapse is both a human event and also a natural process: buildings fall, plants die, and while humans may influence these natural rhythms, we are ourselves a small part of a larger process. Little Sparta also reveals the fragmentary nature of memory, the curious objects we use to produce memory, and the lack of control we ultimately have in curating the memory of our own societies. We can't help but wonder what a visitor from the far future who arrives at Little Sparta without tour guide, informational pamphlet, or prior knowledge of the artist's ironic and oppositional disposition might make of it. What story would these fragmented ruins (a palimpsest of Western civilization in a small garden in central Scotland) tell? These would not be, after all, the only inexplicable standing stones in Scotland. In his discussion of the potential disjunctures between monuments and contemporary knowledge, Guy Middleton notes what a "strange and irrelevant . . . question it would be to ask local English people who built Stonehenge" (2017, p. 248). An ironic homage to homages, Finlay's Little Sparta helps us think about the changing nature of aesthetics and politics in the Anthropocene, ultimately hinting at the fact that, in the end, what we leave behind might say very little about how we lived.

From streams to structures: how to use this book

Taken together, these three discursive streams open up key questions and concerns surrounding collapse: how do different discursive communities imagine and articulate collapse? How does the nature of collapse differ in diverse discursive communities? In what ways do fiction, poetry, visual art, popular media, scientific models, games and simulations, and even social scientific discourses construct various versions of collapse? What happens to collapse when different symbolic tools are used? Does collapse have multiple possible moral valences in different discursive settings? How do different approaches engage or subvert action and/or publics? And to what degree are different approaches more or less reflexive or transparent in terms of how they are using "collapse" vocabularies, metaphors, and ways of thinking?

If, as we said earlier, beginnings are important because they provide a structure and anticipate an ending, where then do our parallel beginnings take us? Carrying forward our discursive streams, we reconstitute them as the three organizational categories that structure this volume: Doc, Pop, and Craft. Chapters in the first section, "Doc Collapse," explore historic and contemporary environmental collapse discourses that focus upon the depiction of and mounting evidence for instances of environmental collapse as a knowable, measurable, and *documentable* phenomena. Chapters in the second section, "Pop Collapse" examine environmental collapse discourses that mass communicate and disseminate various instances of environmental collapse to *popular* audiences. The final section, "Craft Collapse," examines environmental collapse discourses that creatively interpret, frame, and *craft* environmental collapse. We do not intend these categories to create a rigid structure or for them to be followed in a strictly sequential order. In this spirit, we encourage you to choose your own adventure – that is to say, to make connections both within and across the organizing sections of the volume.

"Doc Collapse" consists of four chapters that explore the power and limits of documentation as a mode of articulating collapse as well as the intellectual legacies that shape contemporary understandings of collapse. Michael Egan's "Culture and Collapse: Theses on Catastrophic History for the 21st Century" traces the contemporary fascination with collapse as it arises out of 20th century catastrophes from global wars to nuclear proliferation. Jesse Peterson's "Are Dead Zones Dead? Environmental Collapse in Popular Media about Eutrophication" explores the complex conversations among researchers and stakeholders as they debate the causes of and related responses to sea-based collapses, with a particular focus on the dead zone in the Baltic Sea. Joanna Nurmis's "Can Photojournalism Steer Clear of the Siren Song of Collapse" examines the problems and possibilities associated with photojournalistic depictions of global warming, tuning specifically to the limitations of the still photographic form in the context of a slow-moving and ephemeral problem. Ann Gardiner's "Environmental Collapse in Comics: Reflections on Philippe Squarzoni's *Saison brune*" posits collapse as an environmental and representational crisis to which graphic novels offer an interesting response, examining the adaptation of evidence and perspectives within the form of the graphic novel.

"Pop Collapse" consists of three chapters that explore the popularization of collapse narratives across diverse fields, forms, and audiences – from ecology to popular science and from art and archeology to popular culture. Guy Middleton's "This is the End of the World as We Know it: Narratives of Collapse and Transformation in Archeology and Popular Culture" traces our cultural obsession with narratives of catastrophic collapse from the archaeological records of the Mayans to contemporary historical documentaries and magazines; along the way, he problematizes the tendency in academic and popular communities to construct collapse as singular, apocalyptic event. Jen England's "Survive, Thrive, or Perish: Environmental Collapse in Post-Apocalyptic Digital Games" guides us through the play of two apocalyptic Roleplaying Games (RPGs); focusing on the processes of embodiment and simulation, she suggests that the benefits and opportunities provided by apocalyptic game play are not limited to the virtual world, and may indeed have interesting implications for action and attitudes in the material world. Alison E. Vogelaar and Brack Hale's, "Zooming Out, Closing In: Ecology at the End of the Frontier" explores the changing scope of ecological thinking (as a scientific and popular phenomenon) from the 1960s to the 1990s. Bringing together scientific thought and experiments, popular scientific texts and popular film, this chapter articulates the contours of "spaceship ecology," a discourse that continues to have important influences on the ways in which we think about the planet Earth and our place upon it.

Our final section, "Craft Collapse," consists of three chapters that turn to the entanglement of art and the imagination in collapse discourse. I. J. Macrae's "Imagining the Apocalypse: Valences of Collapse in McCarthy, Burtynsky and Goldsworthy" brings together fiction, photography, and land art, exploring the complex, contradictory, and changing relationships between the natural and the human worlds evoked by three important artists. Matthew Griffiths's "'Something Akin to What's Killing Bees': Colony Collapse as a Motif in Contemporary Poetry" intertwines scientific and poetic responses to Colony Collapse Disorder; engaging with the long tradition of bee poetry, he uses the motif of the bee to explore the fundamental issues of scale and questions of bodily and community health and identity as they articulate key issues of collapse. This collection is sutured with Alexandra Peat's "Salvaging the Fragments: Metaphors of Collapse in Virginia Woolf and *Station Eleven*," which explores the emergence of new metaphors for collapse in the experimental literature of the early 20th century, ultimately questioning how metaphors serve us. She then turns to the interrelated tropes of shipwreck and salvage to explore Emily St Mandel's *Station Eleven* as a narrative of tentative hope in a post-collapse world.

Notes

1 In Roan 2012.
2 This distinction between global and planetary has been provocatively explored by philosophers and theorists including (but not limited to) Gayatari Spivak (2003) and Susan Stanford Friedman (2015).
3 "1) The identity of the social – ecological system must be lost . . . 2) Loss of identity should happen fast . . . 3) Collapse involves substantial losses of social – ecological capital . . . 4. The consequences of collapse must be lasting (5)."
4 The Little Sparta Trust: The Garden of Ian Hamilton Finlay. www.littlesparta.org.uk

References

Bowlby, R., 2016. *Everyday stories*. Oxford and New York: Oxford University Press.

Buell, F., 2014. Global warming as literary narrative. *Philological Quarterly*, 93(3), 261–294.

Burgin, V., 2008. Monuments and melancholy, *Situational aesthetics: Selected writings by Victor Burgin*, ed. Alexander Streitberger. Leuven: Leuven University Press, 315–330.

Crutzen, P.J. and Stoermer, E.F., 2000. The "anthropocene". *Global Change Newsletter*, 41, 17–18. International Geosphere – Biosphere Programme (IGBP).

Cumming, G.S. and Peterson, G.D., 2017. Unifying research on social–ecological resilience and collapse. *Trends in Ecology & Evolution*, 32(9), 695–713.

Davis, H. and Turpin, E., eds., 2015. *Art in the anthropocene: Encounters among aesthetics, politics, environments and epistemologies.* London: Open Humanities Press.

Diamond, J., 2005. *Collapse: How societies choose to fail or succeed.* London: Penguin.

Ehrlich, P.R. and Ehrlich, A.H., 2013. Can a collapse of global civilization be avoided? *Proc. R. Soc. B.* The Royal Society, 20122845.

Foucault, M., 1982. *Archeology of knowledge,* trans. A. M. Sheridan Smith. New York: Vintage.

Friedman, S.S., 2015. *Planetary modernisms: Provocations on modernity across time.* New York: Columbia University Press.

Hance, J., 2016. Why don't we grieve for extinct species. *The Guardian,* November 19.

Heise, U., 2016. *Imagining extinction: The cultural meanings of endangered species.* Chicago and London: University of Chicago Press.

Hoekstra, A.Y. and Wiedmann, T.O., 2014. Humanity's unsustainable environmental footprint. *Science,* 344(6188), 1114 LP–1117. Available at: http://science.sciencemag.org/content/344/6188/1114.abstract.

Holling, C.S., 1973. Resilience and stability of ecological systems. *Annual Review of Ecology and Systematics,* 4, 1–23.

Hunt, E., 2017. 'Sightings' of extinct Tasmanian tiger prompt search in Queensland. *The Guardian,* March 28.

IPCC, 2014. Summary for policymakers, *Climate change 2014: Impacts, adaptation, and vulnerability. Part A: Global and sectorial aspects: Contribution of working group II to the fifth assessment report of the intergovernmental panel on climate change,* ed. C. B. Field et al. Cambridge, UK, and New York, NY: Cambridge University Press, 1–32.

Kermode, F., 1967. *The sense of an ending: Studies in the theory of fiction.* Oxford: Oxford University Press.

Kolbert, E., 2014. *The sixth extinction: An unnatural history.* London: Bloomsbury.

McAnany, P.A. and Yoffee, N., eds., 2009. *Questioning collapse: Human resilience, ecological vulnerability, and the aftermath of empire.* Cambridge and New York: Cambridge University Press.

Meadows, D. H. et al., 1972. *The limits to growth.* New York: Universe Books.

Middleton, G.D., 2012. Nothing lasts forever: Environmental discourses on the collapse of past societies. *Journal of Archaeological Research,* 20(3), 257–307.

Middleton, G. D., 2017. *Understanding collapse: Ancient history and modern myths.* Cambridge and New York: Cambridge University Press.

Roan, S., 2012. F. Sherwood Rowland obituary: Nobel-winning UC Irvine professor who warned of CFCs was 84. *Los Angeles Times,* March 12. Available at: http://articles.latimes.com/2012/mar/12/local/la-me-sherwood-rowland-20120312.

Solnit, R., 2010. *Hope in the dark.* Edinburgh: Canongate.

Spivak, G., 2003. *Death of a discipline.* New York: Columbia University Press.

Steffen, W. Richardson, K., Rockström, J., Cornell, S. E., Fetzer, I., Bennett, E. M., . . . Sörlin, S., 2015. Planetary boundaries: Guiding human development on a changing planet. *Science,* 347(6223), 1259855.

Stewart, S., 2017. Between spoils and gifts. *Edinburgh University,* July 14.

Part I
Doc collapse

1 Culture and collapse

Theses on catastrophic history for the twenty-first century

Michael Egan

I

Perhaps it is suggestive of our contemporary "psychological pandemic" that we are experiencing a renewed interest across the academy in the work of the German intellectual Walter Benjamin.[1] Benjamin is rightly regarded as the twentieth century's greatest prophet of catastrophe, even if his famous "Angel of History" (more on which later) was compelled to look backward into the past rather than forward to the future. At the same time, Benjamin's writings serve as a portal into "catastrophic history," a new way of reading the present apocalyptic fears that resonate throughout mainstream and academic culture in the early stages of the new century. Catastrophic history takes as its foundational premise the argument that natural, technological, and moral catastrophes do not constitute punctuated setbacks in a predominantly progressive history. Rather, they are the norm and invite a more integrated examination of the history of the oppressed, which, Benjamin argues, "teaches us that the 'state of emergency' in which we live is not the exception but the rule" (Benjamin 2007, p. 257, Thesis VIII).

Benjamin's catastrophic worldview was colored by the events and ideas that surrounded him during the first half of the twentieth century. The period was marked by a tension between rapid technological advance and a nostalgia in many quarters for the world being left behind. Globalization and modernity, on the one hand, clashed with traditionalism and newly iterated forms of colloquialism and cultural nationalism on the other. By the late 1920s and early 1930s, economic instability had created an uneasy and untenable situation in the struggling Weimar Republic. As the world followed suit during the economic collapse of the 1930s, Germany's miseries were only compounded. Europe did not experience a series of socialist revolutions, as many radicals hoped and anticipated. Indeed, the socialist promise of the Russian Revolution was already in decline. Instead, much of Europe veered toward fascism. Similarly, the rise of the Third Reich and its persecution of Jews introduced an unprecedented appetite for human annihilation. As the modern world devolved into world war for a second time, barely twenty years removed from the conclusion of the "war to end all wars," the notion of a catastrophic reading of history seemed increasingly persuasive. Benjamin would not survive to reflect on the aftermath of the Holocaust. He committed suicide on the French-Spanish border at Port Bou in 1940, fearing imminent arrest by the Nazis. Nor would he be compelled to reckon with the catastrophic potential of the new atomic age, which so alarmed many of his contemporary philosophers. But he was part of a generation of thinkers that shaped the intellectual context for the mid-twentieth century's "Age of Catastrophe" that spurred an enduring sense of crisis (Hobsbawm 1995). Lest we put too fine a point on the calamitous exterminations that marked the middle of the last century, it behooves us to acknowledge both their variety and their similarity. Günther Anders, Benjamin's cousin and a student of Heidegger's, distinguished between the greater crimes against the human soul that were perpetrated at Auschwitz and the greater threats to humanity as represented from the bombing of Hiroshima. Crimes and threats against soul and humanity constitute the ugly legacy of the twentieth century. As the contemporary philosopher Jean-Pierre Dupuy – the pre-eminent champion of Anders's work – points out: "Nothing in what we call morality or ethics is capable of bearing the enormity of the evil that darkened the century we have just left behind" (Dupuy 2015, p. 38).

Catastrophe is timeless. But the drivers of its cultural anxiety can date themselves. Certainly, the specter of the Holocaust and World War II and nuclear annihilation continue to haunt us. The scars of the twentieth-century contradictions – between innovation and destruction; globalization and retrenchment; unbridled optimism and *ressentiment* – are not sunk beneath the surface of the cultural psyche. These are pasts that are not completely behind us. But thinking catastrophically, these pillars of the "Age of Extremes" seem antiquated in the contemporary context. New political, economic, and environmental problems have since been introduced, colliding with each other in what Christian Parenti (2011) has called "the catastrophic convergence." In place of a binary Cold War, dissident fundamental fractions provoke terror. Geopolitical insecurities are rife. Internal strife and climate change are prompting wave after wave of human migrations, and no political infrastructure is established to accommodate this new refugee crisis. Racial tensions and renewed flirtations with fascism are prevalent, especially in more affluent countries. The economic recession of the past decade mirrors the depression of the 1930s, but its scale and scope are arguably far more severe.[2] Shadow economies are funneling wealth out of circulation and into sheltered bank accounts. New oligarchies are taking more explicit forms of governance, concentrating wealth and power into ever smaller and elite cadres. The planet is getting warmer. Ocean acidification could have a far more significant impact on sea life than the long history of human overfishing. On land and at sea, the earth is undergoing a sixth mass extinction and biodiversity loss at a rate unprecedented since the dinosaurs were wiped out. The litany of these catastrophes and catastrophes-in-waiting pose distinct and severe challenges to the global liberal order that settled in and seemed entrenched after World War II.[3]

The twenty-first-century project involves coming to terms with this fraught, new world, and combobulating a new theory for the catastrophic that would help to explain the current condition. In effect, it means to debunk the concept of catastrophe as an exceptional event. Rather catastrophe is ubiquitous. Catastrophe's consequences and its anticipation govern humanity. A history that reflects this reversal of our understanding of catastrophe and what it means to live in a catastrophic world helps to illuminate the contemporary angst. These theses outline the parameters of that project.

II

The history of the twentieth century remains crucially relevant to a more contemporary catastrophic history, because the last century marks the point at which humanity acquired the capacity (and at times, it seemed, the will) to destroy itself. This constitutes a critical and irreversible turning point in human history. As a result, at the turn of the new century, we have replaced a traumatic past with a catastrophic future (Le Roy et al. 2011). There is a lurking sense – in politics, in economics, in popular culture – that grand-scale social collapse is ominously imminent. In many respects, that sense echoes the burgeoning malaise of modernity that inspired a "crisis of man" literature during the twentieth century (Greif 2015).[4]

This fascination with crisis taught that catastrophe need not be explosive. T. S. Eliot's famous pronouncement in 1925 that the world would end "not with a bang but a whimper" lost currency in the wake of the atomic bomb and the ensuing Cold War, which threatened a more explosive finale (Eliot 1932). By the end of the twentieth century, however, with the collapse of the communist powers, that rhetoric has receded. In its wake is less the prospect of a nuclear conflagration, but a chronic "deterioration of the conditions necessary for [humanity's] survival" (Dupuy 2002, p. 9; as cited in Rousso 2016, p. 11). Whimper seems more plausible again.

Indeed, a recent scholarly pursuit has sought to reveal the nature of slow disasters, those which unfold over a much longer period of time. Slow disasters are typically less visible. Because of their extended timeframes, they attract less public and media attention. The implication that disaster implies an acute condition relegates the importance or urgency of recognizing and addressing more persistent, chronic sources of more prolonged catastrophes. The sociologist Kai Erikson is one of the key pioneers in seeking redress along this avenue of inquiry. "Chronic conditions as well as acute events can induce trauma," he writes, "and this, too, belongs in our calculations" (Erikson 1976, p. 255). Elsewhere, Erikson (1995) iterates important similarities between slow and fast disasters and their impact: "Chronic conditions and acute events can leave much the same human residue and . . . the line separating the chronic from the acute becomes ever more blurred when one looks at that residue" (p. 22).

Slow disaster demands that we take seriously more than just the moment of catastrophic explosion. On the Gulf Coast in August 2005, for example, the devastation that Hurricane Katrina wrought on New Orleans' impoverished Ninth Ward was not a product of storm and floodwaters. Rather, one must consider a much longer history of infrastructural failures to maintain the dykes that girded the city against rising waters. One should also examine the vulnerability of some neighborhoods and not others. And one should look for the deeply ingrained story of institutional racism in the social politics that governed the city's flood planning preparations and operations. Nor should the analyst of slow disaster conclude her or his study with New Orleans underwater. A serious crisis always constitutes an opportunity. The rebuilding of New Orleans has permitted a demographic shift in some of the city's poorer sectors. Gentrification as an expression of affluence has masked the dissolution of old communities and networks and forced previous inhabitants to move even further to the margins. Through the lens of slow disaster, the hurricane is hardly the centerpiece of that story, even if it remains the flashpoint.[5] Per Benjamin: the storm of progress is the real culprit. A more focused analysis of the ubiquity of catastrophic history argues that poverty remains the most enduring slow disaster.

III

Theories of collapse are a longstanding feature of Western thought, especially in the context of economics. The imminent collapse of capitalism – as prognosticated by the German philosopher Karl Marx – heartened and inspired leftist politics. Not all such thought was built from the scaffolding of proletariat revolution. By the 1890s the "Zusammenbruchstheorie" theory of collapse dictated a more terminal breakdown by entropy as new markets to exploit were exhausted.[6]

Through much of the post-World War II period, and with growing relevance since the 1970s, a new form of liberal order – neoliberalism – has merged economic theory with social and political policy. Its ambition was to stimulate global trade and markets through unshackling manufacturing tariffs and the privatization of public services. Over the past forty years, neoliberalism has systematically undermined the welfare policies that preceded it. In their place, risk has been outsourced to the individual. Too: neoliberalism has created a vulnerable labor force – indeed, an emerging class: the precariat – by resolutely championing the invisible hand of the market over local or public goods and welfare. By moving the production of goods to the cheapest manufacturer, frequently in the developing world, where labor and environmental rights are minimized and marginalized, if they exist at all, neoliberalism's capacity to consolidate global markets brings with it a vast alienation of the growing number of those left behind.[7] It is still unclear whether the populist backlash against liberal elitism – as evidenced by the election of Donald Trump in the United States, the Brexit vote in the United

Kingdom, and the hard-right turn in many parts of Europe – represents a serious chink in neoliberalism's global dominance, or whether it is the last-gasp death rattle of older intellectual movements that object to neoliberalism's globalist and cosmopolitan inclinations. The global marketplace threatens not just the working poor, but also the cultural difference that has long been the bulwark of the nation state. If neoliberalism sought to bolster economic growth against collapse, it did so at the expense of local and cultural ties that many were disinclined to surrender. To make matters worse, the market shocks of the first decade of the twenty-first century provoked questions about neoliberalism's unquestioned confidence. The further problem – and pivotal to our contemporary concerns about failing markets – is that the architects of neoliberalism never really accounted for collapse. The market would correct, they promised. Even if it hasn't.

At root, however, is the under-appreciated reality that environmental limits must be accounted for in our economies. The industrial technocracy that has driven human economies for the past 200 years – and become so entrenched that Joel Kovel can suggest that it is easier to imagine the end of the world than the end of capitalism – has been engaged in a frantic race to the outer reaches of these limits (Kovel 2007). Indeed, one persuasive metanarrative of modern history is precisely the struggle for human civilization to shake off the limits imposed by the physical environment. No economic theory, however, provides a viable alternative to air, soil, and water as the lifeblood of human life, social organization, and civilization.[8]

IV

In catastrophic history, a new panoply of analytic vocabulary presents itself. Much of it revolves around risk: precarity, vulnerability, crisis, uncertainty, fear, and anxiety. If one could buy stock in these vocabularies and the frequency of their use, the catastrophist in 2016 would recommend investing in "barbarism." The price seems right (see Figure 1.1).

Barbarism might seem a peculiar vocabulary choice to highlight. But it is extremely pertinent, not least because modern civilization has tamed the traditional barbarian "other" while simultaneously practicing against them the kinds of atrocities no enlightened society could comfortably acknowledge as their own. Syrian refugees. The Calais jungle. Travel bans. The contamination of air, soil, and water. That we put too much emphasis on the progressive history told by the victors, Benjamin (2007) warned, risks neglecting to acknowledge that "there is no document of culture which is not at the same time a document of barbarism" (p. 256, Thesis VII). Too frequently, catastrophe discourse veers toward a kind of fatalist or determinist accounting of events that removes human actions and agency from histories of the catastrophic. Catastrophe and disaster both find their etymological origins in fate and surprise. That natural disasters, for example, are dismissed as "acts of god" ignores the consequences, not to mention the historical processes,

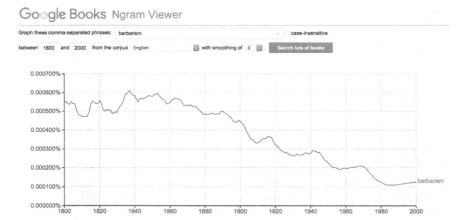

Figure 1.1 Google Books Ngram charting the relative frequency of "barbarism"

of vulnerable sectors of society invariably finding themselves at greater risk. Historian Ted Steinberg points to the important juxtaposition between poor planning and poor luck. The latter is used to excuse the former.[9] Tornadoes being especially drawn to trailer parks is the refashioned fallacy of the adage that insisted that rain follows the plough. Poverty and vulnerability to disasters are frequent companions. This is a fact of history: marginalized groups pushed to the margins.

To the discussion of slow disaster, we should sensibly add "slow violence," the cultural theorist Rob Nixon's term to describe more latent or incremental consequences of environmental deterioration (Nixon 2011). In the control of nature is the control of people. In the destruction of nature is the starting point for catastrophic history.

V

Günther Anders proffers an important binary perspective on the nature of collapse and catastrophe. Appropriately, he presents two such binaries. The first involves the disconnect between action and imagination in the technological age. "The possibility of the apocalypse is our work," he notes. "But we know not what we are doing." Anders identifies a gap between our expanding technical capacity and our diminishing imagination – or, at least, its inability to keep up with technological progress and its repercussions: "We are unable to conceive what we construct; to mentally reproduce what we can produce; to realize the reality which we can bring into being" (Anders 1989, pp. 11–12). Elsewhere, Anders contends with the juxtaposition between a disaster's surprise and its anticipation. It is, first, an event whose consequences and element of surprise invariably challenge the bulwark of social certainties. Its anticipation, however, is present in the concerted building of infrastructure to reduce risk – to prepare for the inevitable (Dupuy 2015). That preparation is necessarily historically situated in the context and information that precedes catastrophe. As the sociologist Robert Wuthnow (2010) observes, when confronting disaster, we act based on previous experience, which is frequently no longer sufficient.

It is important, then, to recall that the human spirit resists the prospect of catastrophe to the bitter end. In trying to explain or justify the Jewish refusal to fathom the reality of industrial genocide – even on the train platform at Auschwitz-Birkenau – Primo Levi recruited the German adage: "Things whose existence is not morally possible cannot exist" (Dupuy 2015, p. 3). Of course, the lesson from history is that the morally possible shifts over time. Though horrors are impossible to conceive of, that doesn't prevent their occurrence. Subsequent history is forever changed, because we cannot undo or unremember past moral reprehensibilities. This would support Benjamin and others in their contention that humanity is on a perpetual slide into catastrophe. Our capacity to imagine catastrophe is constantly expanding, even if it fails to keep pace with our unimagined powers of destruction.

This has broader, biblical – "collaptic" – reverberations, too. The modern understanding of "apocalypse" as a cataclysmic event belies its original meaning as a revelation or a disclosure or an insight. Even in St. John's Revelation – where apocalypse reflected the imminent end of the world (a wholly different kind of collapse) – there came, first, revealing truths. In both definitions, apocalypse provides clarity. We can link Anders's expansion of human horrors and the horrific imagination to a steady march on the revelatory apocalypse.

VI

Things whose existence is not morally possible cannot exist. In 1930, the physicist and Nobel Laureate Robert Millikan asserted that nature was sufficiently resilient to absorb and adjust to whatever environmental trespasses humanity might inflict upon Earth (Hobsbawm 1995).[10] His remarks came on the eve of "the Great Acceleration," a moment that witnessed an incomparable spike in human population growth, in the production and consumption of material goods, and a decided turn toward more wasteful, energy-intensive, and disposable forms of manufacturing. Less than a century later we are entered into a new geological epoch – the Anthropocene – typified precisely by an irrevocable transformation of the earth's crust by human activity. Climate change, mass species extinction, ocean acidification: these are facts that have transcended human history, environmental history, and geological history – wildly distinct units of time.[11]

By extension, the Anthropocene has become, necessarily, the pivotal vantage point for all history. Hannah Arendt (1994) writes: "Whenever an event occurs that is great enough to illuminate its own past, history comes into being" (p. 319). The Anthropocene is a slow disaster – a product of slow violence – that has most assuredly arrived. This is sobering. Arendt continues: "Only then does the chaotic maze of past happenings emerge as a story which can be told, because it has a beginning and an end." The lone certainty of the Anthropocene's future is the fact that Earth's capacity to sustain life as we understand it will be radically and irrevocably changed. Our histories need to be conscious of this. The Anthropocene means that the environment has become an unavoidable category of historical analysis.

VII

The Anthropocene is contemporary history. Living in the Anthropocene will require having access to the most and best information available to us about the world's current condition. Historical context provides critical insight and understanding on the decisions in front of us. This is unequivocally a past that is still with us. "All contemporary history begins with 'the latest catastrophe,'" asserts the historian Henry Rousso (2016, p. 9). Catastrophe provokes hyperbole, which is a distinct hazard of contemporary history, "where the subject of one's narrative is a 'still-there,'" warns Rousso (p. 4). It is too easy, he warns, to be captivated in the immediacy of the present's preoccupations to be able to analyze its causes and effects with clarity. But our recent climate and environmental discoveries force us to rethink these cautions. Whereas historians are still trying to make sense of the political extremism that typified the twentieth century, the new century and its history are forced to contend with the environmental extremism of melting glaciers and strained ecosystems. In that light, new political extremisms are expressions of human desperation. Inasmuch as the Anthropocene is the latest catastrophe: it may also be the last catastrophe.

The enduring challenge, however, is that illuminating events – those that bring history into being – occur with such frequency that it becomes nigh impossible to rationalize each one before it is subsumed by the next. This helps to explain the old adage that any historical treatment of events since the French Revolution is journalism and not history. Indeed, an historian wandering the heated battlefield or snaking between stretchers of wounded soldiers is inadvertently serving as obstacle to the nurse trying to administer care to the sick, hurt, and dying. In other words, the contemporary historian can be an unwelcome – or untimely – presence. Similarly, it seems disingenuous to be inquiring into the causes of an earthquake while interlocutors continue to pick through the rubble for survivors. Indeed, present trauma obscures the lessons history can offer. But historians also reckon with the fact that history hasn't ended. It is right to examine how, when, and why climate warnings were dismissed. And it is important to better understand the mechanisms that got us to here: the Anthropocene shines the torchlight into some underexplored corners of the past. We would do well to examine them.

VIII

It would be to miss the point to establish hard taxonomies of catastrophe. The exercise of trying to parse natural, from technological, from moral catastrophes risks oversimplifying their social, cultural, economic, political, and environmental contexts and intricacies. The famous debate between Voltaire and Rousseau over the concepts of good and evil in the wake of the Lisbon earthquake of 1755 indicate as much. Where earthquake, tsunami, and fire were, for Voltaire, a sign that there was no benevolent god, Rousseau saw instead a more protean series of causes and effects. More recently, Scott Knowles (2012) asks whether the Twin Towers in New York collapsed on 9/11 because of terrorism or fire. Similarly, was Hurricane Katrina a weather event or a technological failure (p. 302)?[12] Further, Jean-Pierre Dupuy (2011) reminds us, in his analysis of the Fukushima nuclear disaster (prompted by a tsunami), that Jews referred to their extermination by the Nazis using the Hebrew word, "*shoah.*" *Shoah* translates as natural catastrophe. We need to reflect on this naturalization of evil, which is a fascinating constant in the history of catastrophe.[13] Catastrophic history demands that we pair the naturalization of evil with the impulse to forget. The literary critic W. G. Sebald (1999) reflected on the manner in which the Allied fire bombing of Germany during World War II is expunged from the German popular memory. Long after World War II, survivors of Hiroshima referred to the thunderclap that destroyed their city as a tsunami.[14]

IX

Because of Walter Benjamin, Paul Klee's *Angelus Novus* has become the perverse muse of history (see Figure 1.2). In his most famous and widely repeated excerpt (Thesis IX), Benjamin described Klee's painting, which he dubbed the angel of history, as capturing the essence of history and of the catastrophic imagination. History, Benjamin argued, was not a series of events but "one single catastrophe, which keeps piling wreckage upon wreckage." One single catastrophe: history is not a series of episodes. Benjamin's angel plays hapless witness to this accumulation as a storm catches its wings and pushes it relentlessly, backward, into the future, "while the pile of debris before him grows towards the sky." This is dishearteningly biblical in its purview. That a golden age should have existed at the beginning of the human chronicle evokes original sin and expulsion from the garden of Eden. It runs counter to more progressive notions of the recent history of human ethics and the broadening scope of social, cultural and economic possibilities in the modern era. But for Benjamin, looking out over what he perceived to be the hopelessness of a European landscape being overrun by fascism, this was consistent with the advance of history. The storm that pushes the angel of history is the storm of progress. "We must base the idea of progress on the idea of catastrophe. Catastrophe is precisely when things carry on as before," he wrote elsewhere (Benjamin 1982, p. 342).[15]

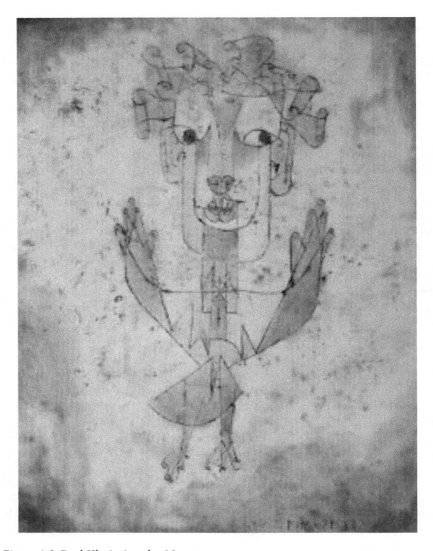

Figure 1.2 Paul Klee's *Angelus Novus*

X

Karl Marx and his -ism have inspired generations of historians to recount histories, wherein market forces and capitalist power structures have foisted upon society a declensionist narrative in which successes have come upon the broken backs of the proletariat or the subaltern or the forsook. The conclusions serve as warnings: that the course of this history is barreling toward a deleterious end, but also that that trajectory need not be wholly determined. As Benjamin notes, the historian's task on the train hurtling into the abyss should be to pull the emergency brake. Even if we cannot change course, we can stop the train. But I don't know that catastrophic history is an extension of the popular jeremiad through which environmental historians conclude with a call to arms and insistence that a glimmer of hope remains. In some macabre sense: catastrophic history works in a post-hope environment. It provides, instead, a record of civilizational collapse. Like Benjamin's angel of history, the historian simply bears witness to the storm.

XI

The historian's task is to brush against the grain, according to Benjamin. In its very suggestion, the history of the future seeks to do just that. The history of the future uses the past as a mirror, reflecting over the shoulder of Benjamin's angel. It examines past cultural visions of what might happen next. Planning for the future – whether on the small scale of a grocery list or the environmental scale of maintaining levees to contain the floodwaters of a major river or the grand scale of human survival in the face of planetary catastrophe – is the one ubiquitous constant of history.

Multiple historians have argued that history is grounded in its own present, and only asks questions of the past that help to explain the contemporary. In this sense, a dizzying logic dictates that "the meaning of the past depends on future actions" (Dupuy 2015, p. 46). History does not propose to predict the future, but it should practice a certain empathy toward futures past. In addition to reading the unfolding of past events, the history of the future should interrogate more closely what past actors thought they were doing. What outcomes did they foresee, or anticipate, or hope for, or hope against? And through this lens, we need to ask the past about catastrophe. There are three moments to an explosion: the second is the moment of detonation. The third is the aftermath: the recovery, the repair, and the lessons learned. This brings our circular chronology to the first moment: preparation for disaster. In learning the lessons from the last catastrophe, we are always planning for the next one.

In short: we know that catastrophe is possible, probable, indeed: inevitable. But we revel in denial (Dupuy 2015, p. 3). At the same time, much of that denial masks a deep history of planning and preparation and the identification and articulation of vulnerabilities. In *Arming Mother Nature*, Jacob Hamblin (2013) relates the efforts of Cold War scientists and officers in their attempts to identify and respond to environmental vulnerabilities. Hamblin also examines the ecologist Charles Elton's "conservation of variety," the idea that abundant biodiversity promotes greater resilience through a series of natural checks and balances.

But also this: if the Anthropocene constitutes an event of sufficient significance to redirect our reading of history, how do we reconcile past events with a history of the future? It is one thing to study a past that has not yet passed, but entirely another to engage with a past that has not yet happened, or may not happen. Or, viewed through a collaptic lens: a future that could erase all history. In its framing of the future, the Anthropocene constitutes our first glimpse at a singular catastrophe that has long been the dominion of Benjamin's angel of history. At its final collapse, it is likely that human civilization's epitaph will read: "Nothing could be done." The catastrophic historian would feel inclined to disagree. There will be no epitaph. "Where there is no one who remembers, there will be nothing left to remember," Anders (1989) asserts in his "Commandments in the Atomic Age." Rather than epitaph, he argues, "the door in front of us bears the inscription: 'Nothing will have been'" (p. 11). Pause and consider the verb tense.

XII

Nowhere is the history of the future's gaze more crystallized than in charting changes and continuities in utopian and dystopian thought. 2016 marked the 500th anniversary of Thomas More's *Utopia* and an American presidential campaign that promised to "make America great again." While there is likely a chasm between More's intent and message and the slogan – and vitriol and divisiveness that accompanied it – that populated the mainstream American airwaves in the lead-up to the fall election, both implied a kind of violence. The Paris Communards, Gabriele D'Annunzio's romanticism, Hitler's nationalism: all traded on utopian visions and violence as means and end (Mishra 2017). All utopias require a fresh canvas. In a new edition of *Utopia* from Verso Books, the fantasy/weird fiction author China Miéville (2016) ruminated on the relationship between idealized society and its history. "A start for any habitable utopia must be to overturn the ideological bullshit of empire," he wrote, "and, unsentimentally but respectfully, to revisit the traduced and defamed cultures on the bones of which some conqueror's utopian dreams were piled up. 'Utopia' is to the political imaginary of bitterness as 'Rhodesia' is to Zimbabwe, 'Gold Coast' to Ghana." But the relationship between idealized past and future is tenuous, Miéville reminds us: "every brutalized, genocided and enslaved people in history have, like the Abraxans, been 'rude and uncivilized' in the tracks of their invaders" (p. 7).[16] History is haunted by its ghosts.

Lest the connections are too subtle, utopia is a sacred prospect, out there or nowhere. Or a direction. Utopia is always an engagement with the future. But it is also in clear but ever-diminishing view of the angel of history, being blown away from Paradise. The history of the future helps to rationalize the sacred and the profane: we cannot hope for the past.

In this space, the Anthropocene offers limited perspective for utopian thought: it possesses the unmistakable imprint of the profane. "Dystopias," the great science fiction author Ursula Le Guin (2016) muses from a contemporary vantage point, "are certainly easier" to write (p. 164). But the neoliberal agenda asserts that one should never let a serious crisis go to waste.[17] In disaster, there is opportunity. In collapse, there is rebirth. For those who survive, a utopian agenda is renewed. Or, perhaps, disaster is a precondition for that utopia's persistence.

XIII

Of course, we have been here before. We have, ingrained in the Judeo-Christian psyche, an origin myth that revolves around environmental collapse and human culpability. The story of Noah and the Flood constitutes an erasing, not just of all life that did not board the Ark, but also of the history of misdeeds and evils that preceded it. Indeed, one interpretation could propose that Noah embarked upon a voyage to a new, but unreached – unrealized – utopia. We know, only, that God was displeased with Man so he brought forth a flood. Noah is at once the lone good human, but also the lone chronicler of the past that preceded this reset. No wonder, then, that his sons should find him asleep in drunken stupor in Genesis 9:21–29, after the Flood. Noah, too, could not unremember the moral reprehensibilities of the past – the misdeeds of men and God's capacity for annihilation.

Noah's Flood is iconic. It represents the cleansing of the civilizational slate by external forces. As a result it is also common in popular culture, not least as an enduring symbol of crisis: social, existential, or civilizational. Indeed, it is interesting to note an increase in references to Noah's Flood in periods of perceived crisis.

Lost in the catastrophic rhetoric, of course, is that civilization did not collapse. Noah built an ark, in which he, his family, and the animals survived. The ark must have been quite the engineering feat, but it also constitutes a remarkable metaphor for the history of the future. Only in the anticipation of catastrophe could its construction be conceived and realized. If there are any grounds for hope in catastrophic history, they rest not with the dove and its olive branch, but in foresighted preparation. And the truth is: we build arks all the time. Amongst the most symbolically grand is the isolated Svalbard Global Seed Vault, tucked underground in one of the most remote places on a well-trammeled planet. Its intent and its claims seem to lack harmony. The seed vault stores and protects the world's largest collection of crop diversity. In the event of a catastrophe, humanity will have the resources to begin anew. This structure preserves the prospect of survival, providing the potential to restore a conservation of variety after a latter-day flood. Much of the literature on and about and from the Svalbard Global Seed Vault insists its security against human and natural disasters is ironclad. At the same time, its inspiration was conceived in preparation for the unimaginable.

XIV

"*Après nous le déluge.*" This delightfully dark claim is attributed to Madame de Pompadour, King Louis XV's lover. There are, of course, multiple ways to interpret Madame de Pompadour's assertion. The first implies culpability: because of our actions, the flood. The second offers a more hedonistic desire: after we have gone, the flood may do whatever it wishes. There is no less a sense of culpability in this second claim. Finally, it is possible to imagine a variation that suggests that without us the deluge is inevitable. In the face of collapse, this third option offers a glimmer of hope. It is our responsibility to withstand or turn back the flood. A world without hope, of course, is a world without civilization. A world without civilization is a world without history: a reversion to prehistory? Certainly an abdication of utopia.

Catastrophic history, however, insists that we do not pause too long on the hopeful interpretation. It depends upon human correction. "Après nous le déluge" also became the motto of the Royal Air Force No. 617 Squadron, most famous for a Ruhr Valley bombing raid in 1943. Operation Chastise used a new piece of catastrophic technology, a bouncing bomb, to breach German dams. The success of the operation entered into the mainstream imagination with the name "Dam Busters." The disastrous flooding that followed was no less destructive or horrific than the fire bombing of Hamburg or Dresden.

XV

"Catastrophe is our bedtime story," asserts Don DeLillo (2016, p. 66) in *Zero K*. The normalization of catastrophe is almost soothing. It gives coherence to the uncertainty of disaster. But in its normalization, we offer a more progressive history, one that paints a more hopeful account of the human past than events warrant. The Anthropocene, as an intellectual tool, suffers a similar limitation, inasmuch as it asserts that we are all in this together. In pulling back its lens to engage with the plight of the planet as a whole, it renders in broad brushstrokes and averages a story that poorly reflects the realities of climate change and resource scarcity. Erikson's slow disaster, Eliot's whimper, Nixon's slow violence, Dupuy's enlightened catastrophism remind us that it is disingenuous to suggest that the entire human species will suffer the Anthropocene in the same way. We are not all in this together. Miéville (2016) again: "We live in utopia; it just isn't ours" (p. 24). Whatever inevitable changes occur, they will be experienced differently in Canada, in Ethiopia, and in the Maldives. More significantly, the poor – in any nation – will feel the bite of rising waters, warming temperatures, and scarcer resources more viscerally than those fortunate enough to live in better-than-subsistence conditions. This is a condition of the "environmentalism of the poor," a term cogently presented by the economist Juan Martinez-Alier (2002), and advanced by Nixon in his work on slow violence.

Catastrophic history is, in its ultimate guise, an analysis of vulnerability and precarity. It takes as its point of focus not the medians and spreadsheets of the economists but a deeper obligation to the Anthropocene's frontline inhabitants: the global poor. That subaltern experience is wont to be washed away in the deluge of global environmental processes. Historians can do more than record its existence before it has disappeared.

"The only historian capable of fanning the spark of hope in the past is the one who is firmly convinced that *even the dead* will not be safe from the enemy if he is victorious. And this enemy has never ceased to be victorious," remarks Walter Benjamin (2007, p. 255, Thesis VI). As a mission statement, catastrophic history shines a light on the darkest recesses of the human experience. It is not enough to look into the abyss. We must inquire into what it is that looks back at us.

Notes

1 "Psychological pandemic" comes from Don DeLillo's *Zero K* (2016, 127). "I told him what was gathering could well be a kind of psychological pandemic. The fearful perception that tends toward wishfulness. Something people want and need from time to time, purely atmospheric. I liked that. Purely atmospheric."
2 See, for example, Paul Mason, *Postcapitalism: A Guide to Our Future* (London: Penguin Books, 2015).
3 For a breathtaking summary of the history of contemporary upset, see Pankaj Mishra, *Age of Anger: A History of the Present* (New York: Farrar, Straus, Giroux, 2017).
4 "Malaise of modernity" was the title given to Charles Taylor's Massey Lectures (Taylor 1991).
5 There is a veritable industry of good new scholarship that treats Hurricane Katrina. See, for example, Craig E. Colten, *Perilous Place, Powerful Storms: Hurricane Protection in Coastal Louisiana* (Jackson, MS: University Press of Mississippi, 2009); Ari Kelman, *A River and Its City: The Nature of Landscape in New Orleans* (Berkeley: University of California Press, 2006); and Douglas Brinkley, *The Great Deluge: Hurricane Katrina, New Orleans, and the Mississippi Gulf Coast* (New York: William Morrow, 2006). See, too, Natasha Trethewey, *Beyond Katrina: A Meditation on the Mississippi Gulf Coast* (Athens, GA: University of Georgia Press, 2010).
6 For a recent discussion, see Gareth Stedman Jones, *Karl Marx: Greatness and Illusion* (London: Penguin Books, 2016), 3.
7 For neoliberalism, see David Harvey, *A Brief History of Neoliberalism* (New York: Oxford University Press, 2005).
8 For a recent investigation of the histories of abundance and limits, see Donald Worster, *Shrinking the Earth: The Rise and Decline of American Abundance* (New York: Oxford University Press, 2016).
9 See, for example, Ted Steinberg, *Acts of God: The Unnatural History of Natural Disasters in America* (New York: Oxford University Press, 2006).
10 Millikan: "One may sleep in peace with the consciousness that the Creator has put some foolproof elements into his handiwork, and that man is powerless to do it any titanic damage" (534).
11 There is a growing literature that works with and against the idea of the Anthropocene as a method of understanding the human relationship with the physical environment. See, as entry point, Christophe Bonneuil & Jean-Baptiste Fressoz, *The Shock of the Anthropocene: The Earth, History and Us* (London: Verso, 2016); Jason W. Moore (ed.), *Anthropocene or Capitalocene? Nature, History, and the Crisis of Capitalism* (Oakland, CA: PM Press, 2016); Ian Angus, *Facing the Anthropocene: Fossil Capitalism and the Crisis of the Earth System*

(New York: Monthly Review Press, 2016); Clive Hamilton, François Gemenne, & Christophe Bonneuil (eds.), *The Anthropocene and the Global Environmental Crisis: Rethinking Modernity in a New Epoch* (New York: Routledge, 2015); and Christian Schwägerl, *The Anthropocene: The Human Era and How It Shapes Our Planet* (Santa Fe, NM: Synergetic Press, 2014).

12 Knowles explains that inquiries into the towers' collapse found that fire prevention measures had been circumvented in their construction. In effect, the World Trade Center should not have fallen down after the planes crashed into them.

13 This chapter eschews (indeed, sheepishly dodges) any direct confrontation with "evil" as an historical idea. For a starting point in that investigation, see Susan Neiman, *Evil in Modern Thought: An Alternative History of Philosophy* (Princeton: Princeton University Press, 2002).

14 Anders: "[Japanese survivors'] resolve not to speak of those who were to blame, not to say that the event had been caused by human beings; not to harbor the least resentment, even though they were victims of the greatest crimes – this really is too much for me, it passes all understanding . . . . The constantly speak of the catastrophe as if it were an earthquake or a tidal wave. They use the Japanese word, tsunami" (Quoted in Dupuy 2015, p. 50).

15 Author's translation: "Il faut fonder le concept de progrès sur l'idée de catastrophe. Que les choses continuent à aller ainsi, voilà la catastrophe."

16 The Abraxans were the forgotten peoples who populated More's Utopia before their conquest by King Utopus. Even More only mentions them in passing. "Utopus, that conquered [the island] (whose name it still carries, for Abraxa was its first name), brought the rude and uncivilized inhabitants into such good government, and to that measure of politeness, that they now far excel all the rest of mankind" (72–73).

17 See, for example, Philip Mirowski, *Never Let a Serious Crisis Go to Waste: How Neoliberalism Survived the Financial Meltdown* (London: Verso Books, 2013); and Naomi Klein, *The Shock Doctrine: The Rise of Disaster Capitalism* (New York: Alfred A. Knopf, 2007).

References

Anders, G., 1989. Commandments in the atomic age. In C. Eatherly & G. Anders, eds. *Burning conscience: The guilt of Hiroshima*. New York: Paragon House.

Arendt, H., 1994. Understanding and politics (the difficulties of understanding). In H. Arendt, ed. *Essays on understanding*. New York: Harcourt Brace.

Benjamin, W., 1982. *Charles Baudelaire*. Paris: Payot.

Benjamin, W., 2007. *Illuminations: The work of art in the age of mechanical reproduction*. New York: Schocken Books.

DeLillo, D., 2016. *Zero K: A novel*. New York: Scribner and Sons.

Dupuy, J.-P., 2002. *Pour un catastrophisme Éclairé: Quand l'impossible est certain*. Paris: Le Seuil.

Dupuy, J.-P., 2011. Une catastrophe monstre. *Le monde*. Available at: www.lemonde.fr/idees/article/2011/03/19/une-catastrophe-monstre_1495592_3232.html.

Dupuy, J.-P., 2015. *A short treatise on the metaphysics of tsunamis*. East Lansing: Michigan State University Press.

Eliot, T.S., 1932. The hollow men. In *Poems, 1909–1925*. New York: Harcourt Brace.

Erikson, K., 1976. *Everything in its path New York*. New York: Simon and Schuster.

Erikson, K., 1995. *A new species of trouble: The human experience of modern disasters*. New York: W. W. Norton & Company.

Greif, M., 2015. *The age of the crisis of man: Thought and fiction in America, 1933–1973*. Princeton: Princeton University Press.

Hamblin, J.D., 2013. *Arming mother nature: The birth of catastrophic environmentalism*. New York: Oxford University Press.

Hobsbawm, E.J., 1995. *The age of extremes: A history of the world, 1914–1991*. London: Abacus.

Knowles, S.G., 2012. *The disaster experts: Mastering risk in modern America*. Philadelphia: University of Pennsylvania Press.

Kovel, J., 2007. *The enemy of nature: The end of capitalism or the end of the world?* London: Zed Books.

Le Guin, U., 2016. A non-Euclidean view of California as a cold place to be. In T. More, ed. *Utopia*. London: Verso.

Le Roy, F. et al., 2011. Introduction. In F. Le Roy et al., eds. *Tickle your catastrophe!: Imagining catastrophe in art, architecture and philosophy*. Gent: Academia Press.

Martinez-Alier, J., 2002. *The environmentalism of the poor*. Northampton, MA: Edward Elgar Publishing.

Miéville, C., 2016. Close to the shore. In T. More, ed. *Utopia*. London: Verso.

Mishra, P., 2017. *Age of anger*. New York: Farrar, Straus and Giroux.

Nixon, R., 2011. *Slow violence and the environmentalism of the poor*. Cambridge, MA: Harvard University Press.

Parenti, C., 2011. *Tropic of chaos: Climate change and the new geography of violence*. New York: Nation Books.

Rousso, H., 2016. *The latest catastrophe: History, the present, the contemporary*. Chicago: University of Chicago Press.

Sebald, W.G., 1999. *On the natural history of destruction*. London: Penguin Books.

Taylor, C., 1991. *The malaise of modernity*. Concord, ON: House of Anansi.

Wuthnow, R., 2010. *Be very afraid: The cultural response to terror, pandemics, environmental devastation, nuclear annihilation, and other threats*. New York: Oxford University Press.

2 Are dead zones dead?

Environmental collapse in popular media about eutrophication in sea-based systems

Jesse Peterson

Environmental collapse in the Baltic Sea

In August 2015, *Svenska Dagbladet*, one of two large daily newspapers in Sweden, published two editorials in which water experts discussed eutrophication in the Baltic Sea. In the first article, experts representing research and technological development interests argued that eutrophication in the Baltic Sea had worsened because low oxygen levels had "activated" a "large internal phosphor[ous] source," meaning that the sea itself impacted eutrophication levels more than any other factor. Two days later, a different group of experts, representing non-profit and governmental interests, published a counter-argument in the same paper. They called into question this "so-called internal load" and argued that the biggest factor affecting eutrophication was still land-based phosphorous pollution (Gustafsson et al. 2015; Stigebrandt et al., 2015). The experts debated what to do about eutrophication, but more importantly, they disagreed about how funds should be allocated to both land-based and offshore research methods and remediation efforts. The ways these two articles frame eutrophication rely as much on expertise, research agendas, market trends and developments, and political alliances as they do scientific certainty (Egan 2015, p. 39).

Though this brief debate was published in a national (Swedish) newspaper, outcomes of eutrophication are transnational. The Baltic Sea – along with its catchment basin – covers about 15 percent of the total area of Europe; rivers from fourteen countries drain into the sea, and nine countries border its coasts. The sea has experienced large-scale eutrophication, the excessive growth of phytoplankton from nutrient enrichment and its effects, for 100 years or more (Bianchi et al. 2000; Zillén and Conley 2010). This "cultural eutrophication" refers to the anthropogenic acceleration of natural processes of eutrophication, caused by long-term nutrient accumulation in water bodies (Rydén et al. 2003; Schindler and Vallentyne 2008; Wassmann 2005; Yang et al. 2008). Experts agree that the anthropogenic acceleration of processes of eutrophication has increased both the size and frequency of the Baltic sea's eutrophic conditions, mirroring similar trends in water bodies around the globe. Today, the hypoxic (or oxygen-depleted) environments – popularly referred to as "dead zones" – in the Baltic Sea affect an area the size of Denmark (Bianchi et al. 2000; Rydén et al. 2003; Zillén and Conley 2010). As the largest dead zone in the world, solutions for eutrophication in the Baltic Sea would have far-reaching consequences, affecting the environment, fisheries, agricultural and marine policies, shipping, and tourism of that region.

It perhaps comes as no surprise that the experts who thought the Baltic Sea's internal phosphorous loads perpetuated the eutrophic conditions described the sea as a collapsed or altered environment. In light of this perspective, they proposed remediating the Baltic dead zones through geoengineering approaches (Stigebrandt et al. 2015). In contrast, the other group of experts – though they note that they could not "recreate" the Baltic Sea of the nineteenth century – described the Baltic Sea as one to be improved and made healthy again. For them, the Baltic Sea had not yet changed into a new, collapsed environment; they sought to prevent systemic collapse. They found the geoengineering solutions presented by the other experts as much of a threat as cultural eutrophication and felt that geoengineering could also send the sea irretrievably into a new environmental regime.[1] Although both groups acknowledged the poor conditions of the Baltic Sea, they understood it differently.

In general, eutrophic water bodies offer an useful example for ecological collapse: a lake is overfed nutrients, becomes eutrophic, and stays that way (Scheffer et al. 2001; Walker and Salt 2006). Thus, the original system "collapses" and shifts into an entirely different steady state. Since scientists explain eutrophication as a process leading to total collapse, narratives about eutrophication in the ocean are implicitly concerned with systemic perspectives that gained popularity among scientists in the latter half of the twentieth century (Egan 2015). The science behind dead zones ultimately frames them as a possible if not inevitable collapse of the entire sea or ocean. Moreover, scientists show us how dead zones in the oceans and sea are dynamic phenomena that exist *within* a larger marine context. For example, eutrophication takes place in the Baltic Sea during the warmer months: in the spring algae grow deeper in the water nearer to the seafloor while in late summer they grow closer to the water's surface. Further, algae first bloom in the southern part of the Baltic where temperatures are warmer. They then move northward as summer progresses, expanding and contracting based on other factors such as salinity. Dead zones are by definition collapsed environments, but what is collapsed shifts based on a dead zone's visibility, seasonality, location, size, and duration.

The debate between the scientists clearly evokes two distinct discursive takes on environmental collapse: collapsed and collapsing. Yet, these two perspectives are often not as clear cut in popular representations of dead zones. Influenced by scientific knowledge about dead zones, popular media texts must negotiate to what extent a dead zone represents a collapsed or collapsing environment. However, whether collapsing or collapsed, dead zones do not always symbolize the same kind of collapse. For example, narratives of eutrophication can describe dead zones as forms of slow-moving destruction while sudden explosions of algae – specifically harmful and toxic cyanobacteria – allow dead zones to be written as narratives of catastrophe (Angus 2013; DeLoughrey 2009; Nixon 2011). As such, how popular media frames dead zones and eutrophication ought to illustrate to some extent what collapse means and for whom. The rest of this chapter explores how dead zones get represented as collapsing or collapsed, noticing how texts complicate these frames and attribute variable meanings to the notion of environmental collapse.

Dead zones in popular media: meanings and struggles

Why do systems collapse? Recent popular narratives about collapse assert that environmental catastrophe precipitates societal collapse, which has led to a healthy discussion and debate (Diamond 2011; McAnany and Yoffee 2009; Middleton 2012). As Guy D. Middleton's exhaustive review of the subject suggests, popular narratives about collapse that hinge on climate change, ecological degradation, or other natural disasters are often not so much concerned with the environment but with understanding how societies change through these processes (2012, p. 258). Perhaps this is one reason why discourses of environmental collapse are seductive. When people talk about the death of the oceans or fish or seals, they are often talking about the death of our species and human ways of life. Talking about a collapse of oceans or water engages in important issues such as origins, duality, archetypes, aliens and monsters, life and death, among many other themes (Alaimo 2016; Bachelard 1983; Glasgow 2009; Illich 2000; Shubin, 2009). Moreover, that seas might *die or be dead* immediately connects to a more embodied, organic, life-centric conundrum than some other forms of environmental collapse narratives such as climate *change*. Therefore, understanding how people talk about environmental collapse in relation to the oceans or seas is not only significant of itself but can also indicate what certain societies perceive to be valuable or meaningful about Earth's waters and how to rethink human-water relationships. In other words, choosing to focus on narratives of environmental or ecological collapse about oceans or seas may reveal a great deal about societies and their struggles to control, understand, exploit, monitor, and heal these environments along with their entangled histories (DeLoughrey et al. 2016, p. 17).

In the sections that follow, I explore media constructions of dead zones as a contemporary and unique form of environmental collapse discourses, focusing on the Baltic Sea and its dead zone. The case of the Baltic Sea is exceptional in that it occupies a liminal space between the more classic cases of eutrophication in freshwater lakes and the dead zone in the Gulf of Mexico.[2] In order to reveal the dominant frames and inherent tensions in this discourse of environmental collapse, this chapter analyzes five texts: the popular scientific texts, *Dead Zones: Why Earth's Waters are Losing*

Oxygen and *Sea Sick: Ocean Change and the Extinction of Life on Earth*, specifically its chapter on oxygen; the second news article, "Sentinels Under Attack," in the Pulitzer-prize winning series on "distressed oceans" first published in the *LA Times*; and the non-profit produced film *Dirty Waters* and book *50 Sätt att Rädda Östersjön* (*50 Ways to Save the Baltic Sea*). This selection includes works that reflect different popular media types and permits varied insights into the portrayal of dead zones. Incorporating many themes found in journalistic reporting, the first three texts underscore the challenges dead zones present for the world's oceans. *Dead Zones*, by Carol Hand, a science writer for young adults, is one of the only books to attempt a comprehensive summary of these phenomena while *Sea Sick* and "Sentinels Under Attack" represent popular and award-winning environmental journalism about changes in the oceans. As such, these sources tell compelling and meaningful stories about dead zones that have been widely distributed and continue to shape public imaginaries about the oceans. The non-profit funded film and book bring in situated knowledge about the Baltic Sea and counterbalance the science journalism with activist lenses. They also represent themes found in more general accounts, such as the Greenpeace funded publication: *Dead Zones: How Agricultural Fertilizers are Killing our Rivers, Lakes, and Oceans*. Baltic Sea 2020 – a non-profit dedicated to increasing knowledge (particularly in relation to fishing and eutrophication) about the Baltic Sea – and its film are particularly well-suited for understanding narratives related to eutrophication in this sea. The text, *50 Sätt att Rädda Östersjön*, put together with help from the World Wildlife Fund and Stockholm Resilience Center (SRC), further illustrates how highly influential institutions interpret environmental collapse in the Baltic, namely in its introduction written by Johan Rockström, the director of the SRC. Together, these five sources illustrate alternative understandings of collapse in the context of dead zones in general as well as, more specifically, the dead zone in the Baltic Sea. Moreover, they present different formats used to discuss and describe dead zones and highlight important crosscutting themes across these formats. The selection helps reveal tensions and contradictions inherent in representing environmental collapse, especially in light of policy decisions that routinely utilize large data sets from the natural sciences to structure social, political, and cultural claims made on or about the state of natural environments (Costanza 2012; Steffen et al. 2015).

What kinds of meanings does environmental collapse assume in this context, and what changes when eutrophication is framed as collapsed or collapsing? To explore these questions, I use the selected sources along with other supporting texts from popular media and focus on how scientific evidence of decreased populations of fishery stocks is evoked to frame collapse as a cascading phenomenon but also one that threatens the status quo of an extractive and economic relationship to the sea. I also provide a glimpse into how texts negotiate oceanic "regime shifts" and show how the notion of a pending collapse invites intervention (Hare and Mantua 2000). I conclude by reflecting on the meanings that dead zones and environmental collapse invoke and argue that this discourse calls for a socio-natural interpretation that sees how such discourses may "collapse" certain environments over others.

Fish populations and fishery collapse

Fears about shifts in humans' economic relationship with the sea, though often cloaked in "ecological" terms, often underpin collapse narratives. *50 Sätt att Rädda Östersjön, Dirty Waters, Dead Zones*, and *Sea Sick* evoke collapse in the loss of economically productive fish, meaning that a reduction in these fish species promotes the growth of dead zones and thereby threatens the entire marine system. Overfishing gets represented as a typical cause or catalyst for systemic collapse, which invites the notion that one collapse precipitates another. Hence, collapse is presented as a cascade effect, implicitly linked to a food chain narrative bolstered by scientific knowledge about "trophic cascades." Sometimes, however, the reverse is articulated – dead zones threaten or cause the collapse of local fisheries. In both cases, fishery collapse symbolizes the health of the marine ecosystem while it complements and sometimes structures declensionist narratives of human livelihoods (Diaz and Rosenberg 2008; Jackson 2008; Malakoff 1998; Mee 2006; Vaquer-Sunyer and Duarte 2008). Collapse suggests a reciprocal and interdependent relationship between fish and dead zones where the desire for a balanced and healthy marine system depends heavily upon how fishery collapse causes dead zones and how dead zones cause fishery collapse.

The amount of fish that can be caught constitutes one indicator for environmental collapse. Overfishing is often pointed to as a direct threat that will lead to "a complete ecological collapse," in part due to its increasingly recognized role in inducing "regime shifts" in the oceans (Klackenberg 2015; Scheffer et al. 2001, p. 595; Worm et al. 2006). NGOs like Baltic Sea 2020 therefore argue that fishing ought to be considered an environmental issue as opposed to one that is purely economic. They point out that overfishing cod can have systemic ramifications for the entire Baltic, particularly in relation to eutrophication.[3] They do so by echoing a "cod is God" discourse and, more importantly, by situating cod within a food chain narrative (Gray et al. 2008, p. 5). When cod is gone, European sprat increases. The sprat eats up zooplankton (and cod larvae and eggs), which would normally eat aquatic plants, including algae. Algae then grow excessively, die, and decompose, consuming large amounts of oxygen in the process. The dead sea beds facilitate the growth of cyanobacteria, which add more nitrogen to the sea (Carlson and Hansson 2009). Effectively borrowing this narrative, Rockström's introduction to *50 Sätt att Rädda Östersjön* adds that when individual species are threatened, the whole ecological balance is at risk, and, before you know it, the Baltic Sea tips over a "threshold," and eutrophication becomes self-reinforcing. A biological balance of fish and minimal eutrophication is the key for keeping the sea healthy (Tell 2015, p. 15). Although framed as an ecological argument where species composition is key for a stable ecosystem, the argument is based in an economic rationale: "We are now right on the threshold of successfully restoring a rich cod population that will allow large, sustainable catches, while contributing to a 'healthier' Baltic. But it is still far too early to say the danger is over" (Carlson and Hansson 2009). Yet, the importance of fish populations can also serve an entirely different imaginary for eutrophic conditions. In *Dirty Waters*, a factory farm manager claims that his company's improved manure management program has contributed "too few nutrients," and now local fishermen have to deal with reduced fish stocks. In other words, vested interests in specific marine communities become critical for imagining sea conditions or quality. Though ecology works as a screen to mask the social, economic, historic, and political workings in these texts, the discourse still cannot escape them. The determining factor for healthy water bodies in such narratives skews toward large (sustainable) catches of fish rather than levels of eutrophication.

Framed in this way, this economic theme reflects a typical "overshoot" narrative that implicitly suggests that the depopulation of cod means environmental collapse (Middleton 2012, p. 262). However, unlike an overshoot narrative applied to social collapse that plays on Malthusian fears, this kind of overshoot narrative uses a sea-based "food chain" logic that also depends upon the amount of fish caught. Situated in this logic, this narrative suggests that the possibility for large catches of economically viable marine life constitutes a "balanced" and "sustainable" environment. The threat of losing cod is not just about the threat of a less-balanced species composition but is also an interruption to the food chain whereby the main anthropogenic food source gets replaced by algae. So, cod – the quantity that can be caught – is used as a fulcrum or as the implicit "threshold" between sustainability and collapse.[4] The potential for large catches of fish, made possible through scientifically informed policies to ensure maximum sustainable yields, becomes equivalent to a "healthy" condition. If the cod fishery collapses, so does the sea or in other words, humans' ability to extract resources from it. This theme invites people to become political and ecological allies with cod, largely to preserve the existing relationship where humans fish large amounts of cod from the sea (Haraway 2015, 2008; Michalopoulos 2016).

Even if we leave aside the implicit conundrum of befriending cod to kill it for capital gain, narratives like this that support cod can ignore or disregard other animals that thrive in their presence, not to mention other lives that may find a cod-less sea much improved. For instance, algae signal environmental collapse in the opposite way to narratives of depopulation. The unprecedented amounts of algae that precipitate dead zones do not constitute collapse to them. Unchecked growth of algae promotes a kind of collapse that favors their own evolutionary adaptations. It also favors entrepreneurs that look or have looked to algae blooms as possible revenue sources and research opportunities, such as the Swedish Algae Factory,

Algoland, Simris, Algix, and others (Gold 2009). Those who seek to incorporate algae into human diets at a large scale can shortcut this food chain
narrative, for example, by reframing an algae-infused ocean as a productive
environment. By shifting from cod as protagonist to algae, an algid food
chain narrative (with humans still at the top) can also make environmental
interventions and claims similar to those texts that utilize a land-based food
chain narrative, which emphasizes the role that terrestrial agriculture plays
in cultural eutrophication.

A land-based food chain narrative questions the implicit good of a large
haul of fish and reflects claims made by those who understand eutrophic collapse as externally rather than internally driven. This time the food chain is
not spoken of in terms of its products but rather in terms of its energy and the
waste it generates. Framed this way, the narrative depicts energy loss in the
food chain as a waste of resources (Hand 2015; Kemmerer 2014). In the film
Dirty Waters, the movie focuses on large-scale animal farms and the manure
their animals excrete, showing the viewer farms and feces in Denmark,
Poland, Belarus, and Russia. Here a narrative of meat consumption mingles
with manure and its flow to the sea, helping to solidify a key argument that
humans ought to change their dietary habits. *50 Sätt att Rädda Östersjön*
and *Dead Zones* also share this narrative. To "save" the Baltic, the non-profit
book lists seven suggestions directly related to food consumption and four
suggestions about food production, including eating less meat, eating less
fish from the Baltic Sea, eating wild animals, eating seasonally, gardening less
intensively, and others. *Dead Zones* covers agriculture impacts to the sea and
improvements to agricultural practices that reduce cultural eutrophication,
and it summarizes scientific and environmentalist reasons for converting to
vegetarian diets. All three texts highlight how a land-based food chain narrative advocates for reductions in meat consumption and vegetarianism as ways
to increase the efficiency of energy distribution of food resources as well as to
improve the conditions of the sea (Mitchell 2009; Rydén 2011; Rydén et al.
2003, pp. 32–33; Tell 2015, p. 113). Even if such actions lead to increased
fish populations, such advocacy undermines the narrative that bounteous
catches of fish equate to a "healthy" sea. Crops replace seafood and meat
products as the most reliable, energetic food source in need of attention and
defense (Hand 2015, p. 32). Yet, though sea-based and land-based food chain
narratives offer different ways of framing collapse, they both agree that food
cultures are intricately tied to the health of the environment. Both kinds of
food chain narratives report that changes in both fish and human diets can
drive ecological change through cascade effects, either by contributing to a
collapsed environment or by saving the environment from collapse.

Though overfishing – the loss of certain species – results in trophic and systemic collapse with the help of food chain narratives, sometimes dead zones
are described as collapsing the fishery. And as with overfishing, narratives
that blame dead zones for killing fish do so with an eye toward fish hauls,
especially since dead zones and algal blooms are reported to become a bigger

factor than overfishing as the greatest threat to fish stocks (Whitty 2006). In *Sea Sick*, Alanna Mitchell mentions that "studies . . . in the Baltic, Black, and Kattegat seas, show that dead zones [in these areas] have destroyed fisheries entirely or caused them to crash" (2009, p. 32). Carol Hand's *Dead Zones* mostly agrees, stating that the Baltic's fisheries have been "wiped out and have not recovered" and that the "lobster industry" in the Kattegat "has collapsed, and bottom-dwelling fish populations have been reduced" (2015, p. 45). Her book begins with anecdotes of struggling fishermen who have had to work elsewhere because of dead zones killing off fish on which the fisherman depended. The book emphasizes the agency of dead zones as well as their economic impacts on fishermen and fisheries. In response to oxygen-depleted conditions, "bottom-dwellers" such as worms, clams, and shrimp reduce reproduction rates, which decreases the amount of available food for fish, lowering catch yields. Plankton are also affected (Suikkanen et al. 2013). But sometimes dead zones do worse than that. Dead zones spur the "total devastation" of "marine species, food sources for humans and animals, and local economies" (Hand 2015, p. 67). As with overfishing, even though this narrative attempts to set aside concern for the collapse of specific species within ecological parameters, the concern usually links to species that constitute food for humans. When Lake Erie was "declared dead or dying" in the 1960s and 1970s, it was partially a result of dead zones "caus[ing] massive fish kills" (Hand 2015, p. 43). Implicitly, the effects that dead zones exert on fish illustrate that Lake Erie had died not just because the fish were dead but also because they were dead in the wrong place. That is, the disappearance of whitefish, walleye, yellow perch, and blue pike from Lake Erie entailed a disappearance from the water body as well as the fisherman's hook and chef's pan. Because any sea's past meshes with human exploitation of that sea, such narratives cannot so readily "express political resistance to modernization and colonization" as might be wished (Heise et al. 2016, p. 7). What can be inferred from this narrative is that a living, healthy environment is irrevocably tied less to living, healthy fish in the water and more to large catches of comestible fish.[5]

Describing fish loss, whether through overfishing or depletion by dead zones, this discursive theme tends to equate a healthy sea with a productive sea. Hence, it reinforces and normalizes a human-sea relationship dependent upon utilization, whether sustainable or not. However, the use of the sea is contested, and therefore, this theme also brings out implicit tensions between ecologic and economic logic, individual versus social responsibility, food systems, and land-based versus sea-based livelihoods and cultures.

Oceanic collapse: uncertain inevitabilities and thresholds

It is not just the collapse of fisheries that indicates systemic collapse; dead zones themselves also fill this function. Because eutrophication is often described as a key ecological shift in these texts, one expects to see a great deal of trepidation and tension – as well as contestation and uncertainty – regarding the state of a eutrophic water body or one that may be in process of eutrophication, especially large ones like the oceans. *Dead Zones, Sea Sick*, and *50 Sätt att Rädda Östersjön* reveal such characteristics while demonstrating various points of view regarding how much of the environment is collapsed.

Hand's *Dead Zones* focuses on nutrient pollution flowing into the sea as a result of farming and the burning of fossil fuels. Hand also references a number of experts to map out the collapsing condition of the seas. Covering problems such as decreases in marine reproduction, animal deformities, fishery collapse, pollution, climate change effects, and oil spills, Hand paints a dire picture. She quotes Ove Hoegh-Guldberg, a marine scientist with the University of Queensland, who acknowledges collapse: "We are changing the way Earth's oceans work, shifting them to entirely new states, which we have not seen before" (Hand 2015, p. 46). In its reporting style, Hand's narrative evokes a persona of the "objective" scientist, reflecting what experts can say with certainty, even as its objective aura deemphasizes the violence that a collapsing environment undergoes. Such reliance upon expert opinion reflects both certainty and uncertainty about the scale of collapse and its occurrence (Beck 2014; Egan 2015, p. 42; MacKenzie 1998). Ultimately, Hand's description of the dead zones and their relationship to collapse suggests that collapse is in process.

Mitchell's *Sea Sick* also displays the uncertainty among popular writers about whether sea eutrophication is best understood as collapsing or collapsed. She acknowledges that "scientists don't yet know the trigger points that would push the ocean into a new regime" and highlights how the long-term effects felt in the oceans is "quite speculative." She paraphrases marine biologist Nancy Rabalais's suggestion that Sweden's waters "may have developed a new, different normal, one that only lightly resembles what was there before," which acknowledges collapse but also minimizes its catastrophic aspect. Here, collapse is not so much a radical disruption as a smooth transitional change to another kind of normal. Moreover, this change appears benign as Mitchell invokes a "great, plastic, endlessly creative nature that will instinctively find a new balance when the old balance is shot," even if this "new balance" seems less desirable in comparison to the "old." At the same time that she invokes a collapsing sea, she also emphasizes that it is already collapsed. For Mitchell, a dead zone is the story of a newly initiated system wrought by humans pushing an ecological system past its limits. She describes the Herculean struggle of one scientist to net fish in the dead zone and contrasts the living seas populated with fish and dolphins with the dead zone that kills off fish, zooplankton, and one-celled organisms. She also points out that a shift in scientific knowledge follows "the switch in the ocean system" (2009, pp. 18, 26, 28–29, 33).

In *50 Sätt att Rädda Östersjön*, Rockström's introduction goes further than the previous texts, describing a collapsed sea. Resilience theory strongly influences the director of the SRC's description of the Baltic Sea. He mentions that the Baltic Sea is a site for large "thresholds," where a (eco)system changes or collapses into another regime, primarily due to the fact that Baltic seawater takes upward of thirty years to get replaced (Tell 2015, p. 14). A slow water exchange means that environmental effects can last longer in the Baltic than other water bodies. But Rockström's framing of the issue also contains a warning. By describing the threshold as large, Rockström describes a Baltic that is difficult to repair rather than one that is merely vulnerable (i.e., has a small threshold) to human-induced change. Utilizing a "large" instead of "small" threshold allows Rockström to present the Baltic Sea as collapsed or just about to collapse as opposed to a sea in decline that needs preventative measures. In some sense, describing collapse as having a large (as opposed to small) threshold allows room for hope and intervention while it also allows him to participate in a tradition of apocalyptic environmental messaging (Heise 2008, p. 133). Rather than making appeals to fear by suggesting the Baltic is vulnerable to human activities, Rockström's narrative suggests reparation is possible, even if difficult. Since the Baltic can be "saved," his declensionist narrative of ecological collapse is wedded to a message of hope that does not undercut the need to redress ecological degradation. At the same time, it also prolongs or delays collapse as a definitive moment in time.

Framing the seas as collapsing or collapsed suggests a wide range of solutions from prevention and symptomatic treatment to complete overhaul and remediation. As articulated in the editorials from *Svenska Dagbladet*, the extent to which a dead zone is envisioned as collapsing or collapsed influences the types of solutions presented and vice versa, and texts deal primarily with reducing nutrient loading and/or geoengineering dead zones back into life. *Dead Zones* surveys various solutions taken to reduce nutrient inputs and offers little by way of advocating one solution over another. If a solution is presented by the author, it is found where Hand urges that "people recognize their role in the interconnections among ecosystems and take action," so the problems with eutrophication can be solved (Hand 2015, p. 67). She defines dead zones as a global problem. There is no call for people to change, merely a mention that such a recognition is a necessary condition for dead zone rehabilitation. As a whole, Hand's focus on agricultural interventions suggests that dead zones are part of a wider oceanic context in which they represent a partial collapse of that system. When the text addresses geoengineering approaches, these solutions do not appear as part of the main narrative but as asides. Indeed, Hand cites another scientist, Daniel Conley,[6] who expresses his fears that geoengineering solutions could provoke an entire systemic collapse of the Baltic (Hand 2015, p. 55).

Nevertheless, geoengineering figures strongly in imagining solutions for eutrophication and dead zones in the Baltic Sea and elsewhere. Such schemes include dredging the sea floor, chemical sedimentation, and giant turbines that aerate deep-sea waters. The search for geoengineering solutions to eutrophication in freshwater systems is well underway and often serves as a starting point for geoengineering solutions in the seas (Lürling et al. 2016). As with the editorials from 2015 I described in the introduction to this chapter, geoengineering proponents generally align themselves with an extreme version of collapse, often precipitated by fears of worsening conditions brought on by climate change. Pointing to a geologic-sized disruptor gives added rationale for geologic scale solutions. Yet, narratives that invoke climate change and geoengineering solutions have yet to reconcile the fact that geoengineering climate change can contradict efforts to improve eutrophic conditions. In *Sea Sick* and *Dead Zones*, both authors point out how the biofuel economy attempts to mitigate climate impacts while simultaneously increasing fertilizer use, thus exacerbating eutrophic conditions (Hand 2015, p. 35; Mitchell 2009, p. 32). Mitchell also notes how algae drive the planet's carbon cycle by taking in carbon dioxide and releasing oxygen. However, she then focuses on what a warming climate will do to algae rather than geoengineering efforts to promote algae growth in the seas.[7] Since growing algae contradicts goals for reducing eutrophication in coastal waters, climate change in these narratives remains a one-sided force that will worsen eutrophic conditions. By discussing algae blooms not algae, this catastrophic collapse narrative eschews a parallel narrative where algae can survive climate change and could mitigate its impacts (Greene et al. 2017; Schlüter et al. 2014).

At first glance, in *50 Sätt att Rädda Östersjön*, the solutions that Rockström's introduction provides do not appear to be geologic either; the solutions are meant to be implemented by the book's readers. Yet, as representative of an imagination that evokes a collapsed sea, this text also smacks of an affinity for geoengineering solutions. If the text is read in this way, Rockström potentially reveals his imagination of the Baltic as collapsed when he says that the solutions to the eutrophication problem actually depend upon bad weather and local pressure on businesses and politicians to act (Tell 2015, pp. 14–16).[8] In other words, natural forces must accompany political interference to save the Baltic rather than individual actions. However, if we take seriously claims made within the Anthropocene discourse, namely that humans are now natural (geological) forces, how Rockström frames the book's solutions becomes more interesting (Crist 2013; Crutzen and Schwägerl 2011). What might be interpreted as simply another ineffective call to individuals to solve global problems can actually be understood as an attempt to sociogeoengineer the Baltic problem by linking the message of individual action to the 90 million inhabitants of the Baltic catchment basin and a global "we," that is all of humanity (Adamson 2016, p. 155; Heise 2008, p. 37; Tell 2015, pp. 15–16). What connects all of humankind in this effort, as he says, is not the water but a warming climate, implying that a reduction in CO_2 emissions would help resolve environmental collapse of the seas. Moreover, in the context of the Anthropocene, a planetary-wide sociological intervention reflects geoengineering aims and its scale. Regardless of the book's actual impact,[9] this appeal to a global society represents how social scientists and humanists concerned with the environment at global scales may find notions of collapsed rather than collapsing environments more favorable. Nevertheless, that geo-engineering is mentioned in many articles about dead zones but still treated cursorily in my sources illustrates that geoengineering has not yet reached a mainstream order of attention in this discourse.

Conclusion

In collapse discourse, information from natural science influences narratives in popular media to negotiate the extent a dead zone and the sea in which it is found are collapsing or collapsed. Such interplay leads to a great deal of uncertainty around collapse and what it means. The five texts I have presented rarely claim that the environment is collapsed even if eutrophication from a scientific perspective suggests systemic collapse. Nevertheless, these texts still narrate environmental collapse, invoking the collapse of fisheries, negotiating positions of proximity to collapse within a broader environmental context, and presenting a wide range of solutions that reflect claims made about the status of the seas.

Narratives about fisheries and dead zones illustrate that whatever marine conditions produce desirable, copious amounts of economically valuable fish constitute a "healthy" sea. This theme rests upon an economic logic, but this logic is supported by both ecologic and culinary concerns. Collapse of the seas relies upon the amount of fish in the sea, the amount of fish that can be caught, the economic productivity of the catch, and how the catch satisfies human appetites. Utilizing a marine-based food chain in this narrative attempts to safeguard human access to a culinary culture of seafood that relies upon top predatory fish as the primary source of food for humans while a counter-narrative that relies on algae challenges this perspective. In addition, eating algae instead of fish mirrors land-based food chain narratives driven by notions of energy budgets, which seek to save the sea from collapse by eating less meat. In these narratives, changes in animal and human eating habits have the power to drive collapse or stop it in its tracks.

Texts dealing with eutrophic collapse also negotiate to what extent the sea is already collapsed or not. In other words, they negotiate both the time-scales of collapse and the extent of collapse. This difference influences a text's privileging of some solutions over others, and the favored solutions generally match the perspective on collapse – the dominant paradigms consisting of preventative measures and engineering solutions. Because current remediation practices are mostly focused on reducing external nutrient loads from agriculture to coastal waters, one may see how those who favor geoengineering approaches might have greater cause to support stronger narratives of collapse. Yet, due to their planetary scale, geoengineering solutions, in particular, represent added fears about the precariousness of seas and their eutrophic environments.

As a result, we get a glimpse of how narratives of eutrophic collapse materialize into struggles, often political, about what relationships are most powerful and in what ways environments, including the human, are pitted for, with, or against each other. Contestations about the reality of environmental collapse often hinge upon what collapse means and for whom. In this case, by looking into texts on dead zones and eutrophication, we can better understand how collapse is socially and culturally constructed even in the case of ecosystems and environments. Such work can show us how certain environments and species get narrated as collapsed while others do not and how these stories might affect human and non-human communities and their relationships to the seas and oceans differently (Hale et al. 2015).

Notes

1 In their article, they argue that geoengineering approaches – specifically chemical sedimentation – represent "irreparable encroachment" and ecosystem collapse (Gustafsson et al. 2015).
2 The Baltic is a shallow, brackish sea that was once a lake. Its natural history and geographical features place it between that of a lake (or freshwater sea) and ocean.
3 Researchers have shown that the presence of top predatory fish, namely perch and pike, affect the scale of macro algae blooms (Eriksson et al. 2009).
4 In this case, being able to effectively monitor cod provides another strong rationale to leave the proper identification of thresholds to natural scientists.
5 Hand acknowledges that a dead zone's impact on marine food sources can be double-sided, that it can be a disaster or a welcomed event. Since her example stems from Marina Del Rey, California, and Mobile, Alabama, respectively, understanding the difference from an environmental justice angle might be elucidating (Dybas 2005; Hand 2015, pp. 8–9).
6 Daniel Conley is one of the authors who advocated for land-based solutions in the editorial that appeared in *Svenska Dagbladet*.
7 In the last decade, for example, private businesses have sought to "seed" the oceans with iron in order to *increase* the amount of plankton in the sea, "greenwashing" their efforts as developing a carbon sequestration source and a more abundant food supply to increase fish stocks (Courtland 2008; McKnight 2013; Moore 2012; "Planktos–Seeding the ocean to capture carbon" n.d.). Of these endeavors, the most recent controversy surrounds a fertilization project off the coast of Chile (Tollefson 2017).
8 Both skeptics and proponents of geoengineering mention that eutrophication solutions may depend on hurricane-strength forces.
9 Being in Swedish, the book's audience is more limited than if it were published in English.

References

Adamson, J., 2016. We have never been anthropos. *Environ. Humanit. Voices Anthr.* 155.
Alaimo, S., 2016. *Exposed: Environmental politics and pleasures in posthuman times*. University of Minnesota Press, Minneapolis.
Angus, I., 2013. The myth of 'environmental catastrophism'. *Mon. Rev.* 64, 15–28.

Bachelard, G., 1983. *Water and dreams: An essay on the imagination of matter.* Pegasus Foundation, Dallas.

Beck, U., 2014. Risk society, in: Morin, J.-F., Orsini, A. (Eds.), *Essential concepts of global environmental governance.* Routledge, Abingdon, UK, pp. 178–179.

Bianchi, T.S., Engelhaupt, E., Westman, P., Andren, T., Rolff, C., Elmgren, R., 2000. Cyanobacterial blooms in the Baltic Sea: Natural or human-induced? *Limnol. Oceanogr.* 45, 716–726.

Carlson, B., Hansson, S., 2009. Irresponsible to approve cod fishing in the Baltic [WWW Document]. *BalticSea2020.* URL http://balticsea2020.org/english/press-room/85-irresponsible-to-approve-cod-fishing-in-the-baltic (accessed 7.28.17).

Costanza, R., 2012. Ecosystem health and ecological engineering. *Ecol. Eng.* 45, 24–29. doi:10.1016/j.ecoleng.2012.03.023

Courtland, R., 2008. Planktos dead in the water. *Nat. News.* doi:10.1038/news.2008.604. URL www.nature.com/news/2008/080215/full/news.2008.604.html.

Crist, E., 2013. On the poverty of our nomenclature. *Environ. Humanit.* 3, 129–147.

Crutzen, P.J., Schwägerl, C., 2011. Living in the Anthropocene: Toward a new global ethos. *Yale Environ.* 360.

DeLoughrey, E., 2009. Radiation ecologies and the wars of light. *MFS Mod. Fict. Stud.* 55, 468–498.

DeLoughrey, E.M., Didur, J., Carrigan, A. (Eds.), 2016. *Global ecologies and the environmental humanities: Postcolonial approaches,* Issued in paperback. Routledge interdisciplinary perspectives on literature. Routledge, New York, NY; London.

Diamond, J., 2011. *Collapse: How societies choose to fail or succeed.* Penguin, London.

Diaz, R.J., Rosenberg, R., 2008. Spreading dead zones and consequences for marine ecosystems. *Science* 321, 926–929. doi:10.1126/science.1156401

Dybas, C.L., 2005. Dead zones spreading in world oceans. *BioScience* 55, 552–557. doi:10.1641/0006-3568(2005)055[0552:DZSIWO]2.0.CO;2

Egan, M., 2015. Confronting collapse: Environmental science at the end of the world, in: B. Hale, C. Kueffer, S. Steinert-Borella, and C. Wiedmer, (Eds.) *Environmental justice, 'collapse' and the question of evidence. Intervalla* 3, 36–43.

Eriksson, B.K., Ljunggren, L., Sandström, A., Johansson, G., Mattila, J., Rubach, A., Råberg, S., Snickars, M., 2009. Declines in predatory fish promote bloom-forming macroalgae. *Ecol. Appl.* 19, 1975–1988.

Glasgow, R.D., 2009. *The concept of water.* RDV Glasgow.

Gold, R., 2009. Entrepreneurs wade into the 'Dead Zone.' *Wall Street Journal.* August 12. URL www.wsj.com/articles/SB125003834803724511.

Gray, T., Hatchard, J., Daw, T., Stead, S., 2008. New cod war of words: 'Cod is God' versus 'sod the cod': Two opposed discourses on the North Sea Cod Recovery Programme. *Fish. Res.* 93, 1–7. doi:10.1016/j.fishres.2008.04.009

Greene, C.H., Huntley, M.E., Archibald, I., Gerber, L.N., Sills, D.L., Granados, J., Beal, C.M., Walsh, M.J., 2017. Geoengineering, marine microalgae, and climate stabilization in the 21st century. *Earth's Future* 5, 278–284. doi:10.1002/2016EF000486

Gustafsson, B., Humborg, C., Elfwing, T., Bonsdorff, E., Norkko, A., Carstensen, J., Conley, D., Gladh, L., Andersson, H., 2015. Det finns ingen mirakelmedicin för Östersjön. *Svenska Dagbladet.* September 1. URL www.svd.se/det-finns-ingen-mirakelmedicin-for-ostersjon.

Hale, B., Kueffer, C., Steinert-Borella, S., Wiedmer, C. (Eds.), 2015. Environmental justice, 'collapse' and the question of evidence. *Intervalla 3*.

Hand, C., 2015. *Dead zones: Why Earth's waters are losing oxygen*. Twenty First Century Books, Minneapolis.

Haraway, D., 2008. *When species meet*. University of Minnesota Press, Minneapolis.

Haraway, D., 2015. Anthropocene, Capitalocene, Plantationocene, Chthulucene: Making Kin. *Environ. Hum.* 6, 159–165.

Hare, S.R., Mantua, N.J., 2000. Empirical evidence for North Pacific regime shifts in 1977 and 1989. *Prog. Oceanogr.* 47, 103–145. doi:10.1016/S0079–6611 (00)00033–1

Heise, U.K., 2008. *Sense of place and sense of planet: The environmental imagination of the global*. Oxford University Press, Oxford; New York.

Heise, U.K., Christensen, J., Niemann, M. (Eds.), 2016. *The Routledge companion to the environmental humanities*. Routledge, Abingdon, Oxon; New York, NY.

Illich, I., 2000. *H2O and the waters of forgetfulness: Reflections on the historicity of "stuff"*. Marion Boyars Publishers Ltd., London.

Jackson, J.B.C., 2008. Ecological extinction and evolution in the brave new ocean. *Proc. Natl. Acad. Sci.* 105, 11458–11465. doi:10.1073/pnas.0802812105

Kemmerer, L., 2014. *Eating Earth: Environmental ethics and dietary choice*. Oxford University Press, Oxford.

Klackenberg, J., 2015. Algae entrepreneur from KTH named Wired fellow. *KTH News Events*. August 28. URL www.kth.se/en/aktuellt/nyheter/algbonde-med-potential-att-forandra-varlden-1.587142.

Lürling, M., Mackay, E., Reitzel, K., Spears, B.M. (Eds.), 2016. Special issue on Geo-engineering to manage eutrophication in lakes. *Water Res.* 97, IFC. doi:10.1016/S0043–1354(16)30271–8

MacKenzie, D., 1998. The certainty trough, in: Fleck, J., Faulkner, W., Williams, R. (Eds.), *Exploring expertise: Issues and perspectives*. Palgrave Macmillan, London, pp. 325–329. doi:10.1007/978-1-349-13693-3_15

Malakoff, D., 1998. Death by suffocation in the Gulf of Mexico. *Science* 281, 190–192. doi:10.1126/science.281.5374.190

McAnany, P.A., Yoffee, N. (Eds.), 2009. *Questioning collapse: Human resilience, ecological vulnerability, and the aftermath of empire*, First edition. Cambridge University Press, Cambridge; New York.

McKnight, Z., 2013. B.C. company at centre of iron dumping scandal stands by its convictions [WWW Document]. *Vancouver Sun*. URL www.vancouversun.com/technology/company+centre+iron+dumping+scandal+stands+convictions/8860731/story.html (accessed 8.2.17).

Mee, L., 2006. Reviving dead zones. *Sci. Am.* 295, 78–85. doi:10.1038/scientificamerican1106–78

Michalopoulos, S., 2016. Commission accused over Baltic cod fishing limits. *euractiv.com*.

Middleton, G.D., 2012. Nothing lasts forever: Environmental discourses on the collapse of past societies. *J. Archaeol. Res.* 20, 257–307. doi:10.1007/s10814-011-9054-1

Mitchell, A., 2009. *Sea sick: Ocean change and the extinction of life on Earth*, First edition. University of Chicago Press, Chicago.

Moore, D., 2012. Greatest risk of ocean experiment is that it will spawn more [WWW Document]. *Geoengin. Monit.* URL www.geoengineeringmonitor.org/2012/10/greatest-risk-of-ocean-experiment-is-that-it-will-spawn-more/ (accessed 8.2.17).

Nixon, R., 2011. *Slow violence and the environmentalism of the poor*. Harvard University Press, Cambridge, MA.

Planktos–Seeding the ocean to capture carbon [WWW Document], n.d. *Planktos Ecosyst*. URL www.planktos.com/ (accessed 8.1.17).

Rydén, F., 2011. *Dirty Waters*. Folke Rydén Production.

Rydén, L., Migula, P., Andersson, M. (Eds.), 2003. *Environmental science: Understanding, protecting, and managing the environment in the Baltic Sea region*. Baltic University Press, Uppsala.

Scheffer, M., Carpenter, S., Foley, J.A., Folke, C., Walker, B., 2001. Catastrophic shifts in ecosystems. *Nature* 413, 591.

Schindler, D.W., Vallentyne, J.R., 2008. *The algal bowl: Overfertilization of the world's freshwaters and estuaries*, Revised edition. Earthscan, London.

Schlüter, L., Lohbeck, K.T., Gutowska, M.A., Gröger, J.P., Riebesell, U., Reusch, T.B.H., 2014. Adaptation of a globally important coccolithophore to ocean warming and acidification. *Nat. Clim. Change* 4, 1024–1030. doi:10.1038/nclimate2379

Shubin, N., 2009. *Your inner fish: A journey into the 3.5-billion-year history of the human body*, First Reprint edition. Vintage, New York.

Steffen, W., Richardson, K., Rockström, J., Cornell, S.E., Fetzer, I., Bennett, E.M., Biggs, R., Carpenter, S.R., de Vries, W., de Wit, C.A., Folke, C., Gerten, D., Heinke, J., Mace, G.M., Persson, L.M., Ramanathan, V., Reyers, B., Sorlin, S., 2015. Planetary boundaries: Guiding human development on a changing planet. *Science* 347, 1259855–1259855. doi:10.1126/science.1259855

Stigebrandt, A., Simonsson, B., Blomqvist, S., 2015. Ny kunskap om övergödning ignoreras. *Svenska Dagsbladet*.

Suikkanen, S., Pulina, S., Engström-Öst, J., Lehtiniemi, M., Lehtinen, S., Brutemark, A., 2013. Climate change and eutrophication induced shifts in northern summer plankton communities. *PLoS One* 8, e66475. doi:10.1371/journal.pone.0066475

Tell, J., 2015. *50 sätt att rädda Östersjön*. Max Ström.

Tollefson, J., 2017. Iron-dumping ocean experiment sparks controversy. *Nat. News* 545, 393. doi:10.1038/545393a

Vaquer-Sunyer, R., Duarte, C.M., 2008. Thresholds of hypoxia for marine biodiversity. *Proc. Natl. Acad. Sci.* 105, 15452–15457. doi:10.1073/pnas.0803833105

Walker, B., Salt, D., 2006. *Resilience thinking: Sustaining ecosystems and people in a changing world*, First edition. Island Press, Washington, DC.

Wassmann, P., 2005. Cultural eutrophication: Perspectives and prospects, in: Wassmann, P., Olli, K. (Eds.), *Drainage basin nutrient inputs and eutrophication: An integrated approach*. University of Tromsø, Norway.

Whitty, J., 2006. The fate of the ocean. *Mother Jones*. March/April. URL www.motherjones.com/politics/2006/03/fate-ocean/

Worm, B., Barbier, E.B., Beaumont, N., Duffy, J.E., Folke, C., Halpern, B.S., Jackson, J.B.C., Lotze, H.K., Micheli, F., Palumbi, S.R., Sala, E., Selkoe, K.A., Stachowicz, J.J., Watson, R., 2006. Impacts of biodiversity loss on ocean ecosystem services. *Science* 314, 787–790. doi:10.1126/science.1132294

Yang, X., Wu, X., Hao, H., He, Z., 2008. Mechanisms and assessment of water eutrophication. *J. Zhejiang Univ. Sci. B* 9, 197–209. doi:10.1631/jzus.B0710626

Zillén, L., Conley, D.J., 2010. Hypoxia and cyanobacteria blooms–are they really natural features of the late Holocene history of the Baltic Sea? *Biogeosciences* 7, 2567–2580. doi:10.5194/bg-7-2567-2010

3 Can photojournalism steer clear of the siren song of collapse?

Joanna Nurmis

Few things are as photogenic as a landscape of collapse. Photographs of cracking ice shelves, eroding coastlines, and billowing wildfires dwarfing miniscule firemen, taken by expert photographers who know how to balance a shot and use light conditions to produce a visually stunning image, often provoke a strong and emotional viewer response. These are the images photo editors and readers alike refer to as "compelling," "haunting," "spectacular," and "disturbingly beautiful." This chapter explores the tendencies for photojournalism to indulge in publicizing images of collapse – either impending or recently occurred – and the implications of such images in the context of reporting on climate change.

Journalistic coverage of climate change is of primary importance in building constructive public engagement (Boykoff and Rajan 2007). Journalism both sets the agenda – deciding which environmental problems are worth paying attention to – and elaborates ways to collectively respond to these problems on the individual and societal level (Luedecke and Boykoff 2017). While journalists work for corporations and may be influenced by shareholders or interest groups, they are also different from policymakers, who represent the government, corporations, whose principal motive is profit, and environmental activists, who often risk "preaching to the choir." Schudson (2013) offers a comprehensive set of six functions journalists fulfill: (1) provide fair and full information on matters of public importance, (2) serve as a watchdog to keep government power in check, (3) analyze and interpret complex issues, (4) build bridges and empathy between people, (5) serve as a public forum for dialogue and the exchange of ideas, and (6) mobilize people in support of particular programs conducive to the public good. Accepting these functions as an underlying framework for understanding the role of the media in communicating climate change means that journalists' responsibility, while different from that of activists or policymakers, goes beyond offering a panel of diverging views on climate change, or even merely presenting the scientific facts of climate change in layman's terms. It means raising awareness of a critical issue that is threatening the public good and that must be acted upon urgently.

Photojournalism can potentially lead to the rich form of engagement needed, as it can communicate both on the cognitive and the emotional level, perhaps more straightforwardly than other media. There are three main reasons for this. First, the human brain has two distinct ways of processing information: the slower one is analytical; it relies on reasoning and linking together abstract concepts, and the quicker, more immediate one is experiential; it interprets new information in accordance with past emotions and memories (Slovic et al. 2004; Marx et al. 2007). Columbia University's Center for Research on Environmental Decisions notes that in climate change communication, it is important to target the experiential information processing system in addition to the analytic one, traditionally more often used: "despite evidence from the social sciences that the experiential processing system is the stronger motivator for action, most climate change communication remains geared toward the analytic processing system" (Shome et al. 2009, p. 16). Visual information, and photographs in particular, are more likely than words to be processed experientially (Williams 2005). In addition, photographs have two main attributes defining their specific way of communicating a news story: (1) they appear more trustworthy than other media because of their indexicality, which means they are an actual "trace" of the object they represent; and (2) they lack propositional syntax (Messaris and Abraham 2001), which means they have suggestive power without the need to spell anything out. Last, photographs are exceptionally memorable. A photograph, commonly referred to as a "freeze frame" or a "snapshot," offers an encounter with an "eternal now" – a moment perhaps even more brief than human perception can acknowledge, a moment that can be experienced by the senses thanks only to its preservation in the photographic format. In other words, "photography interrupts time" (Hirsch 2002). The eternal "now" of the photograph collapses the past and future development of an ongoing process, like climate change, into an instant. While photography's role as bearer of objective truth has certainly been criticized and scrutinized (Ritchin 2009), especially since the proliferation of digital cameras, it is also indisputable that photojournalism can move the public toward specific policy preferences or taking organized action (Perlmutter 1998).

Despite photography's advantages as a medium uniquely posed to activate engagement, there are significant hurdles to communicating anthropogenic climate change using photography. Other environmental issues share this challenge: neither the causes nor the direct effects can easily be photographed – we can't see CO_2 on a photograph, and we can't see rising temperatures. Climate change adds another layer of complexity: the disparity in time and space. The time disparity is known as climate lag: it takes 25 to 50 years between a rise in emissions and the corresponding warming to take effect (Hansen et al. 2005). The spatial disparity occurs because places that cause heavy emissions do not necessarily suffer the consequences, while remote developing countries with near zero emissions per capita find themselves literally on the verge of drowning as a result of rising sea levels. These disparities make climate change an especially challenging subject for a photojournalist to tackle. On the other hand, climate change, not just an environmental problem, encompasses many domains of societal life. A climate change photograph, which can be a photograph of either climate change causes, impacts, or solutions, can depict anything from a person enjoying their steak, to factories emitting smoke, to extreme weather events, to politicians negotiating, to solar panels or wind turbines, to billionaires who fund climate change denial.

In reality, most climate change photographs focus on the adverse effects of climate change that have already been documented. This limited focus might pose a problem for constructive public engagement with the issue. If the primary image of climate change that comes to people's minds is a melting glacier or beachfront houses destroyed by a superstorm, the entire concept of climate change will tend to be past-oriented rather than future-oriented. And one cannot change the past. Such images, while important in communicating the evidence of climate change, perpetuate the notion that losses are already underway and action is futile (Doyle 2009).

Environmental photojournalism, and more broadly, visual communication of the environment in the news, has been criticized as either too pastoral or too catastrophist (Hansen and Machin 2008; Cottle 2009a, b), with not much in between. What is more, many environmental images circulated by the media are highly decontextualized and symbolic, akin to stock photography rather than documentary journalism. Another line of criticism sees environmental images as valuable in setting environmental problems on the public agenda, but notes that often these images stop at encouraging a narrow, consumerist approach to resolving those problems, like buying "green" products or recycling (Dunaway 2015). More specifically, with regard to images of climate change, Walsh (2015) analyzed climate change graphics (including photographs) used by scientists and activists. She showed that they often contain fear appeals and present the challenge of climate change as being above all a distant, complex problem of global dimensions, which makes it seem overly abstract and overwhelming. She concludes that such images lead the public to believe "that climate operates only at a superhuman scale and that climate scientists and agencies occupy elite political positions" (Walsh 2015, p. 366), with regular individuals freed of any responsibility to rethink their way of life or their actions.

Some climate change news photographs relate elegiacally to the past, as if telling the viewer: here is what will soon be lost forever (Jackson 2015). The most typical image of this kind is the sublime image of a receding glacier, or that of a lone polar bear uncertainly staring into the distance (Manzo 2010). Another strand draws attention to the future, even though, as with any photograph, it shows something that occurred in the past. Future-oriented climate change imagery can either depict dire consequences of climate change on human settlements, or renewable energies and lifestyle changes that can be called solutions to climate change. Both types of images say: "This is happening somewhere else, but it could happen here. This will be (or could be) your future, too." It matters whether such images then go on to say: "Collapse is coming" or "Collapse is probably inevitable, unless you act fast."

How can we move beyond collapse?

The 2016 Paris Climate Agreement, while hailed as a major achievement in international climate negotiations, has virtually no chance of preventing the 2 degree warming which climate scientists agree is a threshold beyond which dangerous impacts will be experienced. Even if the Paris Climate Accord were signed and ratified by all countries, and its provisions carried out, scientists warn that dangerous warming beyond 2 degrees will inevitably occur by 2050 (Watson et al. 2015, p. 8; Schiermeier 2015). As a result, measurable degradation of human living conditions, to say nothing of non-human animal habitats, may follow within the current century: sea level rising up to half a meter, multiple crop failures, increased heat waves, drought and flooding in many regions (IPCC 2014, pp. 10–16). Moreover, because we only have a limited understanding of feedback loops and tipping points, a total collapse of important climate elements, such as the Atlantic thermohaline circulation, cannot be ruled out (Crowther et al. 2016; Hamilton 2010; Barnosky and Hadly 2016; Lenton et al. 2008). If a tipping point is crossed, this could lead to abrupt sea level rise that would threaten many coastal cities.

Considering that disastrous climate change is becoming more and more probable, scientists and activists alike have puzzled over the relative inaction on the part of the public and policymakers (Whitmarsh et al. 2011). Despite clear factual evidence of anthropogenic climate change, coupled with the well-known damaging consequences that can be expected within our lifetime, only 48 percent of Americans believe it exists (Funk and Kennedy 2016).

Over a decade ago, Leiserowitz (2006) deplored the lack of engaging images of climate change in the media: "most Americans lacked vivid, concrete, and personally-relevant affective images of climate change, which helps explain why climate change remains a relatively low priority national or environmental issue" (Leiserowitz 2006, p. 55). Around the same time, longtime climate activist and founder of the climate mitigation non-profit, 350.org, Bill McKibben, issued a passionate plea for the emergence of visual climate change art, to help stir imaginations and consciences, and attune them to the gravity of climate change (McKibben 2005). It is fair to say that the past decade of media images, including not just news images but also film, literature, and art, have transformed the visual landscape of climate change. Instead of merely being shown/conceived of as a distant threat to non-human animals and uninhabited landscapes, the threat has been identified as lurking close to Western viewers' homes. The images of Hurricane Sandy's climate refugees and of people made homeless by untamed wildfires in California make the visual case that climate change has "arrived." The connection between extreme weather events and climate change is now made more and more clear by media reports (Placky et al. 2016). Yet, even among those who are profoundly alarmed by the reality of anthropogenic climate change, only about a third have taken any concrete action in the public sphere, like contacting their representatives or signing a petition (Roser-Renouf et al. 2016).

The following analysis of the current climate change iconography in photojournalistic practice and its entanglement with collapse imagery will hopefully yield insight into possible alternatives for climate change photojournalism.

Current photographic coverage of climate change

Metag et al. (2016) recently offered a sweeping meta-analysis of the available literature on currently prevailing photographic depictions of climate change in mainstream media. They showed that three categories of images are most prevalent: (1) photographs showing devastating climate impacts, whether on natural landscapes or human settlements, (2) pictures of talking heads, be it politicians, protesters, or celebrities, and (3) photographs related to energy – whether fossil fuels and the pollution associated with them or renewable energies like wind and solar. This broad categorization of available image themes is based on a decade of research into visual communication of climate change (Rebich-Hespanha et al. 2015; O'Neill and Smith 2014; Rüegg 2015; O'Neill et al. 2013; DiFrancesco and Young 2011; Manzo 2010, and others). Overall, the authors conclude that "visual representations of climate change focus on people and nature being threatened by the impacts of climate change" (Metag et al. 2016, p. 205). They find that the visual representations of climate change in news reporting are rather consistent over time and across geographic boundaries, with a growing tendency to show local impacts, as those are more relevant to local audiences. Another large-scale content analysis of climate change images conducted by Rebich-Hespanha et al. (2015) identified image themes that are missing in climate depictions. One important omission is the individual's role in contributing to climate change. Another is a relative lack of images of positive energy futures. Last, rarely do media show pictures of "bad actors," usually powerful players in industry or politics whose agenda can be summed up in three words: "business as usual." These "gaps" in the imagery have significant consequences, considering what studies on reception of climate images have shown.

A study of the images of climate change circulating in the media is only instructive if we also examine the way audiences read such images. Rare, but important studies on how audience members respond to actual climate change images have been conducted, often using the innovative Q-method (O'Neill and Nicholson-Cole 2009; O'Neill et al. 2013; Metag et al. 2016; Hart and Feldman 2016), asking participants to sort a set of commonly employed images according to two distinct instructions: first, based on how salient they make the issue of climate change, and second, based on how they affect the respondent's self-efficacy, or perception of being able to do something to tackle climate change. The overarching conclusion from these important studies is that images of devastating impacts increase feelings of salience (issue importance), but often leave people feeling helpless and disengaged (O'Neill and Nicholson-Cole 2009; O'Neill et al. 2013). Such images, while often spectacular to behold, "make climate change appear as an overwhelming, forceful natural development, and participants think that they, as individuals, are helpless and cannot do anything to stop it" (Metag et al. 2016, p. 219). On the other hand, images of positive energy futures do make people feel like they can do more. Yet, spectacular, fear-inducing images are used more often than those that increase self-efficiency (Metag et al. 2016).

In analyzing a handful of images that are representative of both past-oriented and future-oriented collapse, I hope to shed light on the practical implications of such a representation of climate change as a challenge facing society. In some cases, I will include text surrounding the image (such as headlines and captions) into the analysis. Indeed, most often, pictures and words work together to produce a signifying media text, and should not be artificially separated in a close reading (Boomgaarden et al. 2016; Horn 1999).

Past-oriented climate change images: pretty pictures of things we've lost

It may be a truism to state that every photograph is a photograph of the past. While that may be true, some photographs emphasize that quality more strikingly by showing something that either no longer exists or is soon to disappear. Some climate change photographs are particularly adept at tapping into this "inherently elegiac" (Hirsch 2002) nature of photography, framing the past as an unattainable, pure, and idyllic state lost forever as a result of climate change. This is most often the case with images related to ice – whether it be receding glaciers, or photographs of Antarctica, or polar bears in the Arctic literally losing ground as ice floes grow few and far between.

The cover of *Time* magazine from April 3, 2006, is a case in point: the cover depicts a lone polar bear solemnly and carefully marching toward an artificially darkened edge of the photo. Similar images of lone polar bears on thin ice have surfaced in almost every media outlet reporting on climate change – for example, in the May 15, 2008, edition of *The New York Times*, a photograph of a lone polar bear in striking golden sunlight by Subhankar Banerjee was accompanied by the headline "Polar Bear Gains Protection as Threatened Species." The *Time* cover is a photo illustration; in other words, the photograph is heavily edited by digital darkroom lighting modification, placing a spotlight on the bear and making the rest of the image ominously dark. The words "Be worried. Be very worried" written in capital letters to the left of the picture conjure up feelings of fear and apprehension. One of the subtitles on that cover, "Earth at the tipping point," refers directly to the possibility of global environmental collapse induced by climate change. The *Time* cover is noteworthy in that the bear is facing the side of the cover that is completely darkened, moving towards a disappearing future. In addition, although the words on the cover also mention how climate change will affect "your kids and their kids as well," this image could not be further removed from such associations. As with other popular climate-change pictures of polar bears, this one is portrayed in complete isolation. Such a portrayal "draws attention to the precariousness of their situation, thus heightening the viewers' sense of the animals' vulnerability to danger and threat" (Manzo 2010, p. 198). If any climate change icon exists, signaling the issue to people without any further explanation, it may well be the image of a polar bear (Manzo 2010).

Another visual trope of climate change-induced collapse is the image of disappearing ice. Such images can be spotted on many newspaper front pages. A recent example is *The New York Times* front page of October 28, 2015, featuring a four-column wide photograph by Josh Haner of a river running through the Greenland ice sheet. The image, taken by drone, is monumentally beautiful, with stark lines and eerie white-blue-green hues. The adjoining headline reads: "A Close-Up Look at Greenland, Melting Away." Doyle's (2007) critique of one type of image often appearing in the media is noteworthy. This image hovers between the temporalities of past and present: like a haunting reversal of the "before and after" TV make-overs, it shows a process of destruction unfolding, with the headline's present continuous use "is melting" even emphasizing this fleeting co-presence of both the past (ice) and the future (water). A more explicit composite before and after image was featured on the front page of *The Washington Post* on November 27, 2015. It shows on the left, a 1920 photograph of Grinnell Glacier in Glacier National Park, Montana, and on the right, the same spot in 2008. Predictably, there is significantly less glacier in the shot on the right. A very similar story ran in the November 23, 2014, edition of *The New York Times*, with a photograph featuring a geologist posing in front of a glacier while holding a tablet in his hand displaying the state of that glacier in 1928.

According to Doyle, "[T]he photographs of a changed landscape due to global warming worryingly position the viewer as looking onto a landscape before climate change and after" (Doyle 2009, p. 290). In other words, the risk of such pairings is that it promotes a reading in which climate change has "already happened," which "renders redundant the potential for present and further preventative action" (Doyle 2009, p. 291). The use of melting ice imagery can also be a form of visual "climate reductionism," defined by Mike Hulme as an intellectual tendency to "privilege climate as the chief determinant of humanity's putative social futures" (Hulme 2011, p. 264). He warns of adopting this narrative of "climate-driven destiny" according to which "the human hand of climate change has replaced the divine hand of God as being responsible for the collapse of civilizations" (Hulme 2011, p. 248). In such a view, humans can merely watch the climate catastrophe unfold, "passively awaiting their climate fate" (Hulme 2011, p. 256). In the context of a global problem of many hands such as climate change, where it is easy to fall prey to the belief that individual action is meaningless (O'Neill and Nicholson-Cole 2009, p. 371), climate reductionism is especially risky.

Future-oriented scenes of collapse: this catastrophe will be your future, too

While some images show elements of nature under threat of destruction, such as the polar bear who may become extinct, others show the direct results of such destruction, be it on natural environments or human settlements. These images are "harbingers" of collapse (Manzo 2010), as their connotative meaning invariably refers to the possibility of whatever dire catastrophe they depict in one part of the world spreading to other parts of the world. Such images prefigure collapse approaching the viewer. It is as if suddenly images coming from developing countries no longer show the past (what life was like before capitalist economic development), but perhaps prefigure the future even developed countries should brace for. Janet Fiskio (2012) notes that such images reinforce the "lifeboat" narrative of global climate change, a social Darwinist approach to the end of civilization in which resources will shrink and only few will survive. The "lifeboat" narrative is what leads countries to delay decisive action in curbing emissions, since it is in their short-term interest not to reduce emissions, even if the long-term interest of all involved is drastic reduction. Responding to climate change becomes a classic case of the prisoner's dilemma, as explained by Stephen Gardiner (2006). Indeed, at an individual level it may be in every nation's interest to continue business as usual, but collectively, this will lead to high levels of warming and impact everyone adversely. Another risk inherent in images of destruction and mayhem inflicted by climate change related causes is that their aesthetic mode fits into a series of events in deep history that were not of our making – as Costello et al. (2011) aptly observe: previous mass extinctions were all caused by "a combination of plate tectonics, supervolcanism and asteroid impacts" (Costello et al. 2011, p. 1868). The cataclysm that could occur if climate change is not halted or at least slowed, on the other hand, is a cumulative result of each and every one of our everyday actions.

We know that a better-informed public does not necessarily result in a public that believes in climate change; on the contrary, ideology and pre-existing beliefs are likely more influential than scientific knowledge. For example, in one recent study, the Pew Research Center found that the level of scientific knowledge about climate change had no effect on the belief in anthropogenic climate change among Republicans in the United States (Funk and Kennedy 2016). Since most of us live in controlled environments in which all goes well, the sun shines and the birds sing, photographs of climate change impacts may serve to raise awareness of what is going on behind the curtain of our curated, user-friendly environment. The philosopher Slavoj Žižek claims that "it is our roots in the natural environment that prevent us from taking seriously things that we already know: that all this normal life we see around us can disappear" (Žižek 2010, p. 161). Photojournalism that concretely shows the dire effects of climate change on human settlements may prove to be instrumental in bridging the gap between knowledge and belief that Žižek and others have identified (Morris and Sayler 2014). Photographs depicting human, relatable climate change victims, may serve as one useful tactic in committing publics to action. Such photographs, according to Nixon (2011), are instrumental in collapsing the threat of climate change, a threat often perceived as distant both in time and in place. Photographers and photo editors hope that viewers will be rattled out of their complacency by images of dire catastrophes occurring ever closer to home. Spectacular front-page photographs of billowing smoke from local wildfires (such as the front page photo of *The New York Times* on August 2, 2015) or the mayhem caused by Hurricane Sandy can thus serve to "bring home" the idea that climate change is a real threat that can likely cause damage to American homes and livelihoods, not a vague and distant global issue to be dealt with by UN officials (see the front page of *The New York Times* dated October 31, 2012).

Like past-oriented collapse images of climate change, these images also carry a certain risk. Cottle (2009b) observed, when studying television images of climate change, that one of the main categories of images is the "spectacular." While he acknowledges the importance of images of climate change impacts as evidence, he also notes the very real risk associated with the repeated exposure to such images:

> The spectacle of climate change visualized through the news media helps to speak to us all about this global threat and marks a crucial development in its media career. When presented in such spectacular ways, however, the news media can all too easily position us as voyeurs only of impending catastrophe.
>
> (Cottle 2009b, p. 91)

This insight calls back to Rancière's observation that in an aesthetic, rather than representative regime of visual meaning making, beauty is no longer the expression of the content, but rises beyond its referent, rendering null any essential relationship to it (Rancière and Elliot 2009, p. 120). I argue that images of climate change that embrace the collapse narrative inevitably slip into the aesthetic regime, breaking loose of the original intention behind photojournalism, which is to provide information that can only be conveyed visually. Instead, such images produce spectacles that are delightful to behold but carry little if any actionable information for the viewer.

Indeed, some of these images can hardly be distinguished from screenshots of apocalyptic films. Since the early 2000s, films have employed climate change as the onset of apocalypse – for example, *Day After Tomorrow* (2004), *Hell* (2011), *Beasts of the Southern Wild* (2012), *Snowpiercer* (2014), or *Interstellar* (2014). In this sense, they may merely strengthen the idea of climate change as assured destruction, and yield in spectators a mixture of awe and terror – the definition of sublime sentiment according to British philosopher Edmund Burke (1821). Climate change, however, is not a singular "event" nor is it a trauma that one can hope to overcome and move on from. Since it is ongoing, and our daily actions continuously influence it, the fact that climate visuals may provide a simile of catharsis may thwart engagement instead of supporting it. The threat represented by climate change is at times compared to, or presented as, equal to the threat of collapse by nuclear war. Most notably, in January 2017 the *Bulletin of Atomic Scientists* presented these two key issues side by side as justifications for moving the "Doomsday Clock" the closest it's been to midnight in over 50 years. Yet preventing nuclear war depends on world leaders *not doing* something: not re-arming, not engaging, not provoking each other, not making an irreversible mistake; preventing climate change induced collapse depends upon world leaders *doing* something: that is, taking bold steps to move away from a fossil-fuel powered economy. If emissions continue to rise, dangerous and wide-reaching impacts can be expected in this century. Thus, just as climate change should not be framed or compared to an event of *force majeure*, it also should not be made analogous with collapse via nuclear war. Nuclear war will not occur if things go on as they are, but climate change will surely reach catastrophic levels if we continue to do "business as usual" in the way we use land and natural resources.

Future-oriented images of hope: an age of human we can look forward to?

Photojournalism has played a major role in documenting the effects of climate change throughout the globe, both on natural remote environments and now increasingly on human settlements. Despite these achievements, the most meaningful aspect of engagement remains elusive: the commitment to action. Research on climate change photojournalism has shown that few images can simultaneously heighten concern and increase the sense that something can be done (O'Neill et al. 2013; Metag et al. 2016). Doherty and Webler (2016) studied the gap between concern and individual action in the public sphere and found that the single strongest predictor of it being bridged is the presence of descriptive social norms – defined as "perceptions of what others do in similar situations" (Doherty and Webler 2016, p. 880). In other words, the awareness of other people taking action leads one to do so as well. The authors suggest that "strategies to elevate descriptive social norms include messages or experiences that highlight the prevalence of targeted actions by friends, neighbors, and other similar individuals" (Doherty and Webler 2016, p. 882).

So, how do we imagine a future in the Anthropocene that is worth living? Can photojournalism get us there? As Pahl et al. (2014) observe in their study of the temporality of climate change, the way society and individuals are used to operating since the late nineteenth century is based on a five- to twenty-year projection at most, making commitment to sustainable behavior, both at the individual and societal scale, a great challenge. The authors explain that "individuals experience less emotive mental imagery with respect to generalized long-term goals (such as living more healthily or sustainably) compared to short-term goals (such as eating a doughnut or driving to the shop)" (Pahl et al. 2014, p. 380). In other words, it is much easier for most people to imagine short-term desirable futures than long-term ones. Photography has a unique opportunity to respond to this gap in mental images and fill it not only with evidence of the irrefutable damage we have done, but also evidence of the inspiring actions many are already taking to effect change. Josh Haner, the *New York Times* photographer who produced front page images of the Greenland ice sheet melting and later American climate refugees, has now turned to photographing sustainable and creative ways in which the Dutch government is preparing for possible flooding as a result of sea level rise. The tide in climate change photography seems to be turning.

Climate change imagery that might inspire viewers by spreading hope and furthering descriptive social norms of action against climate change is rare (Doherty 2014). One example is a front-page photograph by Shiho Fukada of Chinese workers building a wind turbine, which appeared in a prime position above the fold on the January 31, 2010, edition of *The New York Times*. The photograph is intriguing, even playful, and shows people participating in cutting-edge technology, which can potentially inspire envy or at least curiosity in the audience. Similarly, photographs of workers installing solar panels on roofs, like the Al Seib image featured in the *Los Angeles Times* edition of August 9, 2014, can open up visions of renewable-energy powered futures.

Climate Outreach, a UK think tank, produced a research-based guide for communicators using photography to communicate climate change effectively (Corner et al. 2015). In the extensive survey research underlying the guide's recommendation the authors collected responses from over 3,000 people in Germany, the United Kingdom, and the United States and found that communicators needed to strive for authenticity rather than photo opportunities, and to tell "new stories" that move beyond the familiar images of polar bears and smoke stacks. In the survey, images of individuals taking concrete steps to minimize their CO_2 emissions, like rolling out roof insulation or laying solar panels on the roof of a building, scored similarly to other images on understanding (3.83/5 and 3.94/5 respectively) as well as motivation to act (3.04/5 and 3.4/5), but very importantly, they scored much more positive on affect (measuring on a scale of -5 to 5 how the image made respondents feel), while images of causes and impacts invariably scored negatively. Interestingly, the only image in the "solutions" category that also had a negative score in the affect measurement was a photograph of a climate march participant with his face painted blue and a sign behind him saying "Climate Justice NOW." The images of individuals taking concrete steps to diminish their carbon footprint are not breathtaking, compelling, arresting images by any stretch of the imagination, and yet they inspired viewers to learn from, be inspired by, and want to imitate the change that was being modeled. A similar image of a girl sweeping snow from solar panels also produced a positive reaction, as did a photo of a brewery worker in Manchester showing spent grain that would be recycled as fuel. The authors conclude that images of "'real people doing real work'" were "likely to be shared widely as a positive example of a climate solution, across the political spectrum" (Corner et al. 2015, p. 22). Seasoned photographer Gary Braasch also recommends a shift to images showing current actions being taken at all levels to respond to or adapt to climate change:

> Heeding the social scientists' warnings about the helplessness-inducing effects of negative images means that more pictures are needed of specific solutions and adaptations that will shape the world of tomorrow. The future is here. Vast wind turbine fields may still be distant to most people and not very personal, and images of them can be numbing clichés. In contrast, images of a neighborhood of homes with local wind generation, solar panels, electric cars, gardens, and attractive public transit may encourage people to work toward positive goals.
>
> (Braasch 2015, p. 38)

Images of climate change solutions fit in with a narrative of opportunity for people to take charge of their future, rather than helplessly drift toward collapse. However, the collapse narrative can be more visually compelling. A similar dilemma occurs in the photojournalistic depiction of humanitarian disasters: "the right images can arrest our attention, but that is just the first and perhaps the easiest step to take" (Moeller 2006, p. 185). This insight is similar to Cottle's: the images that seem to seal collapse in as a certain event beyond our control are perhaps more entertaining, more engaging in the superficial sense, more likely to win photojournalistic awards, but the ones that show a different, plausible way of functioning without fossil fuels may foster the deeper, more fruitful kind of engagement that communicators should be striving for.

Conclusion

While photographs serve an important role in providing evidence of concrete, mostly undesirable changes brought on by rising emissions, climate change photojournalism has the tendency to embrace collapse imagery, by pointing to that which is already irretrievably lost or our inevitable, tragic fate. The problem with such an approach is that it removes human agency from the picture, even when such agency is implied in the adjacent caption or headline. These spectacular images showcase the collapse brought forth by intensifying climate change as an inevitable impending disaster that we cannot be held accountable for – like an asteroid projected to hit the planet – and that we cannot therefore hope to avoid.

Collapse imagery presents either something valuable under threat of disappearance, or shows the aftermath of destruction on a grand scale. By emphasizing the distance between the viewer and the subject of the photograph, such images take the human out of the collapse equation, presenting collapse as an inevitable *force majeure*. When photojournalism embraces this tendency, it ceases to be the medium of the "now" and instead molds its message to retrospective eulogizing or prospective fear-mongering. No room is left for individual responsibility or agency – the spectator is merely left to stand in awe admiring the image of collapse.

The scale of the human influence on the world's climate is one of the reasons why geologists have now deemed it appropriate to rename the current epoch the "Anthropocene" – marking the fact that for the first time in (deep) history, the influence of human activity on the Earth system is so significant that it will alter the fossil record permanently (Crutzen and Stoermer 2000; Steffen et al. 2015). What this means, in practice, is that "we can no longer look out at nature without looking back at ourselves" (Dryzek et al. 2013, p. 114). In other words, all rhetorical distinctions between nature as pristine, wild, and untouched on the one hand and human society as industrialized, polluted, and messy on the other are rather outdated. We now inhabit an age, as underlined in the Bulletin of the World Meteorological Organization, where even natural disasters are not necessarily natural anymore.

One consequence of acknowledging a geological shift that began in the middle of the twentieth century is a recognition of humanity's center stage role in shaping Earth's ecosystem balance (Szerszynski 2012). Humanity cannot afford to consider environmental collapse as it has traditionally, as an instance of *force majeure*, an asteroid falling to Earth or a deadly volcanic eruption. No, the tables have turned, and humanity itself has become the *force majeure*, aware of itself: "The human is the first geological force to become conscious of its geological role" (Szerszynski 2012, p. 171). This awareness can lead to numbing hubris or to a responsibly proactive relationship with the environment. The latter would imply that instead of sitting back and enjoying the show that is our grandiose self-inflicted collapse, we take reasonable steps to minimizing the harmful effects of climate change while creatively working towards more sustainable forms of social activity, perhaps even moving toward embracing prosperity without growth (Fritz and Koch 2014).

In order for that awareness to sink in, engaging visual climate change reporting cannot stop at raising awareness about the seriousness of our current predicament. Meaningful public engagement on the cognitive, attitudinal and behavioral levels – affecting both knowledge of, attitude towards, and personal behavior as well as voting choices – is necessary

(Whitmarsh et al. 2011; O'Neill et al. 2013). It is important to remember that when news outlets strive for "engagement" with content, they do not necessarily go after what I defined in these pages as "public engagement" with a specific issue – in this case, climate change. While spectacular images of landscapes under threat may lead to higher engagement measured as likes, click counts, shares, or comments, that doesn't necessarily mean those images generate meaningful long-term public engagement with the issue at hand. Indeed, a post-apocalyptic scene of destruction from a hurricane or a sublime landscape now lost to warming or rising sea levels certainly attracts viewers, but it is unclear whether such foster increased understanding of, higher concern about, and willingness to do something to solve the underlying issue reported on: climate change in all its complexity. Clearly, images of indisputable impacts of climate change serve the necessary goal of transforming dry scientific evidence into awareness and concern. However, this aim can no longer suffice, since a large percentage of people are convinced of the reality of anthropogenic climate change but do little to act on their knowledge. What is more, collapse imagery may even disengage publics by presenting ever more catastrophist images that stun the viewer with their artistry, or even beauty, while confirming that collapse cannot be stopped. Photojournalism can and should move beyond past and future-oriented visions of collapse by harnessing the medium's capacity to depict possible alternative futures, not just heart-breaking evidence of loss. Only then can this critical medium succeed in changing hearts, shifting attitudes, and moving people to act both in their individual lives and in the political sphere. Rather than eulogizing an idyllic past now destroyed, or threatening a violent future rife with disaster, resource depletion and conflict, photojournalism can be a vehicle for situating us in the now so as to ask ourselves, what is it that I can do to more responsibly dwell on this Earth that I am every day transforming?

References

Barnosky, A. D., and Hadly, E. A., 2016. *Tipping point for planet Earth: How close are we to the edge?* New York: Thomas Dunne Books.

Boomgaarden, H. G., Boukes, M., and Iorgoveanu, A., 2016. Image versus text: How newspaper reports affect evaluations of political candidates. *International Journal of Communication*, 10, 2529–2555.

Boykoff, M. T., and Rajan, S. R., 2007. Signals and noise. *EMBO Reports*, 8: 207–211. doi:10.1038/sj.embor.7400924

Braasch, G., 2015. Climate change: Is seeing believing? *Bulletin of the Atomic Scientists*, 69, 33–41.

Burke, E., 1821. *Philosophical inquiry into the origin of our ideas of the sublime and beautiful: With an introductory discourse concerning taste, and several other additions.* London: G & W.B. Whittaker.

Corner, A., Webster, R., and Teriete, C., 2015. *Climate visuals: Seven principles for visual climate change communication (based on international social research).* Oxford: Climate Outreach.

Costello, A., Maslin, M., Montgomery, H., Johnson, A. M. and Ekins, P., 2011. Global health and climate change: moving from denial and catastrophic fatalism to positive action. *Philosophical Transactions of the Royal Society of London A: Mathematical, Physical and Engineering Sciences*, 369, 1866–1882.

Cottle, S., 2009a. *Global crises in the news*: Staging new wars, disasters and climate change. *International Journal of Communication*, 3, 24. Retrieved from http://ijoc.org/index.php/ijoc/article/view/473

Cottle, S., 2009b. *Global crisis reporting: Journalism in the global age*. Maidenhead: Open University Press.

Crutzen, P. J., and Stoermer, E. F., 2000. The "Anthropocene." *Global Change Newsletter* 41, 17–18. International Geosphere–Biosphere Programme (IGBP).

Crowther, T. W., et al., 2016. Quantifying global soil carbon losses in response to warming. *Nature*, 540, 104–108.

Difrancesco, A. D., and Young, N., 2011. Seeing climate change: The visual construction of global warming in Canadian national print media. *Cultural Geographies*, 18, 517–536. doi:10.1177/1474474010382072

Doherty, K., 2014. From Alarm to Action: Closing the Gap Between Belief and Behavior in Response to Climate Change. *Doctoral Dissertation*. Antioch: University New England.

Doherty, K., and Webler, T., 2016. Social norms and efficacy beliefs drive the alarmed segment's public-sphere climate actions. *Nature Climate Change*, 6, 879–884.

Doyle, J., 2007. Picturing the clima(c)tic: Greenpeace and the representational politics of climate change communication. *Science as Culture*, 16, 2, 129–150.

Doyle, J., 2009. Seeing the climate? The problematic status of visual evidence in climate change campaigning. In Dobrin, S. I., and Morey, S. (Eds.). *Ecosee: Image, rhetoric, nature*. Albany: SUNY Press. pp. 279–298.

Dryzek, J. S., Norgaard, R. B., and Schlosberg, D., 2013. *Climate-challenged society*. Oxford: Oxford University Press.

Dunaway, F., 2015. *Seeing green: The use and abuse of American environmental images*. Chicago: The University of Chicago Press.

Fiskio, J., 2012. Apocalypse and Ecotopia: Narratives in global climate change discourse. *Race Gender and Class*, 19, 12–36.

Fritz, M., and Koch, M., 2014. Potentials for prosperity without growth: Ecological sustainability, social inclusion and the quality of life in 38 countries. *Ecological Economics*, 108, 191–199.

Funk, C., and Kennedy, B., 2016. The politics of climate. *Pew Research Center*, 4.

Gardiner, S. M., 2006. A perfect moral storm: Climate change, intergenerational ethics and the problem of moral corruption. *Environmental Values*, 397–413.

Hamilton, S. K., 2010. Biogeochemical implications of climate change for tropical rivers and floodplains. *Hydrobiologia*, 657, 19–35.

Hansen, A., and Machin, D., 2008. Visually branding the environment: Climate change as a marketing opportunity. *Discourse Studies*, 10, 777–794. doi:10.1177/1461445608098200

Hansen, J., et al., 2005. Earth's energy imbalance: Confirmation and implications. *Science*, 308, 5727, 1431–1435. doi: 10.1126/science.1110252

Hart, P. S., and Feldman, L., 2016. The impact of climate change–related imagery and text on public opinion and behavior change. *Science Communication*, 38, 415–441.

Hirsch, M., 2002. The day time stopped. *The Chronicle Review*, January 25, B11.

Horn, R. E., 1999. Information design: Emergence of a new profession. in Jacobson, R. (Ed.). *Information design*. Cambridge, MA: The MIT Press, pp. 15–33.

Hulme, M., 2011. Reducing the future to climate: A story of climate determinism and reductionism. *Osiris*, 26, 245–266.

IPCC, 2014. Climate Change 2014: Summary for Policymakers. Synthesis Report. Contribution of Working Groups I, II and III to the Fifth Assessment Report of the Intergovernmental Panel on Climate Change [Core Writing Team, R. K. Pachauri and L. A. Meyer (eds.)]. IPCC, Geneva, Switzerland, 151.

Jackson, M., 2015. Glaciers and climate change: Narratives of ruined futures. *Wiley Interdisciplinary Reviews: Climate Change*, 6, 5, 479–492.

Leiserowitz, A., 2006. Climate change risk perception and policy preferences: The role of affect, imagery, and values. *Climatic Change*, 77, 45–72.

Lenton, T. M., et al., 2008. Tipping elements in the Earth's climate system. Proceedings of the National Academy of Sciences, Online Early Edition. February 4, 2008.

Luedecke, G., and Boykoff, M., 2017. Environment and the media. In Richardson, D., Castree, N., Goodchild, M. F., Kobayashi, A., Liu, W., and Marston, R. A. (Eds.). *The international encyclopedia of geography*. Hoboken, NJ: John Wiley & Sons, Ltd.

Manzo, K., 2010. Beyond polar bears? Re-envisioning climate change. *Meteorological Applications*, 17, 196–208.

Marx, S. M., Weber, E. U., Orlove, B. S., Leiserowitz, A., Krantz, D. H., Roncoli, C., and Phillips, J., 2007. Communication and mental processes: Experiential and analytic processing of uncertain climate information. *Global Environmental Change*, 17, 1, 47–58.

Mckibben, B., 2005. What the world needs now is art, sweet art. *Grist*, April 22. Available at: http://grist.org/article/mckibben-imagine/ [Accessed April 24, 2017]

Messaris, P., and Abraham, L., 2001. Role of images in framing news stories. In Reese, S. D., Gandy, O. H., and Grant, A. E. (Eds.). *Framing public life: Perspectives on media and our understanding of the social world*. Mahwah, NJ: Lawrence Erlbaum Associates.

Metag, J., Schafer, M. S., Fuchslin, T., Kleinen-Von Konigslow, K., and Barsuhn, T., 2016. Perceptions of climate change imagery: Evoked salience and self-efficacy in Germany, Switzerland, and Austria. *Science Communication*, 38, 197–227.

Moeller, S. D., 2006. "Regarding the Pain of Others": Media, Bias and the Coverage of International Disasters. *Journal of International Affairs*, 59, 173–196.

Morris, E., and Sayler, S., 2014. The pensive photograph as agent: What can non-illustrative images do to galvanize public support for climate change action? In Schneider, B., & Nocke, T. (Eds.). *Image politics of climate change: Visualizations, imaginations, documentations*. Bielefeld: Transcript.

Nicholson-Cole, S. A., 2005. Representing climate change futures: A critique on the use of images for visual communication. *Computers, Environment and Urban Systems*, 29, 255–273. doi:10.1016/j.compenvurbsys.2004.05.002

Nixon, R., 2011. *Slow violence and the environmentalism of the poor*. Cambridge, Mass: Harvard University Press.

O'Neill, S., and Nicholson-Cole, S., 2009. "Fear Won't Do It" Promoting Positive Engagement With Climate Change Through Visual and Iconic Representations. *Science Communication*, 30, 355–379.

O'Neill, S. J., Boykoff, M., Niemeyer, S., and Day, S. A., 2013. On the use of imagery for climate change engagement. *Global Environmental Change*, 23, 413–421.

O'Neill, S. J., and Smith, N., 2014. Climate change and visual imagery. *Wiley Interdisciplinary Reviews: Climate Change*, 5, 73–87. doi:10.1002/wcc.249

Pahl, S., Sheppard, S., Boomsma, C., and Groves, C., 2014. Perceptions of time in relation to climate change. *Wiley Interdisciplinary Reviews: Climate Change*, 5, 375–388.

Perlmutter, D. D., 1998. *Photojournalism and foreign policy: Icons of outrage in international crises*. Santa Barbara, CA: Praeger Publishers.

Placky, B. W., Maibach, E., Cullen, H., Witte, J., Ward, B., and Seitter, K., 2016. Climate matters: A comprehensive educational resource program for broadcast meteorologists. *Bulletin of the American Meteorological Society*, 97, 5, 709–712.

Rancière, J., and Elliott, G., 2009. *The emancipated spectator*. London: Verso.

Rebich-Hespanha, S., Rice, R. E., Montello, D. R., Retzloff, S., Tien, S., and Hespanha, J. P., 2015. Image themes and frames in US print news stories about climate Change. *Environmental Communication*, 9, 491–519. doi:10.1080/17524032.2014.983534

Ritchin, F., 2009. *After photography*. New York: W. W. Norton.

Roser-Renouf, C., Maibach, E., Leiserowitz, A., and Rosenthal, S., 2016. *Global warming's six Americas and the election, 2016*. Yale University and George Mason University. New Haven, CT: Yale Program on Climate Change Communication.

Rüegg, I., 2015. Klimawandel visuell. Eine Bildanalyse der Klimaberichterstattung in deutschsprachigen Zeitungen. *Master's Thesis*, Universität Zürich, Zürich, Switzerland.

Schiermeier, Q., 2015. October 30. "Combined climate pledges of 146 nations fall short of 2 °C target", *Nature News*. Available at: http://www.nature.com/news/combined-climate-pledges-of-146-nations-fall-short-of-2-c-target-1.18693.

Schudson, M., 2013. *Why democracies need an unlovable press*. Oxford: Wiley.

Shome, D., et al., 2009. *The psychology of climatechange communication: A guide for scientists, journalists, educators, political aides, and the interested public*. New York: Center for Research on Environmental Decisions.

Slovic, P., Finucane, M. L., Peters, E., and MacGregor, D. G., 2004. Risk as analysis and risk as feelings: Some thoughts about affect, reason, risk, and rationality. *Risk Analysis*, 24, 2, 311–322.

Steffen, W., Richardson, K., Rockström, J., Cornell, S., Fetzer, I., Bennett, E. M., Biggs, R., Carpenter, S. R., De Vries, W., De Wit, C. A., Folke, C., Gerten, D., Heinke, J., Mace, G. M., Persson, L. M., Ramanathan, V., Reyers, B., and Sörlin, S., 2015. Planetary boundaries: Guiding human development on a changing planet. *Science*. doi:10.1126/science.1259855

Szerszynski, B., 2012. The end of the end of nature: The anthropocene and the fate of the human. *Oxford Literary Review*, 34, 165–184.

Walsh, L., 2015. The visual rhetoric of climate change. *Wiley Interdisciplinary Reviews: Climate Change*, 6, 361–368.

Watson, R., Carraro, C., Canziani, P., Nakicenovic, N., McCarthy, J. J., Goldemberg, J., and Hisas, L., 2016. The Truth About Climate Change. *Universal Ecological Fund*. Available at: https://feu-us.org/the-report/.

Whitmarsh, L., O'Neill, S., and Lorenzoni, I. (2011). *Engaging the public with climate change: Behaviour change and communication*. London: Earthscan.

Williams, R., 2005. Cognitive theory. In Smith, K. (Ed.). *Handbook of visual communication research: Theory, methods, and media*. Mahwah, NJ: L. Erlbaum.

Žižek, S., 2010. *Living in the end times*. London: Verso.

4 Environmental collapse in comics

Reflections on Philippe Squarzoni's *Saison brune*

Ann Gardiner

Following the 21st annual United Nations Climate Change Conference of the Parties (COP21) held in Paris from November 30 to December 11, 2015, Emmanuelle Lequeux and Thomas Schlesser (2015) published an article in the French fine arts magazine, *Beaux Arts*, entitled "Les artistes, peuvent-ils sauver la planète?" [Can artists save the planet?]. Therein the authors showcase various artists who have addressed global warming through creative media such as sculpture, film, and photography. They also reference Bruno Latour's forays (2014a, 2014b) into the still-debated concept of the Anthropocene (p. 59) and the "crise de la représentation" [crisis of representation] that he claims surrounds human-induced climate change, a crisis which refers both to: "the representation of things through the intermediary of the laboratory" and to "the representation of citizens through the intermediary of the social contract" (cited in Whiteside 2013, p. 187; see also Latour 1991, p. 43). Latour thus articulates a double-sided crisis: on the one hand problems associated with political representation (citizen involvement and the individuals they elect), and on the other, problems dealing with semiotic representation (how to scientifically visualize or even explain climate change).

This connection between the environmental collapse engendered by climate change and the narrative collapse resulting from its complexity has become an important theme in the literature on environmental degradation.[1] Timothy Morton (2013, 2016) argues that anthropocentric global warming might best be described as a hyperobject that has already "brought about the end of the world" (2013, p. 6), something so vast and complicated that human knowledge can neither adequately document nor describe it. Collectively, scholars across disciplines have explored the narrative side of Latour's representational crisis, often pointing to what Paul Wapner has called "Climate Inc," – "the routinized [and failed] system of response that has evolved to address climate change" (2016, p. 2). Among the different ways to address this narrative collapse, artists have a role to play according to Lequeux and Schlesser because they offer "une autre façon d'éclairer les savoirs" [another way to shed light on knowledge] (2015, p. 59).

One of the works Lequeux and Schlesser highlight is Philippe Squarzoni's documentary comic about climate change, *Saison brune* (2012), which they describe neologistically as a "chef-d'oeuvre écolographique" [ecolographic masterpiece] (p. 68). How Squarzoni tackles both sides of the representational crisis associated with climate change through the medium of comics is the subject of this chapter. In choosing to narrate the story of climate change through this particular medium, which Will Eisner has defined as art that arranges "pictures or images and words to narrate a story or dramatize an idea" (1985, p. 5),[2] Squarzoni offers "another way to shed light" on human-induced climate change, addressing not only the problem of environmental collapse but also, and more importantly, of narrative collapse itself.

Saison brune: not just another comic about climate change

Squarzoni, who has published sixteen comics in France, appears to be little-known in the English-speaking world.[3] Like the US-Maltese comic artist, Joe Sacco, he has specialized in documentary comics, covering various conflict zones around the world. These include the ongoing war in Chiapas between the Zapatista Army of National Liberation and the state of Mexico (2003), the still-unresolved question of Occupied Territories in Palestine (2004), as well as the widely debated problem of US gun violence (volume 1, 2016, volume 2, 2017).[4] As a documentary comic artist, Squarzoni veers toward the unresolved and unsettling, and *Saison brune* is no different: a 475-page black and white comic on the hyperobject that is global warming, translated into English in 2014 by Ivanka Hahnenberger under the title, *Climate changed: a personal journey through the science*. To date, this is the only work of Squarzoni's to have been translated into English.

Comparing the original French title and its English counterpart provides several insights into the multi-layered complexity of the comic. Whereas the English-language title highlights the pragmatic aspects of Squarzoni's project, which charts the author's own subjective attempts to understand the scientific evidence behind climate change, the original title, *Saison brune*, is more abstract. Three quarters of the way through the work, Squarzoni explains that the French title refers to a so-called fifth season in the state of Montana: "brown season" – presumably another term for "mud season" – which the anchor text tells us is "a period between winter and spring, between the freeze and the thaw . . . when the ice starts to melt . . . but spring hasn't announced itself yet" (p. 380).[5] Whereas the English-language title privileges the concrete individual experiences of the author, the French title alludes more collectively to the socio-political crisis humans have put themselves in. It proposes specifically that we currently live in an in-between "brown season" with respect to global warming and that "it's about time we put the necessary policies into place" (p. 381); the use of the past tense, "Climate changed," in the English translation calls into question the historical timing of the phenomenon. While an English introduction by Nicole Whittington-Evans, Alaska Regional Director of the Wilderness Society, begs us to "read this book" (2014, p. 7), the French edition includes a societal caveat on the back cover by the Greek-French philosopher, Cornelius Castoriadis, who claims: "Une société vraiment libre, une société autonome, doit savoir s'autolimiter, savoir qu'il y a des choses qu'on ne peut pas faire ou qu'il ne faut même pas essayer de faire ou qu'il ne faut pas désirer" [a society that is truly free and autonomous must know how to limit itself; it must know that there are things that it cannot do, should not try to do or even desire]. Between Squarzoni's "personal journey through the science," which examines not only what we know about climate change, but also how we know it, and the author's observations about our collective obligations as citizens to live within rather than beyond our environmental means, we have both aspects of Latour's complex "representational crisis" squarely in view.

The ecolographic complexity of Squarzoni's project can also be seen in the actual production of the work itself. Unlike comics that often involve different people scripting, drawing, and even lettering or coloring the work in assembly-line fashion, Squarzoni is at once scénariste [scriptwriter], dessinateur [illustrator], and coloriste [colorist]. He publishes under Editions Delcourt, which Mark McKinney (2008, p. 6) has identified as one of leading comic book publishers in France. In recognition of Squarzoni's efforts at all levels of artistic production, *Saison brune* received numerous prizes the year it was published in the French literary world, including the 2012 "prix du jury" from the Lyon BD Festival as well as the prestigious "prix Léon de Rosen" from the Académie française, a prize that acknowledges single-author creative works including comics that have contributed to our understanding of and respect toward the environment (Académie française, no date). As scholars working in the field of French-language comics have pointed out, these prizes attest to the reputable position of comics in the French literary and visual world (McKinney 2008; Miller and Beaty 2014), as well as to the ways in which the state itself supports the so-called ninth art (Groensteen 2009), which is how the medium of comics or "bandes dessinées" (literally drawn strips) is often referred to in French-language countries. Squarzoni's non-serialized work is published as a softcover with flaps, considered a sign of prestige in the world of French comics, as opposed to a hardcover without flaps, which is how serialized French comics such as *Asterix* are often published. These publication details suggest that *Saison brune* is more than just "an instructional comic"[6] about the facts behind climate change. Instead, as I argue later, one of its aims as a documentary comic is to help the reader understand the representational problems involved in narrating the story of climate change itself.

Documentary narrative strategies in *Saison brune*

The documentary comic genre that *Saison brune* belongs to has attracted considerable scholarly attention over the past decade (Versaci 2007; Nyberg 2012; Mickwitz 2016; Chute 2016). In *Disaster drawn: visual witness, comics and documentary form*, Hillary Chute specifically examines how the genre can visualize catastrophe in ways that images or texts alone cannot. Analyzing works such as Art Spiegelman's *Maus*, Joe Sacco's *Safe Area Goražde*, and atom-bomb manga, she notes the power of comics to "challenge dominant modes of storytelling and history writing through expressing simultaneity, multiple perspectives, shifting temporalities, and paradoxical spaces" (p. 157). Squarzoni takes full advantage of the narrative specificity of this medium – the sequential juxtaposition of text and image, the use of gutters and panels, the spatial layout of the page as well as the role of the narrator (Groensteen 1986; McCloud 1994; Lefèvre 2000; Pratt 2009; Groensteen 2013; Miodrag 2013; Postema 2013) – to offer a thought-provoking alternative to the ways in which the story of anthropocentric climate change has thus far been told.

In *Saison brune*, Squarzoni himself is very present in the narrative. Drawing himself into the comic as both main character and principal narrator, he mirrors certain rhetorical strategies of New Journalism, which challenges traditional ways of news reporting by integrating the reporter's subjective role in creating the story (Wolfe 1975; Boynton 2005). Nyberg (2012) has explored this idea in relation to the comic *Safe area Goražde* (2000) to show how Joe Sacco includes himself in the narrative, intentionally depicting his own often conflicted attempts to document the catastrophic events he is writing about and drawing. This appositional method of comic journalism (Duncan, Taylor and Stoddard 2016), following the French tradition of comics as reportage (Miller 2008), is exactly what Squarzoni uses to address the question of how to tell the story of collapse that climate change has engendered. Exposing the hidden cracks and blank spaces of more objective and factual reporting about climate change, Squarzoni literally stages the collapse of those narratives by inserting himself in the story, pointing out where traditional discourses about climate change conflict with and contradict each other.

The front cover of the English-language translation provides a good example of how Squarzoni's presence in the narrative might interrupt this "routinized Climate Inc." story (Figure 4.1).[7] Here, we see the author with a five-o'clock beard hard at work. Between two drawn likenesses of the earth – one the familiar "blue marble" taken by the Apollo 17 crew in 1972, the other a completely desiccated version of it – Squarzoni sits at his desk, book in hand. He is clearly studying the data. The desk, located in a room that looks like a writer's lair under the roof, is covered with books, with a few sticky-notes on the computer and a blank notebook and pen in front of him. The walls are bare save for a map of the world and a chart with some data on it. The drawn image is striking because we see from the outset the degree to which Squarzoni has integrated himself into the story, as he explains both the evidence behind climate change and the process through which he collected and attempted to make sense of it. He uses the structural aspects of the comics medium (the panels, gutters, images, anchor text, and speech bubbles)

Figure 4.1 Title page of *Saison brune*, English edition

Source: *Climate Changed: A Personal Journey Through Science* by Philippe Squarzoni. English translation copyright © 2014 Harry N. Abrams, Inc. Used with permission of Express Permissions on behalf of Abrams ComicArts, an imprint of Harry N. Abrams, Inc., New York. All rights reserved. www.abramsbooks.com

to craft his own personal encounter with collapse. The reader thus gets an inside view of the author's personal struggles to understand climate change, as well as the day-to-day life he begins to rethink as he increasingly grasps the potential consequences of not taking action. He serves in this respect as a model for the reader herself, inviting her to consider taking the same journey in her own individual context. As one English-language reviewer wrote:

> It is by inserting himself and his personal exploration of responsibilities and choices that Squarzoni makes the most demanding call to action: we cannot address as mere individuals the inequities visited on the planet, but without recognizing our personal responsibility, we can't address it culturally or politically in a timely manner.
>
> (*Booklist* 2014, p. 60)

As a witness to Squarzoni's own witnessing, the reader must also actively participate in the crafting of the story, first by connecting the panels laid out on individual pages (what Scott McCloud (1994) calls closure in comics) and second by connecting successive pages into a cohesive story. Unlike many book-length prose narratives, there are no distinct chapters in Squarzoni's project. Although blank pages do occasionally separate the 475-page work into smaller units, each large unit covers a broad spectrum of material, weaving together a dizzying array of narrative moments that include the author's personal memories, his present attempts to fathom climate change, scenes from his day-to-day life, interviews with scientists, excerpts from other works about climate change, and visualizations of climate change data. The narrative montage formally begins with a prologue-like series of panels describing Squarzoni's musings on narrative beginnings from his own personal favorites, from Flaubert's *Salammbô* to the children's movie *Peter Pan*, the apocalyptic novel *Watermelon Sugar* by Richard Brautigan to the great epic film *Ran*, directed by Akira Kurosawa. With a borderless panel opening the comic, Squarzoni's literal first words are: "there are many ways to start a book" (p. 9, panel 1).

Opening a narrative about climate change with a declarative statement about narrative beginnings alerts readers immediately to the idea that Squarzoni is interested not simply in the facts related to climate change, but also in the question of how to tell the story about it.[8] Beginnings, however, as Brian Richardson (2008) has shown, are not as simple as they might seem; and we see Squarzoni apparently struggling to start this project (Figure 4.2). The prologue is filled with images of blank notebooks and blank computer screens; as on the front cover of the English translation, he clearly has not started yet. Ultimately, at the close of the prologue, Squarzoni decides that he will start with a memory, which significantly emerges as a drawn image between a blank notebook and a blank computer screen. "For this book" (Figure 4.2, panel 5), the author concludes "it's not the beginning that is the most difficult." The last panel of the page (panel 6), stark in its use of white

Figure 4.2 Reflecting on narrative beginnings and endings

Source: *Climate Changed: A Personal Journey Through Science* by Philippe Squarzoni. English translation copyright © 2014 Harry N. Abrams, Inc. Used with permission of Express Permissions on behalf of Abrams ComicArts, an imprint of Harry N. Abrams, Inc., New York. All rights reserved. www.abramsbooks.com

anchor text boxes set against a totally black background, points specifically
to the representational crisis in which he and by extension the reader find
themselves as both citizens and interpreters of the narratives about climate
change. Addressing not only the semiotic problem of how to tell the story of
climate change but also the political question of what we do with that story
once it is told, he closes the prologue with the observation that "the hardest
thing . . . [with this book] is how to end it."

With the reader as yet unaware of how he will, in fact, end the comic,
Squarzoni's observation articulates the larger looming aesthetic and political problem of how to end a text about the end. Recalling Morton's concept
of global warming as a hyperobject that has already brought about the end
of the world, it would nonetheless be misleading to classify *Saison brune* as
an apocalyptic narrative. Although there are plenty of moments in the text
in which environmental collapse emerges as the logical consequence of our
present wasteful capitalist practices – for example when Squarzoni relates
his interviews with scientists – the work itself does not strictly articulate,
as Frank Kermode would put it, *The sense of an ending* (1967). For Kermode, Apocalypse and its related themes are "strikingly long-lived" in fiction (p. 29) as they "underlie our ways of making sense of the world from
where we stand, in the middest" (p. 29).[9] Challenging this sense of an ending,
Squarzoni instead introduces several narrative and generic uncertainties, first
by beginning a non-fiction comic on climate change with narrative openings
from fiction, and second by starting the comic with a discussion about ending it. This focus on the difficulty of ending the story, which replicates in
uncanny fashion the difficulty of addressing the potential collapse associated
with climate change, is what the reader is left with as she begins the comic.

By the conclusion of the work 475 pages later, through a kind of endless
deferral (Höpker 2014), we are no closer to ending than we were at the
beginning. The narrative logic is thus circular, which implies non-ending or a
kind of narrative stasis despite how the story has unraveled in the meantime.
The closing panels show the same writer's lair depicted on the front cover of
the English-language edition, this time with his partner also sitting at a desk,
both of them pondering how to end the narrative (p. 466, panel 1). They
have been having a conversation about an article in the paper about "Earth
Overshoot Day," which we passed this year on August 2, 2017, and which
pinpoints the day that "we will have used more from nature than our planet
can renew in the whole year" (Earthovershootday, no date). Several panels
later, still considering how to finish the comic, he quotes one of Woody
Allen's stand-up endings, telling his partner and by extension the reader: "I
wish I could think of a positive point to leave you with. Will you take two
negative points?" (p. 466, panel 2). His partner, out of the frame in the next
panel, asks through a speech bubble: "Are going to end your book like that?"
(panel 3). "No," says Squarzoni in panel four, which, significantly, constitutes the last written word of *Saison brune*, offering thus an ending, but at
the same time stepping away from it. The final images, textless, show both

Squarzoni and his partner back at work in the same writer's lair pictured on the front cover of the English-language translation.

In a sense, we have come full circle, except not quite. Squarzoni's beard is longer than it was on the front cover, the reader's perspective of the writer's lair has changed, and the "No" of the previous panel is indeed not the end of the comic since there are six additional wordless panels to view. This ambiguous refusal to end a work about the end with a "No" leads the reader to consider several questions about the possibility of narrating climate change at all. Is climate change ultimately unnarratable because "it defies the powers of the narrator" (Prince 1988, p. 1); "disnarrated" because the ensuing collapse has not quite happened yet (Prince 1988), or are we are dealing with a "failure of the grammar of the ordinary" (Das 2007, p. 7)?[10] Squarzoni's "No" may also be read as a rejection of "end of world" narratives themselves as this "last word" seems not only to refuse to end the book project per se, but also deny apocalyptic scenarios that could lead to pessimism and inaction. Although the English-language edition in particular, with its title, *Climate changed*, suggests that the end has already happened, Squarzoni's ambivalence about ending the comic, already announced at the beginning of the narrative, echoes Morton, who argues, that

> this [end] does not mean that there is no hope for ecological politics and ethics. Far from it . . . . the strongly held belief that the world is about to end 'unless we act now' is paradoxically one of the most powerful factors that inhibits a full engagement with our ecological coexistences here on Earth.
>
> (2013, p. 6).

Squarzoni, by not ending this comic about the end, seems ultimately to reject the use of apocalyptic stories to transform readers, asking readers instead to question those very narratives.

With this emphasis on the impossibility of telling the story of climate change, Squarzoni draws, not simply from the narrative strategies of New Journalism, but also from those found in documentary film.[11] In particular, *Saison brune* incorporates modes of address seen in Al Gore's *An inconvenient truth* (2006) and more recently Leonardo DiCaprio's *Before the flood* (2016). The shared mode of address in all three of these examples, which largely functions through pathos, is what ecocritic Mark Minster (2010) calls a modern rhetoric of conversion. Helen Smith (2010) dates the emergence of personal conversion narratives as a genre specific to the seventeenth and eighteenth centuries, noting they typically involve individuals proclaiming their own spiritual rebirth within a new faith. Caldwell (1983) has suggested, furthermore, that they have a particular place in subjective and collective identity formation during times of great crisis. Within the debate about climate change, it is easy to see how a secularized narrative about conversion – "I was blind but now I see" – might be seductive.

In Squarzoni's comic, as with Gore's film, this conversion narrative relies significantly on personal memories. Just as we hear Gore reminiscing about growing up on a tobacco farm in Tennessee or remembering the death of his sister due to cancer – both indicating a kind of complicity in the problem – *Saison brune* begins, after much hesitation, with the author's memories of his childhood home. Using a technique that recalls that of a zoom lens on a camera, Squarzoni starts with an image of the village where he grew up in Southeastern France, "between the plains of the Ardèche and the Ibie river" (p. 16). He then slowly proceeds panel by panel to the house, with successive images of the road out of the village, the dirt track through the vineyards, and finally of the house itself, which clearly looks abandoned. The textual descriptions accompanying these images are anchor texts (framed in rectangular boxes as opposed to actual speech bubbles), and serve, as Roland Barthes noted (1964), to "anchor" or fix the meaning of images, which as floating signifiers would otherwise be difficult to interpret. In comics, they can function somewhat like a voice-over in film, in the sense that they are often extra or meta-diegetic, and therefore not part of the present mimetic narrative moment.[12] Complicating traditional notions of storytelling, Squarzoni often includes his personal, unvoiced reflections and memories in the comic as a way to contextualize the mimetic moment taking place in different panels, sharing thus his inner thoughts with the reader. On a single page or even within a single panel, there are thus often several temporal moments and types of narration at play between diegetic anchor text and mimetic speech bubbles (Figure 4.3).

The story of the author's personal introduction to and gradual understanding of the scientific issues around the problem of global warming illustrates a modern conversion narrative for a time of crisis. He admits at the beginning of the work that he does not "really know a whole lot about environmental issues" (p. 27). Here, the reader finds Squarzoni and his partner, Camille, planning to spend part of the summer at her parents' chalet in the French Alps. In this section, the author provides us with the impetus for the book itself: he is finishing another comic on the consequences of "liberal policies during French President Jacque Chirac's second term [2002–2007]" and has one aspect left to cover: "the government's environmental policies" (p. 27). What he finds, he tells us in anchor text, "isn't great" (p. 27). His main problem, he notes several pages later, is that he does not "really know what [he is] talking about" (p. 31). In fact, it is his partner Camille, we learn during one of their walks in the countryside, who suggests that "it will mean doing a whole new book" (p. 33). Although Squarzoni denies this possibility, we soon see him in a bookstore in Grenoble, his partner telling him "I can tell, you're circling about the idea of a new book" (p. 36). Squarzoni's transparency about how the idea for his own comic about climate change came about suggests that the comic begins even before its formal beginning. The author's confession that he knows little about the topic also helps him connect with his readers, who may not know much about climate change themselves, or

Figure 4.3 Memetic v. diegetic time in comics

Source: Climate Changed: *A Personal Journey Through Science* by Philippe Squarzoni. English translation copyright © 2014 Harry N. Abrams, Inc. Used with permission of Express Permissions on behalf of Abrams ComicArts, an imprint of Harry N. Abrams, Inc., New York. All rights reserved. www.abramsbooks.com

have been put off by the routinized response of "Climate Inc." and the elite nature of the evidence in the scientific debate.

Drawing evidence

As a documentary comic about Squarzoni's "personal journey through the science," the author/narrator spends considerable time grappling with the actual scientific evidence behind climate change, as did both Gore and DiCaprio in their respective films. The drawn aspect of the medium, however, distinguishes Squarzoni's work from the films mentioned previously. In *Saison brune*, even the text counts as drawn since it is hand lettered (the lettering in the English translation was carried out by a third party) and therefore the drawn deserves careful attention. As Johanna Nurmis (2017) in this volume shows, images, specifically photographs, may communicate environmental collapse more compellingly than words. The drawn, I would argue, adds another layer to the idea that images may help readers understand climate change better than words alone. In *Disaster drawn*, Chute (2016) devotes many pages to this particular aspect of comics, starting with the idea that many people have trouble believing that a drawing can be objective, as opposed, say, to a photograph. What she argues, however, is that the drawn can actually be meta-objective in the sense that it "calls overt attention to the crafting of histories and historiography" (p. 2). She thus suggests that the drawn can provide a critical take on the act of visually documenting; creative invention, she moreover claims, "is not the opposite of accuracy" (p. 2). In *Saison brune*, Squarzoni uses the meta-objective nature of the drawn to critically comment on traditional visual documentation of climate change, encouraging the reader not only to learn about how scientists document the phenomenon, but also consider its narrative failures. The drawn or "ecolographic" aspect of the comic is how Squarzoni presents "another way to shed light on knowledge."

We see a surplus of panels featuring drawings of more traditional scientific ways to provide evidence: maps, charts, and tables, among others. Evidence itself is a complex concept, particularly when coupled with global warming (Hale et al. 2015), and through his drawings of evidence Squarzoni seems to play with the very notion of evidence itself. The word, etymologically, is intimately connected with the idea of witnessing,[13] which Nyberg (2012) has noted plays such a prominent role within the context of documentary or journalistic comics. Chute (2016, p. 2) has moreover argued that the very medium of comics "calls attention to itself as evidence, [making] a reader access the unfolding of evidence in the movement of its basic grammar by aggregating and accumulating frames of information." As drawn images, the maps, charts, and tables that we see proliferating in Squarzoni's project are thus one step removed from those actual visualizations. They are, in other words, meta-representations, adding a new twist to the already problematic nature of visually representing data. As the master of data visualization,

Edward Tufte (1990, 1997, 2001, 2006), points out, and as more recent scholarship has shown (Smelik 2010), representing data in the form of evidence necessarily transforms it. If representing the data in the form of a table or chart already modifies it, in the sense of Magritte's famous image of a pipe, under which he has written "ceci n'est pas une pipe" [this is not a pipe], then drawing those visualizations goes one step further, suggesting likewise that "ceci n'est pas une preuve" [this is not proof]. By calling attention to the very nature of climate change evidence through drawings of that evidence, Squarzoni addresses the problem of how to visualize the data. Benefitting from the meta-representative nature of drawn images, he not only asks the reader to consider the evidence about the ensuing destruction of our planet, but also, in so doing, asks the reader to question its very nature as evidence.

Open *Saison brune* to any page and the reader is likely to see drawn reproductions of various visualizations of climate change evidence (Figures 4.4 and 4.5). In this series of panels, we see a successive layering of different ways to explain the phenomenon of global warming. Squarzoni begins with a simple map, asking in the anchor text "what does tomorrow's world look like?" (p. 272). In successive panels, he then overlays the map with other kinds of data visualization: a line chart representing rising temperatures, various bar charts showing changes in precipitation, 3-D drawings of weather patterns, and so on. The end result is a cacophony of evidence (panel 6), which suggests not only that we have an abundance of evidence at our disposal, but also that visualizing this evidence may be part of the problem of explaining it. This layered surplus in drawn form calls attention to the evidence itself as evidence, asking readers to question simultaneously what constitutes evidence, and how we produce it, who creates it, and most importantly, how it is narrated (Hale et al. 2015). Viewing this cacophony, which contrasts sharply with the use of blank space in other panels, we are left with an unsettling feeling of too much or too little, invited to witness the semiotic crisis of representation that is climate change and the ensuing narrative collapse that such a crisis engenders.

Squarzoni takes the reader through a visual grand tour of evidence. In addition to drawings of the actual scientific data, we also see images of how scientists have collected that data, in the laboratory, for example, as well as numerous drawings of the media through which this evidence is shared to a wider community: newspaper headlines, articles, books, and newscasts, among others. Often, the image in the panel is clearly a graphic reproduction of another medium, headlines from the title page of *Le Monde*, for example (p. 289). Sometimes, however, it is difficult to distinguish Squarzoni's drawing from the actual media involved. In one series of panels, Squarzoni asks his partner, Camille, what she is reading (pp. 168–169). She explains that she is "flipping through your Al Gore book about global warming" (p. 168, panel 3), revealing again how transparent Squarzoni is in telling the backstory to his story. Successive panels show images of Gore's book, functioning in essence as critical or meta commentary on the work, gradually zooming

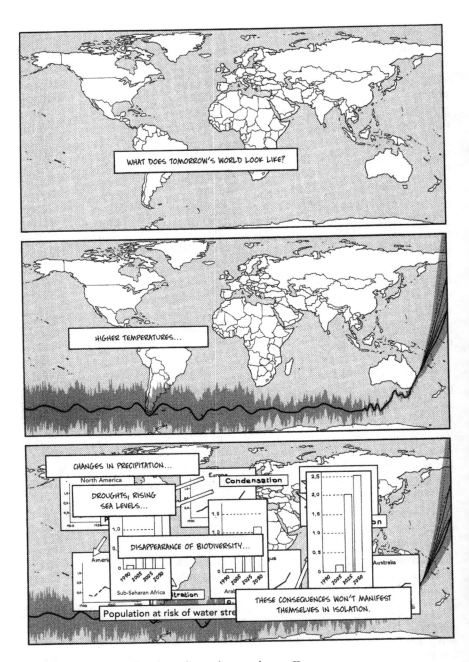

Figure 4.4 Representing data about climate change II

Source: *Climate Changed: A Personal Journey Through Science* by Philippe Squarzoni. English translation copyright © 2014 Harry N. Abrams, Inc. Used with permission of Express Permissions on behalf of Abrams ComicArts, an imprint of Harry N. Abrams, Inc., New York. All rights reserved. www.abramsbooks.com

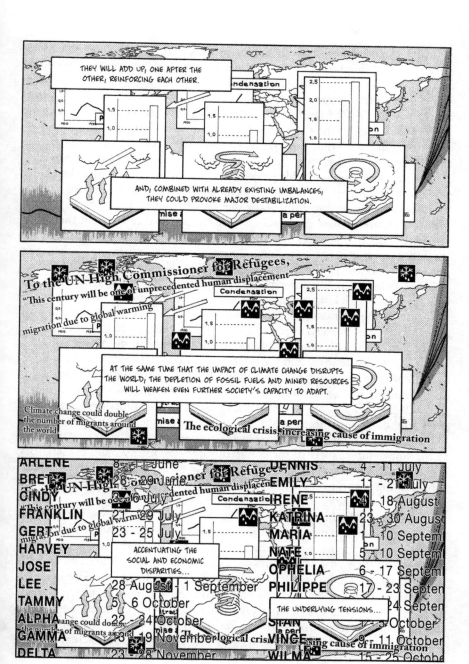

Figure 4.5 Narrating interviews

Source: *Climate Changed: A Personal Journey Through Science* by Philippe Squarzoni. English translation copyright © 2014 Harry N. Abrams, Inc. Used with permission of Express Permissions on behalf of Abrams ComicArts, an imprint of Harry N. Abrams, Inc., New York. All rights reserved. www.abramsbooks.com

in on the famous "blue marble" image of the earth, with the accompanying anchor text "Ninety-nine times out of a hundred, when we see a photo of earth, it's this one" (p. 170). The reader is hard pressed to know whether this is the actual photograph, or Squarzoni's drawing of the photograph, and it causes readers, in Tuftian fashion, to reflect upon the messages behind the images belonging to the routinized story of climate change.

Yet another way that Squarzoni visually narrates the story of climate change involves the series of interviews that he undertook with climate specialists in connection with this project. In the English translation, the reader gets the biographies of the nine experts he interviewed, from well-known members of the Intergovernmental Panel on Climate Change (IPCC) such as Jean Jouzel, "renowned climatologist and the director research at the Laboratory for Climate Sciences and the Environment" (p. 469) to lesser known specialists such as René Passet, "economist, a development specialist, and professor emeritus at the Sorbonne" (p. 470). These interviews, or rather excerpts from them, are interspersed throughout the work, each adding a new layer of convincing testimony to the debate about climate change. The inclusion of these interviews shows the reader how big that debate is, how many disciplines are involved, and what the potential effects are: biological, economic, social, ethical, and political. Squarzoni, moreover, includes both the actual interview and the interview process. The interview with Bernard Laponche, nuclear physicist, allows Squarzoni to share what he learns about energy, from personal travel and home heating to shipping freight (pp. 370–375, Figure 4.6). The reader, in each of these interview segments, is privy to the mimetic moment of testimony, with images of the specialist and the use of speech bubbles, as well as the diegetic moments that relate more to the storytelling aspect of the comic through anchor text and explanatory images. In this sense, illustrating the narrative possibilities of comics, Squarzoni initiates a three-way conversation that includes the specialist, himself as narrator, and the reader.

It is perhaps fitting to close this chapter with a few observations on the semiotics of Squarzoni's images. Like many comic artists, he predominantly uses the iconic mode, which for Groensteen is the *sine qua non* of comics (2009) and for McCloud specifically allows "amplification through simplification" (1994, p. 30). According to McCloud, the iconic mode emphasizes certain details of an object to reduce that object to its essential meaning. In the images analyzed throughout this chapter, we see just enough details – the writer's lair, the return to Squarzoni's childhood home and other images of personal memories, the interviews with scientists, the data itself presented as evidence – to recognize what that image is referring to, but for McCloud, as well as for Groensteen (2007, p. 10), it is precisely this iconic reduction that allows the reader to connect with the image. McCloud posits that the reader's active participation in creating meaning through the sequences of images is what defines the "arthology" (Groensteen 2007) or semiotic system of comics. There is no narrative per se in

Figure 4.6 Representing data about climate change I

Source: *Climate Changed: My personal Journey Through Science* by Philippe Sqarzoni. English translation copyright © 2014 Harry N. Abrams, Inc. Used with permission of Express Permissions on behalf of Abrams ComicArts, an imprint of Harry N. Abrams, Inc., New York. All rights reserved. www.abramsbooks.com

the individual panels, but the sequential succession of panels on the page, connected by means of the gutter, leads the reader herself to create the narrative (Groensteen 2013). In this way, the reader of comics acts herself as a participant in the story. By choosing the iconic mode, emphasized all the more by the absence of color in the comic, Squarzoni invites the reader to participate in the narrative of environmental collapse that unfolds, panel after panel, throughout the work. This comic's "alternative way to shed light on knowledge" (Lequeux and Schlesser 2015, p. 59) ultimately performs the very collapse he is writing about. Echoing Judith Butler's ideas on performative acts, which she claims "produce what they name" (1993, p. 23), *Saison brune* calls to mind more specifically Derek Attridge's ideas on literature as ethical event (2016), particularly where the reader is concerned. By producing the collapse that the comic names, while at the same time refusing to end a story about that end, *Saison brune* becomes far more than a factual documentary comic about climate change. Instead the work asks us as readers to participate in a narrative that embodies the forms of both New Journalism and documentary film; a narrative that questions both sides of the representational crisis surrounding climate change, not only the political crisis we face as citizens, but also, and perhaps more importantly, the semiotic crisis inherent in explaining it. Most importantly, *Saison brune* is a work illustrative of a medium that requires reader participation in order for it to make sense. This work, as Lequeux and Schlesser (2015, p. 59) have argued, is indeed an "ecolographic masterpiece"; the narrative strategies used to address collapse, both political and semiotic, present us with a complex story about the end, placing the reader at the heart of the double-sided crisis of climate change.

Notes

1 See for example, Daniels and Endfield 2008; Spoel et al. 2008; Lejano, Taveres-Reager and Berkes 2013; Mayer and von Mossner 2014; Bristow and Ford 2016; Bushell et al. 2017; Segal 2017.
2 In the field of comic studies, the very definition of comics has been hotly debated. For more on this debate, see Meskin 2007 and Groensteen 2015. Interestingly, the debate about formal definitions of comics depends partially on cultural and historical context, with US theories tending to focus on the sequential nature of comic images, and French theories focusing more on the semiotic relationships between text and image.
3 He is not mentioned, for example, in the recently published Routledge companion to comics (Bramlett, Cook and Meskin 2017) and articles devoted to his work do not show up in any major databases.
4 This multi-volume comic re-interprets journalist David Simon's investigative reports (1991) about his experiences shadowing police officers in the Baltimore homicide unit.
5 Page numbers refer to the English translation throughout.
6 The use of comics in teaching and learning has received increased critical attention in recent years (Tilley and Weiner 2017) and the English language publisher of *Saison brune* has, in fact, published a teacher's guide (Gutiérrez 2014).

7 Interestingly, and in contrast to the English-language edition, the French cover shows an abstract image of a tilted hourglass running out of sand, suggesting metaphorically that time is literally running out with respect to our planet. Again, as with the title, and taking into account how translations need to adapt to different cultural audiences, we see that the paratext of the English-language edition has privileged the subjective experience of the author whereas that of the French edition seems to privilege abstract ideas.

8 These forays into the storytelling process ruffled the feathers of one English-language reviewer (Yoshioka 2015), who clearly wanted a more straightforward and factual approach to the problem of climate change. The narrative focus nonetheless adds depth to the work as a whole, as Squarzoni's overall goal is not merely to explain climate change, but also to question the failed attempts to make sense of it.

9 Drawing from Kermode, David Dowling has discussed the difference between probability and plausibility in *Fictions of Nuclear Disaster* (1987) suggesting that nuclear disasters must be plausible in the minds of readers.

10 Robyn Warhol's concept of the "neonarrative" (2005), which refers to how film can articulate the unnarratable in new ways, seems particularly relevant in the context of comics.

11 In this regard, *Saison brune* recalls larger scholarly debates about whether the medium of comics belongs to the textual or the visual world. Several scholars have specifically suggested that the storytelling processes of documentary comics resemble the representational practices of documentary film (Woo 2010; Lefèvre 2007). Mickwitz (2016), drawing from Meskin (2010) argues for a compromise by suggesting that documentary comics might best be understood as kind of "cross-medium" (p. 7).

12 The term diegetic comes from the Greek, "diegesis," which literally means to tell a story. As Prince (1987) has shown, it refers to the telling or recounting part of narration, as opposed to mimesis, from the Greek, *mimeisthai*, to imitate, which refers to the direct enactment of the story.

13 According to the Oxford English Dictionary, the word stems from the old French, *evidence*, which in turn stems from the Late Latin *evidentia* or proof. In classical Latin, the word referred to "distinction, vivid presentation, clearness," while the root term *evidens* meant "obvious or apparent" (OED). Around 1300, in English, *evidence* denoted "appearance from which inferences may be drawn," evolving into "grounds for belief" from the late fourteenth century, and replacing the concept of witness, or "one who furnishes testimony" in the 1590s.

References

Académie française, No date. *Prix Léon de Rosen*. Available at www.academie-francaise.fr/prix-leon-de-rosen [Accessed 19 January 2017].

Attridge, D., 2016. The literary work as an ethical event. In M. Middeke and C. Reinfandt, eds., *Theory matters*. London: Palgrave Macmillan. pp. 219–232.

Barthes, R., 1964. The rhetoric of the image. In J. Evans and S. Hall, eds., 1999. *Visual culture: The reader*. Thousand Oaks, CA: Sage Publications. pp. 33–40.

Before the flood, 2016. [film]. Directed by Fisher Stevens. National Geographic, U.S.A.

Booklist, 2014. Climate changed: A personal journey through the science (Review). *Booklist* (June 1 & 15), p. 60.

Boynton, R. S., 2005. *The new journalism: Conversations with America's best non fiction writers on their craft*. New York: Vintage Books.

Bramlett, F., Cook, R. T. and Meskin, A., 2017. *The Routledge companion to comics*. London and New York: Routledge.

Bristow, T. and Ford, T. eds., 2016. *A cultural history of climate change*. London and New York: Routledge.

Bushell, S., Satre Buisson, G., Workman, M. and Colley, T., 2017. Strategic narratives in climate change: Towards a unifying narrative to address the action gap on climate change. *Energy Research & Social Science* 28(June), pp. 39–49. http://dx.doi.org/10.1016/j.erss.2017.04.001.

Butler, J., 1993. *Bodies that matter*. London and New York: Routledge.

Caldwell, P., 1983. *The puritan conversion narrative: The beginnings of American expression*. New York: Cambridge University Press.

Chute, H. L., 2016. *Disaster drawn: Visible witness, comics and documentary form*. Cambridge: Harvard University Press.

Daniels, S. and Endfield, G. H., 2009. Narratives of climate change: Introduction. *Journal of Historical Geography* 35(2), pp. 215–222. https://doi.org/10.1016/j.jhg.2008.09.005.

Das, V., 2007. *Life and words: Violence and the descent into the ordinary*. Berkeley: University of California Press.

Dowling, D., 1987. *Fictions of nuclear disaster*. London: MacMillan.

Duncan, R., Taylor, M. R. and Stoddard, D. eds., 2016. *Creating comics as journalism, memoir, and non-fiction*. London and New York: Routledge.

Earthovershootday. No Date. Available at www.overshootday.org/ [Accessed 14 July 2017].

Eisner, W., 1985. *Comics and sequential art*. Principles and practices of the world's most popular artform. Guerneville, CA: Poorhouse Press.

Groensteen, T., 2007. *The system of comics*. Translated by B. Beaty and N. Nguyen. Jackson, MS: University of Mississippi Press.

Groensteen, T., 2009. Why are comics still in search of cultural legitimization? In J. Heer and K. Worcester, eds. *The comics studies reader*. Jackson, MS: University of Mississippi Press. pp. 3–11.

Groensteen, T., 2013. *Comics and narration*. Translated by A. Miller. Jackson, MS: University of Mississippi Press.

Gutiérrez, P., 2014. *Teacher's guide to climate changed: A personal journey through the science by Philippe Squarzoni*. [pdf] Abrams Books. Available at www.abramsbooks.com/pdfs/academic/ClimateChanged_TeachingGuide.pdf [Accessed 25 February 2017].

Hale, B., Kuepfer, C., Steinert-Borella, S. and Wiedmer, C., 2015. Environmental justice, 'collapse' and the question of evidence. *Intervalla* 3, pp. i–vi, [online] Available at www.fus.edu/intervalla/volume-3-environmental-justice-collapse-and-the-question-of-evidence [Accessed 20 February 2017].

Höpker, K., 2014. A sense of an ending–risk, catastrophe and precarious humanity in Margaret Atwood's *Oryx and Crake*. In S. Mayer and A. W. von Mossner, eds., *The anticipation of catastrophe: Environmental risk in North American literature and culture*. Heidelberg: Universiätsverlag Winter. pp. 162–180.

An inconvenient truth, 1996. [film]. Directed by Davis Guggenheim. Paramount Classics, U.S.A.

Kermode, F., 1967. *The sense of an ending: Studies in the theory of fiction*. New York: Oxford University Press.

Latour, B., 1991. *Nous n'avons jamais été modernes*. Paris: La Découverte.

Latour, B., 2014a. Agency at the time of the Anthropocene. *New Literary History* 45(1) (Winter), pp. 1–18.

Latour, B., 2014b. *The Anthropocene and the destruction of the image of the globe.* Gifford Lecture, University of Edinburgh. Available at www.artandeducation.net/ classroom/video/66319/bruno-latour-the-anthropocene-and-the-destruction-of-the-image-of-the-globe [Accessed 30 January 2017].

Lefèvre, P., 2000. Narration in comics. *Image & Narrative* 1(1). Available at www.image andnarrative.be/inarchive/narratology/pascallefevre.htm [Accessed 14 July 2017].

Lefèvre, P., 2007. Incompatible visual ontologies? The problematic adaption of drawn images. In I. Gordon, M Jancovich and M.P. McAllister, eds., *Film and comic books.* Jackson, MS: University of Mississippi Press. pp. 1–12.

Lejano, R. P., Taveres-Reager, J. and Berkes, F., 2013. Climate and narrative: Environmental knowledge in everyday life. *Environmental Science & Policy* 31(August), pp. 61–70. http://dx.doi.org/10.1016/j.envsci.2013.02.009.

Lequeux, E. and Schlesser. T., 2015. Les artistes peuvent-ils sauver la planète? *Beaux Arts,* 378(December), pp. 56–69.

Mayer, S. and von Mossner, A. W. eds., 2014. *The anticipation of catastrophe: Environmental risk in North American literature and culture.* Heidelberg: Universiätsverlag Winter.

McCloud, S., 1994. *Understanding comics: The invisible art.* New York: Harper Perennial.

McKinney, M., 2008. Representations of history and politics in French-language comics and graphic novels. In M. McKinney, ed., *History and politics in French-language comics and graphic novels.* Jackson, MS: University Press of Mississippi. pp. 3–24.

Meskin, A., 2007. Defining comics? *The Journal of Aesthetics and Art Criticism* 65(4), pp. 369–379.

Meskin, A., 2010. Comics as literature? *British Journal of Aesthetics* 49(3), pp. 219–239. https://doi.org/10.1093/aesthj/ayp025.

Mickwitz, N., 2016. *Documentary comics: Graphic truth-telling in a skeptical age.* Basingstoke and New York: Palgrave Macmillan.

Miller, A., 2008. Bande dessinée as reportage. In M. McKinney, ed., *History and politics in French-language comics and graphic novels.* Jackson, MS: University Press of Mississippi. pp. 97–116.

Miller, A. and Beaty, B. eds., 2014. *The French comics theory reader.* Leuven, Belgium: Leuven University Press.

Minster, M., 2010. The rhetoric of ascent in *An inconvenient truth* and *Everything's cool.* In P. Willoquet-Maricondi, ed., *Framing the world: Explorations in ecocriticism and film.* Charlottesville: University of Virginia Press. pp. 25–42.

Miodrag, H. ed., 2013. *Comics and language: Reimagining critical discourse on the form.* Jackson, MS: University Press of Mississippi.

Morton, T., 2013. *Hyperobjects: Philosophy and ecology after the end of the world.* Minneapolis: University of Minnesota Press.

Morton, T., 2016. This is not my beautiful biosphere. In T. Bristow and T. H. Ford, eds., *A cultural history of climate change.* London and New York: Routledge. pp. 229–238.

Nurmis, J., 2017. The siren song of collapse and ways forward for climate change photojournalism. In A. Vogelaar, B. Hale and A. Peat, eds., *The discourses of environmental collapse: Imagining the end.* London and New York: Routledge.

Nyberg, A. K., 2012. Comics journalism: Drawing on words to picture the past in *Safe area Goražde*. In M. J. Smith and R. Duncan, eds., *Critical approaches to comics*. London and New York: Routledge. pp. 116–128.

Postema, B., 2013. *Narrative structure in comics: Making sense of fragments*. Suffolk: Boydell Press.

Pratt, H. J., 2009. Narrative in comics. *The Journal of Aesthetics and Art Criticism* 67, pp. 107–117. http://dx.doi.org/10.1111/j.1540-6245.2008.01339.x.

Prince, G., 1987. *A dictionary of narratology*. Revised edition 2003. Lincoln and London: University of Nebraska Press.

Prince, G., 1988. The disnarrated. *Style*, 22(1), pp. 1–8. Available at www.jstor.org/stable/42945681 [Accessed 14 July 2017].

Richardson, B. ed., 2008. *Narrative beginnings: Theories and practices*. Lincoln and London: University of Nebraska Press.

Sacco, J., 2000. *Safe area Goražde*. Seattle: Fantagraphic Books.

Segal, M., 2017. The missing climate change narrative. *South Atlantic Quarterly* 116(1), pp. 121–128. http://dx.doi.org/10.1215/00382876-3749370.

Simon, D., 1991. *Homicide: A year in the killing streets*. New York: Houghton Mifflin.

Smelik, A. ed., 2010. *The scientific imaginary in visual culture*. Göttingen: V & R Unipress.

Smith, H., 2010. What is a conversion narrative? *Conversion narratives in early modern Europe*. Available from: https://europeanconversionnarratives.wordpress.com/2010/12/01/what-is-a-conversion-narrative/ [Accessed 3 January 2017].

Spoel, P., Goforth, D., Cheu, H. and Pearson, D., 2008. Public communication of climate change science: Engaging citizens through apocalyptic narrative explanation. *Technical Communication Quarterly* 18(1), pp. 49–81. http://dx.doi.org/10.1080/10572250802437382.

Squarzoni, P., 2003. *Zapata, en temps de guerre*. Paris: Delcourt.

Squarzoni, P., 2004. *Torture blanche*. Paris: Delcourt.

Squarzoni, P., 2012. *Saison brune*. Paris: Delcourt.

Squarzoni, P., 2014. *Climate changed: A personal journey through the science*. Translated from the French by I. Hahnenberger. New York: Abrams.

Squarzoni, P., 2016–2017. *Homicide: une année dans les rues de Baltimore*. 2 vols. Paris: Delcourt.

Tilley, C. and Weiner, R., 2017. Teaching and learning with comics. In F. Bramlette, R. T. Cook and A. Meskin, eds., *The Routledge companion to comics*. London and New York: Routledge. pp. 358–366.

Tufte, E. R., 1990. *Envisioning information*. Cheshire, CT: Graphics Press.

Tufte, E. R., 1997. *Visual explanations: Images and quantities, evidence and narrative*. Cheshire, CT: Graphics Press.

Tufte, E. R., 2001. *The visual display of quantitative information*. Cheshire, CT: Graphics Press.

Tufte, E. R., 2006. *Beautiful evidence*. Cheshire, CT: Graphics Press.

Versaci, R., 2007. *This book contains graphic language: Comics as literature*. New York: Continuum.

Wapner, P., 2016. Introduction. In P. Wapner and H. Elver, eds., *Reimagining climate change*. London and New York: Routledge. pp. 1–13.

Warhol, R. R., 2005. Neonarrative; or how to render the unnarratable in realist fiction and contemporary film. In J. Phelan and P. J. Rabinowitz, eds., *A *companion to narrative theory*. Malden, MA and Oxford: Blackwell Publishing. pp. 220–231.

Whiteside, K. H., 2013. A representative politics of nature? Bruno Latour on collectives and constitutions. *Contemporary Political Theory* 12(3), 185–205. http://dx.doi.org/10.1057/cpt.2012.24.

Whittington-Evans, N., 2014. Introduction. In P. Squarzoni, ed., *Saison brune*. Translated from the French by Ivanka Hahnenberger. New York: Abrams. pp. 6–7.

Wolfe, T., 1975. *The new journalism*. London: Picador.

Woo, B., 2010. Reconsidering comics journalism: Experience and information in Joe Sacco's *Palestine*. In D. Hassler-Forest and J. Goggin, eds., *The rise and reason of comics and graphic literature: Critical essays on the form*. Jefferson, NC: McFarland. pp. 166–177.

Yoshioka, J. 2015. *Climate changed: A personal journey through the science* [Book Review]. *American Meteorological Society* (November), p. 173.

Part II
Pop collapse

5 This is the end of the world as we know it

Narratives of collapse and transformation in archaeology and popular culture

Guy D. Middleton

Collapse lies at an interface between academic research and popular culture; it is a subject for serious analysis by archaeologists, historians, and academics in other fields, as well as for entertainment, sermonizing, and spectacle. It has become a boom industry, with many authors, magazines, and documentary and feature film makers "cranking out collapse porn," as Phillips puts it (2015). We are gleefully bombarded with apocalyptic images illustrating our impending doom, which will come about either through the damage we have done to the earth since the industrial revolution, through unchecked population growth, extensive misuse of the land, the poisoning of the oceans, our thirst for fresh water, or in the form of human-caused climate change. As Steve Almond (2013) wrote in the *New York Times*, "as a culture, we've become obsessed with creating and consuming visions of the apocalypse." Our society is haunted by narratives of a catastrophic collapse that has not yet happened.

There is no doubt that (some) human societies have, over the past two centuries, abused our shared planet to the extent that it is now in a critical condition. As is almost universally accepted, we face increasing climate instability because of the effects of our greenhouse gas emissions since the industrial revolution, and we also have serious environmental problems caused by unprecedented population levels, mass urbanization, and the industrialization of agriculture, energy, and food supply. The forests, which soak up carbon dioxide and provide us with oxygen, are disappearing and the oceans, the home of oxygen-producing marine flora, are becoming warmer, more acidic, and less oxygenated. There is a horrifying level of marine plastics pollution, a direct result of modernity, which is not going anywhere except into the food chain. We may be facing Earth's sixth great extinction event – and it may well be "our" fault (Barnosky et al. 2011; Hance 2015). Gaia may well take her revenge (Lovelock 2007).

These images of a possible future global environmental collapse are often projected back in time, applied to past societies, whose histories are transformed into horror stories in which thousands, even millions die and cities are consumed by desert or jungle, only to be rediscovered by intrepid (and usually Western) explorers. We hear stories of plagues, of societies propelled by a combination of overpopulation, climate change and environmental damage into famine, violence, death, and even cannibalism; they fall from a state of civilization into one of barbarism and savagery. These graphic depictions of apocalyptic collapse have been popularized over recent decades by bestselling and respected non-fiction authors such as Lester Brown (2011); Jared Diamond (2005); Paul Ehrlich (1968); Ehrlich and Ehrlich (2013); and Clive Ponting (1991, 1994, 2007) and in popular science magazines such as *New Scientist* and *Scientific American* (Figure 5.1). These authors are not

Figures 5.1a and 5.1b Collapse makes the headlines in popular science magazines

Source: With kind permission of *New Scientist*

Figures 5.1a and 5.1b (Continued)

archaeologists, but they use the supposed fates of past societies as warnings to contemporary audiences.

Collapse makes good material for television documentary makers too, who can combine academic talking heads with dramatic and exotic shots of jungle or desert and dramatic historical reconstructions. Diamond's book inspired a National Geographic film, *Collapse*, which portrays future archaeologists of the twenty-third century picking over the ruins of lost American cities – "the greatest civilization in history." It poses the question "how could a civilization that mastered the planet, suddenly collapse?" The video, presumably produced with a US audience in mind, has much to say about how great and powerful Western (or American) civilization is and also makes it clear how destructive and unsustainable human urban development, especially in California and the southwestern United States, is.

Of past collapses there are also examples. The BBC documentary *Ancient Apocalypse: The Maya Collapse* opens with a shot of the misty jungle at dawn or dusk, grand stone pyramids and monuments can be seen rising through the tree canopy, birdsong and flutes flutter in the tranquil calm. Then we see the wise careworn face of an elderly Maya person and a pensive child, followed by a shot of sinister carrion birds, which suggest the impending doom that we know that the story will reveal to us. The narrator explains the mystery, clearly setting out the problem to be solved in the film:

> Twelve hundred years ago, a catastrophe struck. One of the most extraordinary civilizations the world has ever known disappeared. Millions of people died. Some were savagely murdered. Why it happened is a mystery.

The History Channel's alarmingly titled *Who Killed the Maya?* also dwells lovingly on the apocalyptic and the catastrophic; the title clearly emphasizes death and destruction and presents the Maya as victims whose civilization and people vanished after thousands of years. As with the BBC documentary, a mysterious aura is created to draw us in.

It is not only the Maya who receive apocalyptic treatment. Another History Channel documentary, this time about the collapse in at the end of the Late Bronze Age in the Eastern Mediterranean, entitled *Secrets of the Aegean Apocalypse*, begins in a similarly melodramatic way; in a sonorous voice, replete with dramatic pauses, the narrator declaims:

> Armageddon, the apocalypse, the end of the world, predicted thousands of times, but in 1200 BC it actually happened. And no-one saw it coming. Some of the greatest civilizations of the age were wiped out in a single generation.

However, the story of the Late Bronze Age collapse is a lot more complicated, as Eric Cline and others have demonstrated (Cline 2014; Middleton 2010). It is certainly true that the palace states of Mycenaean Greece and the Hittite empire in Anatolia collapsed, and major sites such as Ugarit were destroyed, but it was not the end of the world – in Greece the Mycenaean culture continued for more than a century and in the east Neo-Hittite states developed, some, such as Carchemish, were ruled by descendants of the Anatolian

Hittite royal family. Egypt did not collapse and on Cyprus destruction was followed by growth.

The Smithsonian channel's film *Perfect Storms: Dark Age Volcano* is another example of "catastrophist" thinking; it tells the story of the effects of a volcanic super-eruption in Mesoamerica in AD 536, which "set off a lethal chain of events, from climate change to the Bubonic plague." It even led, so the film claims, to the collapse of the Roman Empire (though the western empire fragmented across the fifth century and the eastern empire survived for another thousand years, despite plague, war, and civil strife, until it was destroyed by the Ottomans in 1453).

These examples demonstrate a tendency to see collapse as apocalyptic and catastrophic. People and civilizations were wiped out suddenly, under mysterious circumstances. While the archaeologists involved in such television programs usually present more nuanced perspectives, the shows are edited to be dramatic and entertaining, as well as educational and informative; they fit well into the genre of "edutainment" or "infotainment" (Thussu 2007). Such stories, whether intended as educational or just as entertainment, tie in with our cultural expectations and at the same time shape our understanding of and beliefs about what happened in the past and how human societies work.

This chapter examines our popular discourse of collapse as apocalypse and sets this beside the views of archaeologists who study and write about collapse. To begin with, I suggest that we come to collapse with ready-made cultural frameworks of collapse as apocalypse which are deeply embedded in our heritage. I then turn to the reporting collapse in the news media and non-fiction writing. After that, I examine how archaeologists have responded to the challenge of the environmental discourse of collapse. I briefly look at how archaeologists understand the wider role of archaeology and its importance. Finally, I return to the example of the Classic Maya collapse and to why questioning the now traditional environmental collapse narratives is important.

Apocalyptic collapse as cultural heritage

Those growing up in and influenced by "the Western tradition" are socialized into particular views of collapse from stories that have long been embedded in the western culture and worldview. To start with, we can refer to the many episodes of destruction in the Bible, where God destroys the people who displease him. Perhaps the most well-known of these is the flood, sent to "cleanse" the earth, which is described in Genesis:

> The Lord saw that the wickedness of man was great on the earth, and that every intent of the thoughts of his heart was continually only evil. The Lord was sorry that He had made man on the earth, and it grieved Him in His heart. So the Lord said, "I will destroy man, whom I have created, from the face of the earth – both man and beast, and

the creeping things, and the birds of the sky, for I am sorry that I have made them."

Then there is God's judgement and destruction of the cities of Sodom and Gomorrah, also described in Genesis:

the Lord rained brimstone and fire on Sodom and Gomorrah. It was from the Lord out of heaven. So He overthrew those cities, all the valley, all the inhabitants of the cities, and what grew on the ground.

Despite the increasingly secular nature of western society and the decline, in many areas, of (at least a strong) Christianity, these stories remain well known. The story of Sodom and Gomorrah was also (loosely) retold by Hollywood director Robert Aldrich in 1962 in a film starring Stewart Granger that was popular but not noted as particularly good. More recently, in 2014 Darren Aronofsky released his Hollywood epic *Noah*, starring Russell Crowe in the title role, which garnered generally positive reviews and did well at the box office. That such a film got made in the first place testifies to the interest and audience that could be expected. Far from seeing the story as "true," Aronofsky suggested that "the Noah story is something metaphorical and mythic, a beautiful fiction that points towards truth, rather than simply reporting it" (Collin 2014). Themes of apocalyptic destruction by a powerful superhuman force as a result of "sin" evidently still have some cultural weight and this way of thinking (or representing) translates easily into a context in which humanity's mistreatment of Earth, our modern sin, results in the destruction of human civilization and possibly humanity itself by the earth, the environment, or nature. Indeed, one recent book on collapse focuses on the hubris of societies that fail to recognize their own problems and adapt accordingly (Johnson 2017).

From the classical heritage there are also well-worn stories of apocalyptic collapse. The best known must be Plato's Atlantis story, told in the *Critias* and *Timaeus* (fourth century BC). This story has caught the modern imagination, with "believers" of all stripes; classicist Alan Cameron noted in 1983 that some 20,000 or more books on the topic had been published – a number which has continued to rise in the past three decades. In the story, Atlantis was an ideal state located on a large island somewhere beyond the Mediterranean; it was populated by a virtuous race of people. However, the Atlanteans fell into wickedness and greed; they embarked on wars of conquest and enslaved their defeated enemies. The Athenians then led an alliance of Greeks against them and defeated them. Afterwards "there were earthquakes and floods of extraordinary violence, and in a single dreadful day and night all your fighting men were swallowed up by the earth, and the island of Atlantis was similarly swallowed up by the sea and vanished" (Plato 1977, p. 38).

People tend to forget the details of the story but remember the apocalyptic fate of Atlantis (Figure 5.2). While many have tried, one way or another, to

Figure 5.2 Destruction of Atlantis (note the inspiration of Maya rather than Greek architectural style), Robert Stacy-Judd (1936).

Source: Courtesy of the Art, Design & Architecture Museum at the University of California, Santa Barbara

"prove" the story, it is clearly a political allegory invented by Plato, who, we should recall, devised other "ideal" states in his *Republic* and *Laws* (Morgan 1998). The Atlantis story is not then a Greek myth, as such, but is rather a Platonic myth. For its fourth century BC audience, it would have recalled the surprising defeat of the Persian superpower by the Athenians and other Greeks in the fifth century BC and would have conveyed a message that overweening ambition, corruption, and greed – imperialism – carried with it the potential for utter destruction; the Athenians of an earlier age were virtuous and thus victorious. The story is moral and didactic, not a distorted and almost lost memory of ancient history. As Cameron (2004, p. 124 n.5) noted, "it is only in modern times that people have taken the Atlantis story seriously; no-one did so in antiquity." This conclusion does not really matter here, for as Russell (2004, p. 99) said, "the myth is of even more importance, historically, than the reality" – it is the story itself that matters, that is popular, that speaks to us, and that in turn promotes an apocalyptic vision of collapse. We, like the Atlanteans, may be punished for our arrogance and greed by some terrible catastrophe.

Such visions of apocalyptic collapse are not only to be found in the deep roots of Western culture, in religious or philosophical texts, the nineteenth century, with its progress in science and technology, transformed and popularized images of collapse into "images of degeneration, catastrophe, total war, the collapse of civilization and the extermination of life," found in both fiction and non-fiction genres (Bulfin 2015, p. 82). The genre of "last man" science fiction, still popular today, was born from the fertile imagination of Mary Shelley, whose novel *The Last Man*, in which plague ravages the world causing death, migration, and conflict, was published in 1826. In a serious article entitled "How will the world end?," published in *Pearson's Magazine* in July 1900, Herbert C. Fyfe explored contemporary ideas "held by men of learning and repute" about the end of days – "the annihilation of our planet by sudden catastrophe, or by gradual decay, or else the disappearance of human life from the face of the globe."

These catastrophe theories included running out of oxygen, the destruction of the atmosphere, destruction by comets (Biela's Comet had been a particular worry), the rise of "lower" animals such as giant predatory crabs, cuttlefish and octopi (Figure 5.3), perhaps because of changes in ecosystems that held their numbers in check, climate change and the spread of germs and micro-organisms that "could destroy the entire human race in a month." Sir William Crookes calculated that the bread-consuming population would outstrip wheat production by 1931, while the Belgian General Brialmant suggested that "in less than 180 years [thus by 2080] the population of the globe would be so dense that the earth could no longer nourish its inhabitants, and that hundreds of millions of human beings must die yearly of hunger" (Fyfe 1900).

The Victorian discourse on apocalyptic collapse is not too dissimilar to our own. Paul and Anne Ehrlich, for example, have been particularly prominent in popularizing a coming apocalyptic collapse with their 1968 book *The Population Bomb*, although as Rubin (1998, p. 78) has pointed out, the book, when it appeared, was not novel in its idea of overpopulation bringing famine, disease, conflict and war. A fairly recent volume entitled *Global Catastrophic Risks*, aimed at an academic audience, revisits themes of cometary impact, climate change, human and animal evolution, volcanic eruptions, plagues and pandemics, as well as describing new dangers from artificial intelligence and bio- and nanotechnology (Bostrom and Cirkovic 2008). The British cosmologist Martin Rees has written, for a broad "popular" audience, on the potential imminent end of humanity due to its own scientific and technological "progress"; Rees thinks that "the odds are no better than fifty-fifty that our present civilization on Earth will survive to the end of the present century without a serious setback" (Rees 2003, p. 8).

Just as the themes Fyfe wrote about were well known to the Victorian public, as Bulfin (2015) makes clear, the topics addressed in Bostrom and Cirkovic and Rees's books are well-known subjects of twentieth and twenty-first century news, popular science literature, and science fiction books, films, and documentaries. Harry Harrison's *Make Room! Make Room!* later filmed as *Soylent Green* (1973), and John Wyndham's novels *The Kraken Wakes* and *The Day of the Triffids* come to mind, dealing in turn with serious

Figure 5.3 "A sudden appearance out of the sea of a race of amphibious monsters, capable of sweeping men out of existence"

Source: Illustration from Herbert C. Fyfe's article "How will the world end?" in *Pearson's Magazine* 1900 (July), page 9; illustration by Warwick Goble.

overpopulation and food and water shortages, an alien threat from the sea, and the perils of genetic engineering for human society. Films such as *Armageddon* (1998), *Contagion* (2011), *San Andreas* (2015), and *The Day After Tomorrow* (2004) reprise these themes and others too. Like the Victorians, we are caught between a narrative of progress and one of peril and collapse. The discourse on and images of collapse that we have and the panic that seems so urgent are not at all new.

The outlook in 1900 was not hopeless though. Then as now, there was a secular faith that science and technology could come to the rescue – a belief in the power of progress (Kelly 2013). The various authorities Fyfe introduced proposed, for example, that air could be manufactured and carried around in diver-style tanks, that agriculture could be improved to remove more "carbonic acid gas and to release sufficient new oxygen" to support life and also to increase the agricultural yields necessary to feed the growing population, "waves, waterfalls, solar energy, the wind, the ether, atmospheric electricity" could "be made to supply the energy that we require for daily needs." Apart from the oxygen tanks, we would not need to look far to find the same faith in science and even the same suggestions presented as solutions to contemporary problems. Yet some see science and technology as part of the problem – that our overdevelopment may contain the seeds of our own destruction.

While these are visions of global collapse, archaeologists are usually interested in specific cultures and societies; they are most often not describing or seeking to explain an apocalyptic collapse, or to reveal so-called ancient doomsday prophecies. However, it remains the case that our cultural heritage hardwires us to think about these collapses in an apocalyptic way and to accept simple sweeping explanations of collapse. This is particularly apparent in the way that collapse is dealt with and reported in the news and in popular non-fiction writing.

The public face of collapse: news and non-fiction

Periodically, research on ancient collapse is reported in the popular press, where it is commonly presented as a problem-solution narrative in which scientists "solve" the problem of collapse, very often, in recent years, by finding evidence for past climate changes. Thus we can read headlines such as "Climate change killed off Maya civilization, study says" (*National Geographic News* 13 March 2003); "Climate change may be responsible for the rise and fall of Roman empire, scientists find" (*The Telegraph* 16 January 2011); "Climate killed Harappan civilization" (*The Times of India* 29th May 2012); and "Did climate change kill the Mayans"? (*Time* 9 November 2012). In an article entitled "Climate change: The great civilization destroyer," which appeared in *New Scientist* in 2012, Marshall suggested that the list of civilizations laid low by climate change was an ever-growing one as more palaeoclimatic data was gathered.

Other scholars prefer to lay the blame for collapse on human societies themselves. The most well-known of this group is Jared Diamond, who wrote the bestselling book *Collapse: How Societies Choose to Fail or Succeed* (2005). What Diamond attempted to show was that human societies had collapsed because they had damaged their environments; his book built on an earlier paper on this theme, which considered isolated island societies (Diamond 1994). However, his research suggested that this position was certainly not the case in many examples of collapse; thus he wrote that he knew of no "case in which a society's collapse can be attributed solely to environmental damage" and even that "it would be absurd to claim that environmental damage must be a major factor in all collapses" (Diamond 2005, pp. 11, 15). Yet throughout the book, the original position, which seems in origin based on his earlier theories about small isolated societies, is maintained. Thus "deforestation was a or *the* major factor" in the collapse of the Ancestral Puebloans, the Classic Maya, Easter Island, and the Greenland Norse (Diamond 2005, p. 487). Added to this, he sees overpopulation as a key factor in each example, since this made societies more vulnerable to ecological changes that would affect subsistence production and social stability. This style of argument is known as the "overshoot" model and it has been soundly critiqued by Joseph Tainter, who argues that there "does not presently appear to be a confirmed archaeological case of overshoot, resource degradation, and collapse brought about by overpopulation and/or mass consumption" (Tainter 2006, p. 71).

Population and resources are major factors for others too, for example Ehrlich and Ehrlich, mentioned previously. In one newspaper article in 2011, Paul Ehrlich was labelled as "the modern day equivalent of Malthus, the eighteenth-century English clergyman who popularized the idea that the number of people would eventually outstrip food production" (Jowit 2011). *The Population Bomb* has been regarded as "a masterful work of popularization," one that does not "attempt to convince intellectually" but emotionally. In the scholarly press, they have reasserted their ideas, suggesting that "for the first time, humanity's *global* civilization – the worldwide, increasingly interconnected, highly technological society in which we all are to one degree or another, embedded – is threatened with collapse by an array of environmental problems" (Ehrlich and Ehrlich 2013). Diamond and the Ehrlichs's work have in common a neo-Malthusian slant – for both, population and resources are key, and collapse apocalyptic.

As this chapter was being completed, new research on collapse reached the news. *The Daily Mail Online* (1 September 2016) reports this under the headline "How to spot if society is DOOMED: Researchers reveal the signs that show civilization is set to collapse" (Macdonald 2016). The article opens with the statement that "it has been seen all throughout human history – a bustling community experiences a population boom and technological advancement until, seemingly overnight, it plummets into total collapse." A story could hardly be more apocalyptic.

For Diamond and others, collapse is primarily a matter of a "drastic decrease in human population size . . . over a considerable area, for an extended time" (Diamond 2005, p. 3). The "society is DOOMED" article reports on research published in the *Proceedings of the National Academy of Sciences* (Downey et al. 2016; Scheffer 2016), which investigated whether early warning signs could be detected prior to "population collapse" in Neolithic societies. This is a very specific type of collapse best known from biology and population studies in which populations in a given ecosystem "collapse." However, in defining collapse, archaeologists are not usually thinking primarily of population. Tainter, in perhaps the most influential work on archaeology and collapse, argues that "collapse . . . is a *political* process. It may, and often does have consequences in such areas as economics, art, and literature, but it is fundamentally a matter of the socio-political sphere" (Tainter 1988, pp. 4–5). Another archaeologist, Glenn Schwartz, notes that:

> In the archaeological literature, collapse usually entails some or all of the following: the fragmentation of states into smaller political entities; the partial abandonment or complete desertion of urban centers, along with the loss or depletion of their centralizing functions; the breakdown of regional economic systems; and the failure of civilizational ideologies.
> (Schwartz 2006, pp. 5–6)

Indeed, Tainter (2006) and Maya archaeologist Arthur Demarest (2001) have suggested that many arguments about collapse are caused by a lack of terminological clarity – it is assumed that we all know what "collapse" signifies, though in reality it means different things to different people; even in archaeology.

It would be wrong to suggest that environmental narratives of collapse are in any sense "made up" or that they are not based on archaeological and other, especially palaeoclimatic, evidence; each is based on published scholarly studies in respectable journals and books. Yet sometimes it is interpretations that are repeated or cited as evidence or conclusion – or as fact. When information crosses genres or scholarly fields its nuance and context is easily mislaid or replaced. The dynamic nature of archaeological and historical interpretation is frequently lost and very often there is a lack of attention paid to exactly "what" is collapsing as well as to what "collapse" means in any particular instance, as if reconstructions of the societies or groups in question or the historical processes which they underwent were clear and unproblematic.

Diamond's work piggybacked on previous environmental histories that saw anthropogenic environmental damage as a key to explaining collapse. In 1991, Clive Ponting's *Green History of the World* took a very bleak look at the catalogue of environmental problems caused by ancient societies – starting with Easter Island and including Mesopotamia and the Classic Maya. The book was republished in 1994 and, following the commercial success of Diamond's book, again in 2007 with a new subtitle "The Environment and the Collapse of Great Civilizations." Another influence was archaeologist Paul Bahn and John Flenley's popular archaeology book *Easter Island, Earth Island* (1992). In their view, Easter Island declined into collapse after AD 1500 "economically and demographically" in a vicious cycle where increased *moai*-carving created an imbalance between food producers and non-food producers (Bahn and Flenley 1992, p. 208). The population grew, which meant the islanders had to cut down more trees to grow more food, yet with the unintended consequence that this reduced crop yields: "clearly the islanders brought disaster on themselves by gradually destroying a crucial resource" (Bahn and Flenley 1992, p. 210). They drew a wider moral message about greed, selfishness, and sustainability from their Easter Island narrative, which many have followed – using archaeological and historical examples as parables, warnings for today.

In addition to Bahn and Flenley's crossover book on Easter Island, for example, Diamond was also influenced by Charles Redman's 1999 *Human Impact on Ancient Environments*, which began with an ecocide/overshoot narrative of Easter Island's collapse. Marshall's 2012 article on climate change and collapse followed and expanded on an influential 2001 paper published in *Science*, in which archaeologist Harvey Weiss and climatologist Raymond Bradley had listed twelve "societies" that they thought had collapsed because of climate change: Natufians; Uruk; Akkadian Empire, Old Kingdom Egypt, Harappa IIIB; EBA III Palestine, LBA Greece, Crete; Moche; Tiwanaku; Classic Maya; and the Ancestral Puebloans.

As for the Classic Maya collapse, archaeologist Gyles Iannone and colleagues counted forty-three major articles on the megadrought model published between 1978 and 2012, with the majority appearing between 2000 and 2012 (Iannone et al. 2014, pp. 51, 53–57). The important volume in which their paper appears clearly demonstrates that archaeologists do accept the validity and usefulness of palaeoclimatic data and the reality of historic climate change (Iannone 2014). However, the archaeological evidence for some Maya regions, especially the southern Peten, demonstrates our "ability to very specifically reconstruct events and processes of the southwestern Peten collapse in terms of chronology and *layers* of causality *before* and *without* drought" (Demarest 2014, p. 206).

Clearly news sources and a section of environmental non-fiction present very particular views of collapse which portray it as apocalyptic, sometimes caused by nature and sometimes by humanity's short-sighted abuse of the environment, and often with an emphasis on population numbers. These views tie with our inherited images of apocalypse and collapse – they are popular and believable precisely because they fit in with our preconceptions. However, we should remember that there is no simple divide between popular sensationalist apocalyptic stories of collapse and serious scholarly interpretations, one being "true" and the other "false"; within archaeology, there are many scholars who give prominence to environmental factors in collapse – and many who see these arguments as deterministic, overstated, simplistic, unproved, or just wrong. The wider discourse on collapse spans academic and popular culture, science, fiction, and moralizing texts, each influencing the other in the wider social milieu. As a result, it is important always to question the stories we are told about collapse.

The archaeologists strike back

Although less likely to be reported in the wider press, some archaeologists have mounted a spirited defence of more complex and nuanced views of past collapse. An extended review of Diamond's *Collapse*, and the discourse it could be seen to represent, was written by collapse doyenne Joseph Tainter, though not in a place likely to be seen by non-archaeologists and anthropologists. This cutting review pointed out the inconsistencies in Diamond's argument, the fact that he wanted to blame collapse on human-caused environmental damage, but realized it was more complex, yet still went on to make the argument anyway, and concluded that the book was a "banal muddle" (Tainter 2008, p. 348). Later, in 2010, a conference entitled "Crisis, what Crisis? Collapses and Dark Ages in Comparative Perspective" was held at The McDonald Institute for Archaeological Research at Cambridge, reported on in *Science* (Lawler 2010). At the conference, participants stressed that collapse was rarely sudden or total, and that some episodes labelled as collapse had been exaggerated and oversimplified and could be better envisioned and labelled as "transformation."

Two examples discussed at the Cambridge conference were Old Kingdom Egypt and the Classic Maya, both often seen as environment-caused collapses. The Old Kingdom collapse in Egypt, that led to the First Intermediate Period (sometimes labelled a "dark age" in older literature), for example, is now beginning to be seen the result of a longer scale set of social and political transformations and not just a disaster caused by a lower Nile. The Egyptologist Miroslav Barta argued that "there was no collapse" and that "the peasants may never have noticed the change" (quoted in Lawler 2010, p. 908). Many Maya archaeologists question the notion of a sudden and catastrophic Maya collapse. James Aimers in a 2007 review of the archaeological work on the Maya collapse has stated that "there is now a consensus that Maya civilization as a whole did not collapse, although many zones did experience profound change" (Aimers 2007, p. 329). Elizabeth Graham sees continuity in the Maya sites of Belize, with "no sign of crisis" (Lawler 2010, p. 908). They do not deny at all that many Classic Maya *states* collapsed, which they did at different times, but the Maya *civilization* as a whole transformed over some three centuries. As Lawler reported "this emphasis on transformation rather than abrupt fall represents something of a backlash against a recent spate of claims that environmental disasters, both natural and human made, are the true culprits behind many ancient societal collapses" (Lawler 2010, p. 907).

An edited book entitled *Questioning Collapse* was also published in 2010, in response to Diamond's views on history and especially of collapse (McAnany and Yoffee 2010a). Specialists on Easter Island, the Greenland Norse, the American southwest, the Classic Maya and Mesopotamia, amongst others, presented their own interpretations. In each case, they problematized simplistic narratives of collapse and stressed the resilience of human communities. In a very odd episode, this book was reviewed by Diamond in the influential journal *Nature*, and he very clearly did not approve – the authors responded to this clear (yet undeclared) conflict of interests in a letter to the journal (Diamond 2010; McAnany and Yoffee 2010b). In 2012 three other archaeologists identified and took issue with the environmental turn, querying the turn to catastrophism and environmental determinism apparent in contemporary discourses of collapse (Butzer 2012; Butzer and Endfield 2012; Middleton 2012). A new book *Understanding Collapse: Ancient History and Modern Myths* also questions many of the current popular narratives of collapse that have become dominant and seeks to give a voice to the many archaeologists working on collapse in different areas (Middleton 2017).

As I outlined earlier, archaeologists are not generally climate sceptics, nor are they unaware of human impacts on the environment; archaeology has been at the forefront of understanding ancient environments and the human impact on them. Many would admit that there is evidence for climate change at some times of collapse – but, they would also remind us that coincidence is not causation, that chronological resolution is often not very precise, and that there are instances of collapse without climate change and instances of climate change without collapse. As we can clearly see from the present day and from recent history, change can be actively driven by people and groups from within societies and is not something that is always just a result of external factors; this is as true for the ancients as well as for us. A majority would question simplistic silver bullet theories of collapse of the sort often reported. These neither provide sufficiently complex pictures of the society in question nor of the changes that we label "collapse."

A recognition of collapse as a complex process is not new; the renowned archaeologist Mortimer Wheeler explained in 1968 (p. 126), writing of the Indus Valley collapse, that: "the fall, like the rise, of a civilization is a highly complex operation which can only be distorted and obscured by easy simplification." However, the degree of complexity involved, and the difficulty in adequately describing let alone "explaining" collapse, is increasingly and rightly being emphasized. Eric Cline, addressing the eastern Mediterranean collapse at the end of the Late Bronze Age, stated that

> there is little doubt that the collapse of the Late Bronze Age civilizations was complex in its origins. We do know that many possible variables may have had a contributing role in the collapse, but we are not even

certain that we know all of the variables and we undoubtedly do not know which were critical.

(Cline 2014, p. 170)

Even more recently, historian John Haldon has similarly written, though in a more academic setting, that

> differentiating between the various effects of the structural dynamics of a set of interconnected or overlapping socioeconomic or cultural systems – let us call them the dialectics of the system – is complex enough in itself, before we begin to build in the impact of environmental stressors . . . Simplistic one-to-one determinisms are, of course, entirely inadequate: human social organization is incredibly complex, and societal reaction to change can rarely be understood from a monocausal perspective.
>
> (Haldon 2016, p. 191)

These may seem disappointing as answers to questions about historical change – they are not as satisfying to some people as headlines such as "climate killed the Maya" and are less likely to be more widely reported or to grab headlines. Thus archaeology may be seen as not giving us the concrete results – the "real" reasons for collapse – that other harder sciences or maverick investigators, whose exciting results are better reported, seem capable of providing, and archaeological perspectives on collapse and transformation may therefore remain less visible to wider society.

Can archaeology help us today?

Archaeology is the study of the past through material culture, and, in non-prehistoric times, texts as well. As we have seen previously, many popular writers and researchers in the sciences make use of archaeological data and interpretation to make their own points about our present day environmental situation – very often in the form of exhortations to better, more sustainable behavior, or warnings about current norms and practices. This kind of appropriation of the past for moral purposes is not what we would generally think of as "history," though it seems often to pass for it, but what do archaeologists themselves think about the use of the past and do their views present any further problems?

One interdisciplinary group of archaeologists, environmental scientists, and sustainability thinkers meeting at Dahlem have argued that we must integrate the story of human history with "the rest of nature," a socioecological perspective, to "help clarify the options for managing our increasingly interconnected global system" (Costanza et al. 2007b, p. 522; Costanza et al. 2007a). Rather than providing simple analogies, though, they see "the past" as providing "the means to test the models upon which we depend for future projections and scenarios: for climate, key ecological processes, changing socioenvironmental conditions, and the intensity of impacts." Thus archaeology and history can play a role not only in understanding the present but in predicting potential futures through "simulation games and scenario analysis" (Costanza et al. 2007b, p. 525). Archaeology can provide data for futurologists and others to work with. Yet the group also admitted that using archaeology in this way is not a simple task because multiple factors were always involved and interacted on each other and, in addition, individual choice and agency must be taken into account.

While the intentions are good, this approach raises other issues. For example, the Dahlem group also suggested that "if we continue to operate in ignorance or denial of this integrated historical understanding, we run the very real risk of mirroring the paths of the Easter Islanders, the Classic Maya, or the Roman Empire" (Costanza et al. 2007b, p. 522). But this again suggests an uncritical attitude to the societies in question and to what "the thing we call collapse" actually was, as well as an assumption that it was "a bad thing." Were collapses always "bad?" A number of scholars have suggested that past collapses mostly involved the rejection of particular elite and ruling ideologies and symbolism – the rejection of specific people and regimes; for us, these symbols (whether *moai*, palaces, or pyramids) are often the characteristics of a particular "civilization" that we admire (Lawler 2010, p. 907; Tainter 1999). But was it a bad thing that Easter Islanders stopped making *moai*? Was it a bad thing that a particular form of divine kingship based in urban centres in the Maya lands ended? Was it a bad thing for an oppressive totalitarian dictatorship, the Western Roman Empire, stretching across western Europe and North Africa to have fallen apart? Would it be bad if global capitalism and consumerism were rejected, along with the privileged political and business elites that often benefit from them?

Using "the past" really means using "history," which is evidence-based description, interpretation, and explanation of the past (on the distinctions, see Arnold 2000). There is not one single history of the past, rather there are multiple histories and multiple narratives, some of which are more dominant and influential than others. When researchers seek to describe and explain collapse, it is necessary to take this multiplicity of histories and perspectives into account. For whom was collapse bad – and who might have benefitted? If we accept that collapse primarily involved human choices in social settings (which sometimes may well have been responses to environmental change), we need to try to understand people's motivations and actions in these settings. Many archaeologists aspire to constructing this kind of more nuanced and multifaceted view as opposed to sweeping generalizations and overly simple "answers." This is one way in which archaeology and history, as social sciences, really can help us today.

Others similarly see archaeology as serving a wider social and intellectual function in contemporary society. In an article from 2014, a group of archaeologists stated that:

> Archaeology is a source of essential data regarding the fundamental nature of human societies. Researchers across the behavioral and social

sciences use archeological data in framing foundational arguments. Archaeological evidence frequently undergirds debate on contemporary issues.

(Kintigh et al. 2014, p. 879)

These archaeologists set out to devise a list of "grand challenges" for archaeology; to do so they surveyed archaeologists in North America and Europe and held a follow-up workshop in Santa Fe in 2012 (Kintigh et al. 2014). In the workshop, they decided that "the problems should have global significance." They identified five key areas: A) emergence, communities, and complexity; B) resilience, persistence, transformation, and collapse; C) movement, mobility, and migration; D) cognition, behavior, and identity; and E) human-environment interactions; for each area, a list of questions was also proposed. Area B refers directly to collapse and transformation and resilience and persistence and the following research questions were generated:

1   What factors have allowed for differential persistence of societies?
2   What are the roles of social and environmental diversity and complexity in creating resilience and how do their impacts vary by social scale?
3   Can we characterize social collapse or decline in a way that is applicable across cultures, and are there any warning signals that collapse or severe decline is near?
4   How does ideology structure economic, political, and ritual systems?

Area E also contains questions potentially related to collapse such as 6) "how do humans respond to abrupt environmental change" and 7) "how do humans perceive and react to changes in climate and the natural environment over short- and long-terms?"

These categories and questions reflect recent concerns in archaeology (and wider society) as well as setting challenges to guide it. To some extent they serve as strong claims by archaeologists for the importance of the discipline in the face of pressure on the humanities. Research on climate change and environmental issues seems much more pressing and relevant than archaeology, and so such pre-emptive defences are understandable. What is certain is that issues of collapse and sustainability, of resilience and transformation, are, and will remain, important concerns for archaeologists now and in the coming years, and the data and narratives generated by archaeology can be of use more widely.

Again this points up the central issue of terminology. When considering resilience too, and sustainability, precision of thought and expression is important – are researchers discussing biological, cultural, or political resilience? Does resilience mean a political entity enduring in the same form or being flexible enough to change? Is resilience or the replication of a given social order always desirable? States may collapse but populations survive (as in the collapse of the Western Roman Empire) while populations may collapse but states survive (as in the Black Death in Europe, for example). There is a danger of talking at cross purposes, and when collapse is reported in the news, a lack of clarity over terminology can easily lead to the conflation of quite different ideas and images of collapse and resilience. Archaeology as a discipline can help us address these issues.

Archaeology can then provide a chronologically deep and culturally and geographically diverse data set that can be drawn on by researchers across disciplines. It is not unproblematic, but it is there for us to interrogate and to use with caution. In addition, archaeologists can provide interpretation, context, and nuance, which can enrich the available data and enable more realistic and sophisticated understanding of historical circumstances, which in turn can be used in scenario-building for the present and future.

As useful as archaeology can be as a source of knowledge and ideas, do environmentally concerned authors really need to use the past to find "lessons" on sustainability or to hijack people's histories for moral guidance? I would argue not. It seems to me that this use of "the past" is really an "abuse" of history. Archaeologists and historians have a social and ethical responsibility to question popular narratives of past collapse and to promote their own views. The damage that industrial civilization has wreaked across the planet is clear to us through modern scientific research; the problems of overpopulation do not need to be projected back onto pre-industrial societies for us to understand the difficulties that they present now and in the future. We can see around us poverty, inequality, hunger, conflict, and any number of environmental problems that, however caused, we must try to mitigate.

So what did happen to the Maya?

At the start of this chapter we saw that past collapses, especially but not only the Classic Maya collapse, have been the subject of documentary films and news headlines which have fed apocalyptic stories of collapse into popular culture. It seems right at this point to say just a little more about what happened to the Maya.

The Maya, of course, never disappeared; millions of modern Maya people live in the same lands inhabited by their ancestors in Belize, El Salvador, Honduras, and Mexico (Leventhal et al. 2012). The Classic Maya collapse, if we choose to call it that, was a transformation, a set of changes, that took place over around three centuries (hence archaeologists call this whole period the "Terminal Classic"), in which the Maya rejected some forms of their society (most notably divine kingship) and adopted new ones (Middleton 2017). Individual states did collapse, but at different times across the Maya regions – some states grew at the same time; some, at least, seem to have collapsed in conflict with rival states (sometimes ruling families were executed). There was no single Maya collapse "event" (even if there were droughts in some parts of the Maya lands) and millions of people did not die all at once, so no single cause can be assigned to explain what happened. When

Europeans arrived in the early 1500s, they found literate Maya living in organized societies in cities with stone buildings and temples. The Europeans brought disease, but they also set out deliberately to erase traditional Maya culture by collecting and burning Maya books and by forcibly "re-educating" Maya people, especially children, compelling them to convert to Catholicism. The last independent Maya kingdom, the Itza kingdom of Nojpeten, was conquered by Europeans only in 1697 – around eight centuries after the Classic collapse supposedly killed the Maya off. Yet the Maya culture and people survived – they are a prime example of resilience in the face of multiple pressures over a very long period of time.

The Maya people have continued to fight for, and increasingly to gain, political representation and civil rights to this day; for too long they have remained a marginalized underclass in colonial states. A narrative of apocalyptic collapse, narratives in which the Maya were killed off by climate change or ruined their own environment, can be seen to support a colonialist discourse that shifts attention from the actual actions of Europeans to the supposed shortcomings of the ancient Maya (or the ancient Easter Islanders). The modern Maya play little or no role in this discourse – they are rendered invisible by it. For this reason, we have to question our narratives of collapse and the descriptions and explanations that we find in both popular and academic culture.

Conclusion

In this chapter, I have tried to show how our cultural inheritance influences the way we think about collapse, encouraging us to see it as apocalyptic and catastrophic – and presenting collapse as a kind of divine punishment that is inflicted by greater powers (gods, nature . . .). I have tied this into how collapse is reported in the news, in documentary films, and in non-fiction writing, and to how ideas on collapse are translated from archaeology into wider social arenas and discourses (and vice versa), usually through simplification and through constructing a dramatic and often apocalyptic narrative. I then examined the responses of archaeologists to the environmental turn in collapse discourses, in which such views are being increasingly scrutinized in terms of the data generated and how this links to societal change. Archaeologists are trying to put people back at the heart of collapse narratives as active, deliberate, and thoughtful agents of change rather than passive victims of disaster; as knowledgeable, resourceful and resilient, rather than ignorant or imprudent.

Clearly archaeology can bring something to the table when it comes to considering the "success or failure" of societies (to borrow Diamond's sub-title), but we must consider what we mean by success and failure and who we are thinking about when we imagine and characterize collapse. By success do we simply mean "longevity" – how long a society endures in a particular form – or can we be more sophisticated in the questions we ask and the answers we construct? As a more thorough investigation of the Classic Maya collapse and the fate of the Maya peoples shows us, we need to question the apocalyptic narratives of collapse that surround us.

Acknowledgments

I would like to thank Ailise Bulfin and Arthur Demarest for sharing with me some of their recent work and Alison Vogelaar for kindly inviting me to participate in this fascinating and timely project.

References

Aimers, J. J., 2007. What Maya collapse? Terminal Classic variation in the Maya Lowlands. *Journal of Archaeological Research*, 15, 329–377.

Almond, S., 2013. The apocalypse market is booming. *The New York Times Magazine* (www.nytimes.com/2013/09/29/magazine/the-apocalypse-market-is-booming.html?_r=0) Accessed 1 August 2016.

Arnold, J. H., 2000. *History: A very short introduction*. Oxford University Press, Oxford.

Bahn, P. and Flenley, J., 1992. *Easter Island, Earth Island*. Thames and Hudson, London.

Barnosky, A. D., Matzke, N., Tomiya, S., Wogan, G. O., Swartz, B., Quental, T. B., Marshall, C., McGuire, J. L., Lindsey, E. L., Maguire, K. C., Mersey, B. and Ferrer, E. A., 2011. Has the Earth's sixth mass extinction already arrived? *Nature*, 471, 51–57.

Bostrom, N. and Cirkovic, M. M. eds., 2008. *Global catastrophic risks*. Oxford University Press, Oxford.

Brown, L., 2011. *World on the edge: How to prevent environmental and economic collapse*. Norton, New York.

Bulfin, A., 2015. The natural catastrophe in Late Victorian popular fiction: "How will the world end"? *Critical Survey*, 27, 81–100.

Butzer, K. W., 2012. Collapse, environment, and society. *Proceedings of the National Academy of Sciences*, 109, 3632–3639.

Butzer, K. W. and Endfield, G. H., 2012. Critical perspectives on historical collapse. *Proceedings of the National Academy of Science*, 109, 3628–3631.

Cameron, A., 1983. Crantor and Posidonius on Atlantis. *Classical Quarterly*, 33, 81–91.

Cameron, A., 2004. *Greek mythography in the Roman world*. Oxford University Press, Oxford.

Cline, E. H., 2014. *1177 BC: The year civilization collapsed*. Princeton University Press, Princeton.

Collin, R., 2014. Darren Aronofsky interview: "The Noah story is scary". *The Telegraph* (www.telegraph.co.uk/culture/film/10739539/Darren-Aronofsky-interview-The-Noah-story-is-scary.html) Accessed 1 August 2016.

Costanza, R., Graumlich, L. J. and Steffen, W. eds., 2007a. *Sustainability or collapse? An integrated history and future of people on Earth*. Dahlem University Press and Massachusetts Institute of Technology, Cambridge.

Costanza, R., Graumlich, L. J., Steffen, W., Crumley, C., Dearing, J., Hibbard, K., Leemans, R., Redman, C. and Schimel, D., 2007b. Sustainability or collapse: What can we learn from integrating the history of humans and the rest of nature? *Ambio*, 36, 522–527.

Demarest, A. A., 2001. Climatic change and the Maya collapse: The return of catastrophism. *Latin American Antiquity*, 12, 105–107.

Demarest, A. A., 2014. The Classic Maya collapse, water, and economic change in Mesoamerica, in Iannone, G. ed., *The great Maya droughts in cultural context*. University Press of Colorado, Boulder, 177–206.

Diamond, J., 1994. Ecological collapses of past civilizations. *Proceedings of the American Philosophical Society*, 138, 363–370.

Diamond, J., 2005. *Collapse: How societies choose to fail or succeed*. Penguin, London.

Diamond, J., 2010. Two views of collapse. *Nature*, 463, 880–881.

Downey, S. S., Haas, W. R. and Shennan, S. J., 2016. European Neolithic societies showed early warning signals of population collapse. *Proceedings of the National Academy of Sciences*, 113, 9751–9756.

Ehrlich, P. R., 1968. *The population bomb*. Ballantine Books, New York.

Ehrlich, P. R. and Ehrlich, A. H., 2013. Can a collapse of global civilization be avoided? *Proceedings of the Royal Society*, B 280, 20122845.

Fyfe, H. C., 1900. How will the world end? *Pearson's Magazine*, 10(55), 3–12.

Haldon, J., 2016. Cooling and societal change. *Nature Geoscience*, 9, 191–192.

Hance, J., 2015. How humans are driving the sixth mass extinction. *The Guardian* (www.theguardian.com/environment/radical-conservation/2015/oct/20/the-four-horsemen-of-the-sixth-mass-extinction) Accessed 1 August 2016.

Harrison, H., 1966. *Make room! Make room!* Orb Books, New York [2008].

Iannone, G. ed., 2014. *The great Maya droughts in cultural context*. University Press of Colorado, Boulder.

Iannone, G., Yaeger, J. and Hodell, D., 2014. Assessing the great Maya droughts, in Iannone, G. ed., *The great Maya droughts in cultural context*. University Press of Colorado, Boulder, 51–70.

Johnson, S. A., 2017. *Why did ancient civilizations fail?* Routledge, New York.

Jowit, J., 2011. Paul Ehrlich, a prophet of global population doom who is gloomier than ever. *The Guardian* (www.theguardian.com/environment/2011/oct/23/paul-ehrlich-global-collapse-warning) Accessed 1 August 2016.

Kelly, M. J., 2013. Why a collapse of global civilization will be avoided: A comment on Ehrlich and Ehrlich. *Proceedings of the Royal Society*, B 280, 0131193.

Kintigh, K. W., Altschul, J. H., Beaudry, M. C., Drennan, R. D., Kinzig, A. P., Kohler, T. A., Limp, W. F., Maschner, H. D., Michener, W. K., Pauketat, T. R., Peregrine, P., Sabloff, J. A., Wilkinson, T. J., Wright, H. T. and Zeder, M. A., 2014. Grand challenges for archaeology. *Proceedings of the National Academy of Sciences*, 111, 879–880.

Lawler, A., 2010. Collapse? What collapse? Societal change revisited. *Science*, 330, 907–909.

Leventhal, R. M., Espinosa, C. C. and Coc, C., 2012. The modern Maya and recent history. *Expedition*, 54, 46–51.

Lovelock, J., 2007. *The revenge of Gaia*. Penguin, London.

Macdonald, C., 2016. How to spot if society is DOOMED: Researchers reveal the signs that show civilization is set to collapse. *Mail Online* (www.dailymail.co.uk/sciencetech/article-3767950/How-spot-society-DOOMED-Researchers-reveal-signs-civilization-set-collapse.html) Accessed 1 September 2016.

Marshall, M., 2012. Climate change: The great civilization destroyer. *New Scientist*, 215, 32–36.

McAnany, P. A. and Yoffee, N. eds., 2010a. *Questioning collapse: Human resilience, ecological vulnerability, and the aftermath of empire*. Cambridge University Press, Cambridge.

McAnany, P. A. and Yoffee, N., 2010b. Questioning how different societies respond to crises. *Nature*, 464, 977.

Middleton, G. D., 2010. *The collapse of palatial society in LBA Greece and the postpalatial period*. Archaeopress, Oxford.

Middleton, G. D., 2012. Nothing lasts forever: Environmental discourses on the collapse of past societies. *Journal of Archaeological Research*, 20, 257–307.

Middleton, G. D., 2017. *Understanding collapse: Ancient history and modern myths*. Cambridge University Press, Cambridge.

Morgan, K. A., 1998. Designer history: Plato's Atlantis story and fourth-century ideology. *Journal of Hellenic Studies*, 118, 101–118.

Phillips, L., 2015. *Austerity ecology and the collapse-porn addicts: A defence of growth, progress, industry and stuff*. Zero Books, Alresford.

Plato., 1977. *Timaeus and Critias* (translated by Lee, D.). Penguin, London.

Ponting, C., 1991. *A green history of the world*. Sinclair-Stevenson, London. Republished (1994). *A green history of the world: The environment and the collapse of great civilizations*, new edition. Penguin, London, and again (2007). *A new green history of the world: The environment and the collapse of great civilizations*, revised edition. Penguin, London.

Redman, C. L., 1999. *Human impact on ancient environments*. University of Arizona Press, Tucson.

Rees, M., 2003. *Our final century: Will civilisation survive the twenty-first century? Will the human race survive the twenty-first century?* Arrow, London.

Rubin, C. T., 1998. *The green crusade: Rethinking the roots of environmentalism*. Rowman and Littlefield, Lanham.

Russell, B., 2004. *History of western philosophy*. London, Routledge.

Scheffer, M., 2016. Anticipating societal collapse: Hints from the Stone Age. *Proceedings of the National Academy of Sciences*, 113, 10733–10735.

Schwartz, G. M., 2006. From collapse to regeneration, in Schwartz, G. M. and Nichols, J. J. eds., After collapse: the regeneration of complex societies. University of Arizona Press, Tucson, 3–17.

Tainter, J. A., 1988. The collapse of complex societies. Cambridge University Press, Cambridge.

Tainter, J. A., 1999. Post-collapse societies, in Barker, G. ed., *Companion encyclopedia of archaeology*. Routledge, London, 988–1039.

Tainter, J. A., 2006. Archaeology of overshoot and collapse. *Annual Review of Anthropology*, 35, 59–74.

Tainter, J. A., 2008. Collapse, sustainability, and the environment: How authors choose to fail or succeed. *Reviews in Anthropology*, 37, 342–371.

Thussu, D. K., 2007. *News as entertainment: The rise of global infotainment*. Sage, London.

Weiss, H. and Bradley, R. S., 2001. What drives societal collapse? *Science*, 291, 609–610.

Wheeler, M., 1968. *The Indus civilization*. Cambridge University Press, Cambridge.

6 Survive, thrive, or perish
Environmental collapse in post-apocalyptic digital games

Jen England

Heat and decay. Mutations and disfigurements. Death and destruction. This is what welcomes players to the worlds of *Wasteland* and *Fallout*. These popular American post-apocalyptic roleplaying games (RPGs) present an Earth nearly destroyed from nuclear catastrophes. Through their avatars – Desert Rangers in *Wasteland* and Vault Dwellers/Overseers in *Fallout* – players traverse open worlds of murderous survivors, grossly mutated plants and animals, and severely depleted natural resources. This chapter explores how *Wasteland* and *Fallout* embody and enact a long-held Western fascination with post-nuclear narratives, specifically those that depict environmental collapse. As Noël Sturgeon (2009) explains:

> The environmental themes that begin to appear in almost every arena of popular culture in the post-cold war era are complicated phenomena. They are useful and flexible tropes . . . that tell powerful stories about who we (in the United States) are, what our history has meant, and what direction we should take the world.
>
> (p. 7)

By focusing on concepts of embodiment and simulation in game play, I show how players are faced with issues central to collapse. How would we react if the environment as we know it collapsed? How would we survive? How would we rebuild? Ultimately, these games force players to confront the lengths to which they're willing to go to thrive, survive, or perish as they rebuild a simulated (virtual) civilization in the United States. Thus, these games become both a reflection of and preparation for environmental collapse.

In *Wasteland* and *Fallout*, players make choices that are deeply connected to issues of identity and community, economics and politics, morals and ethics. Whether it's fighting radioactive people and animals, re-starting water purification efforts, or growing crops to feed small settlements of survivors, players' decisions impact how they will navigate through the virtual communities they must rebuild. These decisions also impact the livelihood of the virtual worlds themselves. Players must think critically and strategically about how environmental collapse has shaped these virtual worlds and what role it might play in shaping their futures. While game play might not provide practical solutions, it engages players in cognitive work valuable for understanding actions and practices that can lead to collapse not only in the virtual world but, importantly, in the material world too.

Background on the *Wasteland* and *Fallout* Series

Wasteland and *Fallout* are pioneering and critically acclaimed examples of post-apocalyptic RPGs.[1] The original PC-based *Wasteland* (Electronic Arts 1988) has been called "the godfather" of post-apocalyptic RPGs (Kickstarter n.d.). Produced by Brian Fargo, *Wasteland* is set in a futuristic American Southwest following a meteoric impact event that unintentionally triggered a global nuclear war. In the game, a surviving team of former US Army engineers are rebranded as the Desert Rangers and are tasked with rebuilding and maintaining civilization. However, reconstruction proves difficult as they face human, animal, and technological hurdles to success. More than 25 years later, Fargo released the highly anticipated sequel, *Wasteland 2* (in Xile Entertainment 2014), which picks up the story 15 years later. *Wasteland 2* follows the original game closely, with Desert Rangers traveling from Arizona to California to complete a variety of new survival-based missions, including battling murderous pre-war artificial intelligence and fixing science experiments gone awry. Fargo is presently developing *Wasteland 3*, which is set for release in 2019.

Fargo also developed *Wasteland*'s "spiritual successor," *Fallout* (Plunkett 2012; Falero 2015). While Fargo is attached to *Fallout* (Black Isle Studios 1997) and *Fallout 2* (Black Isle Studios 1998), he was not involved in the remainder of the series: *Fallout 3* (Bethesda Game Studios 2008), *Fallout: New Vegas* (Obsidian Entertainment 2010), and *Fallout 4* (Bethesda Game Studios 2015).[2] The *Fallout* universe is largely destroyed from a nuclear arms race that sparked several global wars. In this series, the US government partners with a high-tech company to build underground shelters called vaults to keep the population safe. However, the government knows many citizens have no chance of survival, which is why they *actually* create the vaults for social experimentation on select populations. Survivors, called Vault Dwellers or Overseers (depending upon the game), must find ways to restore the radioactive land to a minimal liveable order through a variety of means: combat, barter, settlements, and resource management.

Post-apocalyptic storytelling: embodiment and simulation in digital games

Post-apocalyptic narratives in RPGs like *Wasteland* and *Fallout* are often products of the ebb and flow of American Cold War fears of global nuclear war. Michael Falero (2015) suggests American post-apocalyptic digital games are influenced by the "popular focus on nuclear warfare, MAD, and fallout shelters [that] overlapped with the advent of video game technology" in the 1970s and 1980s (para. 11). Jerry Määttä (2015) claims that we've seen a rise in "interesting" post-apocalyptic narratives since those times, pointing to events such as September 11, 2001, that have "given new possibilities for depicting especially large-scale or even global disasters" (p. 421).[3] While drawing inspiration from contemporary technologies and catastrophic events, digital games' post-apocalyptic narratives also are rooted in historical literary traditions, such as, for example, Mary Shelley's early nineteenth century science fiction novel *The Last Man* (Falero 2015; Määttä 2015), which confronts the limits of scientific (and technological) inquiry and humankind. Digital games often combine "elements of earlier post-apocalyptic literary tradition – a narrative focus on people dealing with social breakdown and lacking the basic necessities to survive – with the interactive elements of the video game, such as decision-making, fighting threats, and an immersive visual experience" (Falero 2015, para. 12). The interactivity and immersiveness of RPGs make their post-apocalyptic narratives so compelling – and so different from other media – as players must actively participate in the games' narratives. RPGs demand players make choices and take action to navigate and advance through the game. Bianca Batti (2015) suggests digital games have great narrative potential due to what their "modes of storytelling and representation have to offer us in the way we think about how it is we interact with a text and what such interactions might tell us about ourselves" (para. 8). Following scholars such as James Paul Gee (2008);[4] Bonnie Nardi (2009),[5] Celia Pearce (2011);[6] and Souvik Mukherjee (2015),[7] I argue players' embodiment of avatars – particularly in RPGs – drives this interactivity and leads to an immersive experience within virtual (or simulated) worlds. Avatars create opportunities for players to interact with and feel part of the devastated environments in post-apocalyptic RPGs, allowing players to grapple with the complexities of environmental collapse in meaningful ways.

An avatar, however, is more than a navigational tool; rather, it is an "extension of the player's real-life persona, even if it instantiates in ways that digress significantly from her real-world personality or life roles" (Pearce 2011, p. 198). A player and avatar thus have a unique relationship, which Gee (2008) calls a surrogacy. This surrogate relationship creates an embodied experience in which avatars' "virtual minds and virtual bodies . . . become the player's surrogate mind and body" (p. 258). Tom Tyler (2009) expands upon Gee's work, claiming that, through an avatar, players are immersed in "an environment that molds their actions, prompts their responses, and works them over" while at the same time "shap[ing] their environment, actively modifying their surroundings, [and] pursuing the tilling of the virtual landscape" (p. 266). In other words, to successfully play digital RPGs, players must "become" their avatars; they must understand avatars' capabilities and limitations, the choices they can and cannot make, and how decisions and actions can impact virtual worlds.

Player-avatars also must become part of the virtual worlds they inhabit during the game. As Sven Cavalcanti (2008) asserts, though game worlds "imply a flight from reality into a dream world," they also must "be understood as an extension of present societies" (p. 131). Virtual worlds, in other words, can reflect and project our material-world realities. This creates what Peter Berger (2008) calls a "virtual-but-real" simulation (p. 47) of places and spaces players might have experienced in the material world. For example, because *Fallout 4* is set in what was previously Massachusetts, when my husband, who is from the East Coast, plays the game he often identifies familiar landmarks like the Boston Public Library, Boston Common, and Old North Church. Even if players (like myself) have not actually visited particular virtual-world places in the material world, they are likely somewhat familiar with them through other media. Berger (2008) argues players will draw from these experiences and "readily project their knowledge" into the virtual world (p. 47), lending a materiality to virtual worlds that players connect with cognitively and emotionally. Through their avatars, players are able to experience deeper connections with the virtual worlds they inhabit, which can lead to a palpable embodied experience of game play, and ultimately create a sense of real urgency for rebuilding collapsed societies and environments.

Post-apocalyptic games not only provide extensions of present societies, but they also can reimagine past societies and simulate potential future societies. What is particularly interesting about the *Wasteland* and *Fallout* series is how they simultaneously do both. While the extreme environmental collapses in *Wasteland*'s and *Fallout*'s post-apocalyptic worlds might seem outlandish to some, they are modeled on previous nuclear threats that are then set in virtual futures. Steven Messner (2015) argues these simulations are not farfetched when we consider what we already know about how "the strain of a global nuclear war on the ecosystem would be so severe that the blasted landscape" of these games is within reason (para. 10). These games are part remembrance and part warning: players must confront historical wrongdoings, trace their damage along a timeline that advances into the future, and adjust to a new normal in collapsed worlds. These games are a call to not forget and to be prepared.

Representations of environmental collapse in *Wasteland* and *Fallout*

Wasteland and particularly *Fallout* have earned the attention of scholars who use game play to explore moral decision making (Schulzke 2009),[8] ethical design and game play (Sicart 2010),[9] and history and cultural heritage (Owens 2010).[10] What is missing from this scholarship is an examination of the ways *Wasteland* and *Fallout* represent environmental issues and concerns in their virtual worlds. Some recent scholarship has begun this work in digital games more broadly. For example, Shawna Kelly and Bonnie Nardi

(2014)[11] discuss scarcity and sustainability narratives, Odile Blanchard and Arnaud Buchs (2015)[12] explore sustainable development through roleplay, and Karen Schrier (2015)[13] examines ethical decision-making related to sustainability. However, there is a gap in scholarship that addresses macro-level environmental issues through micro-level analysis of game play. This chapter responds to this gap by advancing a conversation explicitly about how players engage with representations of environmental collapse in post-apocalyptic RPGs *Wasteland* and *Fallout*. Given the series' vast open worlds and replayability, each game easily can take 100 hours to play. My discussion will focus on one of my playthroughs of games from each series and therefore cannot cover all applicable aspects of the entire series – notably, biomedical research, which deserves attention in future work. I focus my discussion on nuclear catastrophes and envirotechnical failures, aspects that a casual gamer not attuned to the scholarship might notice and reflect upon throughout the games.

Nuclear catastrophes

In both series I find myself in alternate (retro)futuristic societies where Earth has been practically destroyed by nuclear catastrophes. Through cutscenes and conversations with non-playable characters (NPCs), I learn *Wasteland*'s nuclear holocaust was triggered by a meteoric impact event. This event set off nuclear weapons in the United States and Soviet Union, and both countries blamed each other rather than the meteor, retaliating by launching more nuclear weapons. I join the Desert Rangers, the remaining Army Corps of Engineers battalion, who survived because they were isolated in the American southwest desert doing construction work when the nuclear blast occurred (Gamepedia n.d.a.). As a Desert Ranger I must complete "quests" to investigate disturbances and to maintain safety in this volatile landscape. This landscape is, frankly, gross. Debris is everywhere, and it's often hard to tell what is in the piles. Barrels filled with trash burn throughout the land. According to my game play and the *Wasteland 2*'s vision document, this land is the

> antithesis of the clean, futuristic society that it once was. Wasteland is a world in decay. The once glimmering cities of glass and steel lie in ruin. Rusted hulls of cars litter the urban environment as a reminder of the world that once was.
>
> (Wasteland Wiki n.d., "Pillars")

My team and I must travel carefully among the ruins and the "wastes" – the remaining small establishments and communities. We diligently monitor the nuclear hotspots on our map and check our biometric reader to make sure we are not poisoned by dangerous levels of radiation. I quickly learn the hard way that radiation poisoning causes a fit of strangled breathing and then death (followed thankfully, for the player, by regeneration).

In the *Fallout* series, the nuclear event was explicitly triggered by a nuclear war. The game establishes an alternative history where political unrest, energy crises, oil wars, and military invasions led to global tension; China invaded the United States, and vice versa. Thus began the "Great War." The nuclear launches were so powerful they caused "Earth's fault lines to shift, creating mountain ranges and oceans where there were none" (Hall 2015, "Oct. 23, 2077"). According to *Fallout*'s backstory, I survived the war by being government-selected to live in one of 122 underground vaults (Fallout Wiki n.d.b). Those not lucky enough to have shelter were exposed to such high levels of radiation that they mutated, turning ghoulish and often violent. When I emerge from the vault many years later, it's dirty and dark: even when there's sunlight, the sky has a lingering hazy quality. People are separated from their families and their homes. Devastation is everywhere, and this bleakness mirrors my struggles to bring back some semblance of a functioning community in order to survive in this harsh new world. As Guy Middleton (2012) points out, "warfare, violence, relocation and resultant trauma from dislocation are noted as features of many collapses" throughout history in the material world (p. 264). This is clearly represented in the virtual worlds of *Wasteland* and *Fallout*. Survival requires taking appropriate actions to secure shelter, resources, and safety; it also demands working through the emotional and traumatic experience of being a healthy survivor when there's so much suffering around me.

That *Wasteland*'s and *Fallout*'s nuclear catastrophes caused such profound environmental collapse is not surprising. Nuclear events – from producing and testing weapons, to experiencing perceived and real threats of war, to actually dropping atomic bombs – have resulted in a "nuclear legacy" in America (Taylor and Kinsella 2007). This legacy is now a part of the American consciousness, often provoking anxieties and confusion about nuclear capabilities and applications. These games tap into this cultural fear. As players, we have no choice but to confront our fears head on and to embrace the chaos caused by collapse while we "play out" different scenarios and consider multiple strategies for survival. Importantly, the games' post-apocalyptic narratives offer hope for rebuilding after collapse. Life has been altered, but it also carries on.

Grappling with the logistical and emotional aspects of collapse is the important work of post-apocalyptic narratives. Määttä (2015) explains many "post-apocalyptic narratives deal with subject matter that is related to some of our deepest emotions, anxieties, and fears – of death, powerlessness, separation, and abandonment – but also to fantasies of belongingness, fellowship, and survival, or even sadistic desires and feelings of guilt" (p. 428). RPGs are particularly well suited to this task. *Wasteland*'s and *Fallout*'s virtual worlds rely on America's material-world nuclear legacy to depict alternative narratives in which nuclear catastrophes lead to an environmental collapse we fear might actually occur. As simulations of the material world, they create space for players to embody the role of a survivor as a way to come to terms with what collapse might mean for humanity – and how we might survive and rebuild.

Envirotechnical disasters

Wasteland's and *Fallout*'s narratives also engage the role envirotechnical systems[14] play in catastrophes and environmental collapse. Sara Pritchard (2012) defines envirotechnical systems as the "complex, dynamic, porous, and inextricable configuration of nature, technology, and politics" (p. 233) in which "environmental processes shape and are shaped by technologies" (p. 229). Central to survival (or death) in both series, water filtration and purification systems hold social and political significance in surviving communities. Importantly, both series also treat these systems as envirotechnical disasters, making explicit the impact that failing systems have in times of catastrophe. I see this as a virtual world intervention: in the material world, we often do not realize this impact until a disaster strikes and the systems fail. For example, in the United States we did not pay much attention to levees and other structural barriers until Hurricanes Katrina, Harvey, and Maria wreaked havoc on them or to BP's Deepwater Horizon until it spilled millions of gallons of oil into the Gulf. We also remain largely ignorant of nuclear-based envirotechnical systems until tragedy unfolds like it did with Chernobyl, Three Mile Island, and the Fukushima Daiichi nuclear power plant. By building water filtration and purification systems into the narratives of *Wasteland* and *Fallout*, the games challenge us to become more aware of the inherent connection between environment, technology, and humanity (Pritchard 2012; Hindmarsh 2013).

As a player in *Wasteland* and *Fallout*, I cannot sit back and allow envirotechnical systems to further fail and destroy the virtual worlds. Instead, I must actively engage in quests and missions to repair damaged systems. In the *Fallout* series, the nuclear war either damaged or destroyed the usual systems that filter and supply clean water to the surviving communities. This is particularly devastating because almost all major water sources, including the Potomac River, have become irradiated from nuclear fallout. I join a group of scientists and select citizen survivors who are developing massive-scale technology capable of bringing clean, potable water to the wasteland (Fallout Wiki n.d.a.). My job is to combine this technology with a terraforming device that contains the agricultural components needed to regenerate health and plant and harvest crops. In *Wasteland*, I am sent to Highpool, a surviving community in the wastes that has maintained a reservoir providing water to most of the region (Gamepedia n.d.b.). Although largely spared from the nuclear event, the reservoir has developed some structural weaknesses. These weaknesses are targeted by a group of raiders, who plan to exploit the deficiencies in order to flood the community and take control. I take my team of Desert Rangers to Highpool not only to stop this destruction but also to rebuild the technology responsible for sustaining life in the wasteland.

Prior to the nuclear catastrophes in both virtual worlds, water was taken for granted because the technologies that supported its purification and distribution functioned. When the virtual envirotechnical systems failed after catastrophes, water became not only a scarcity but also a political commodity. This is of course not limited to virtual worlds. The ongoing water crisis in Flint, Michigan, is a material-world example of an envirotechnical failure. Although the Environmental Protection Agency has awarded $100 million USD to Flint for "drinking water infrastructure upgrades" to remediate damage (lead poisoning, Legionnaire's outbreaks, and other devastating illnesses) caused by decades long impoverishment of water infrastructures in the city (CNN Library 2017, "Timeline"), citizens and civil rights activists argue this does little to address the "deeply embedded institutional, systemic and historical racism . . . at the root of this crisis" (Michigan Civil Rights Commission 2017, p. 9). As Flint shows, like the virtual worlds of *Wasteland* and *Fallout*, our material world has politicized water and other basic human needs. Faced with ongoing and recent humanitarian crises, the US government has done little to help its citizens and survivors, often acting antagonistically toward rebuilding necessary infrastructures. In another material-world example, in the aftermath of Hurricane Maria, raw sewage has flooded into rivers, reservoirs, and other water sources in Puerto Rico;[15] the US government's (lack of) response has left the majority of these American citizens still without clean water weeks later. Unfortunately, the "apocalyptic damage" to Puerto Rico (Lifton 2017; Narayan 2017) and the fight for clean water on the island and in Flint highlight how the material world and virtual world resemble one another in a fight for survival.

Whether in the virtual or material world, envirotechnical systems, failures, and disasters often contribute to and/or exacerbate environmental and societal collapse. Analyzing these systems raises important questions, including: "Whose goals do these technologies serve? What political and economic interests shape the design and use of complex technological systems? And what assumptions about the natural world and human – natural relations are embedded in these technologies?" (Pritchard 2012, p. 221). RPGs like *Wasteland* and *Fallout* provide players opportunities to explore these questions and seek answers in low-stakes environments. By challenging assumptions and making mistakes, players can learn to see environment and technologies as integral aspects of our humanity – and perhaps they can grow more comfortable advocating against environmental and social injustices before more systems collapse and more people's lives are devastated.

Bridging the virtual and the material worlds

The virtual worlds of the *Wasteland* and *Fallout* series present particular representations of environmental collapse. However, it is highly unlikely the series were developed with a clear definition of collapse in mind; after all, as popular mainstream non-educational RPGs, their first priority is to entertain not to educate. Yet, they do present opportunities to learn. They require critical thinking, decision making, and problem solving. They help players to see the material world in the virtual world and vice versa, and to embrace this interconnectedness as they make sense of a post-apocalyptic society. And they allow players to feel what it might be like to live in a world that has collapsed. This, according to Gee (2007), is what games do best:

> [T]he power of video games is not in operating an avatar per se. Rather, it is in situating one's body and mind in a world from the perspective of the avatar . . . What video games do – better than any other medium in my view – is *let people understand a world from the inside.*
>
> (p. 16, emphasis added)

The way in which *Wasteland* and *Fallout* situate player-avatars in virtual worlds mirrors science popularizer Jared Diamond's[16] notion of collapse as a "drastic decrease in human population size and/or political/economic/social complexity, over a considerable area, for an extended time" (2005, p. 3). Furthermore, *Wasteland*'s and *Fallout*'s particular collapse narratives also represent "ecocide," defined by international lawyer and advocate Polly Higgins as "the extensive destruction, damage to or loss of ecosystem(s) of a given territory, whether by human agency or by other causes, to such an extent that peaceful enjoyment by the inhabitants of that territory has been severely diminished" (as cited in Wood 2011). This again suggests that though the post-apocalyptic narratives in *Wasteland* and *Fallout* are fictional, they are grounded in material-world realities of environmental destruction. These games, therefore, allow players to make sense of the world(s) and how they understand environmental and societal collapse.

Digital games like *Wasteland* and *Fallout* provide productive opportunities for virtual-world learning that is applicable to and complementary of material-world engagement with environmental concepts. Kelly and Nardi (2014) claim digital games that

> narrativize scarce resources, promote competitive and collaborative social interaction, and foreground survival goals . . . have the capacity to convey the complexity of future research to wider publics who can attain new insights and devise solutions, as well as *generate new ways of thinking about the future.* As global population and consumption habits continue to strain existing social and economic infrastructures, a [gaming] community that has explored conditions of scarcity and adaptations will be of growing relevance and importance.
>
> (para. 7, emphasis added)

What Kelly and Nardi (2014) suggest about the capacity of games is compelling, and my own game play certainly supports their claim. While it is impractical to assume game play will solve our environmental crises, digital games – particularly RPGs – can create problem solvers. In encouraging critical and creative thinking, such games can shape players who "cultivate imaginative responses and encourage players to think outside the box" (Kelly and Nardi 2014, para. 7). And thinking is, in fact, important work. What is more, digital games are representative of how the human mind processes information:

> Humans think and understand best when they can imagine (or simulate) an experience in such a way that the simulation prepares them . . . to understand and make sense of things, but also to help prepare for action in the world . . . [so] the mind is a simulator, but one that builds simulations to prepare purposely for specific actions and to achieve specific goals.
>
> (Gee, n.d. pp. 8–9)

By embodying avatars (surrogates), players experience games' virtual (simulated) worlds in ways that make them confront the beliefs and attitudes they hold toward the environment, and consider the choices they would make (or not make) in response to its collapse. Games like the *Wasteland* and *Fallout* series prompt players not only to ask but also to enact how they will solve life-threatening problems, whom they will help, and for what they are thriving, surviving, or perishing. Importantly, this embodied experience of game play might influence players' ability to address and communicate about these questions beyond the virtual world. At a time of rising nuclear tensions and largely human-caused environmental problems, perhaps a willingness to experiment and think creatively through both game design and game play could help us develop social and global awareness that can be harnessed for doing environmental good in the world and lead to positive material-world change.

Notes

1 *Wasteland* secured spots on IGN's top 25 PC games of all time and the Smithsonian American Art Museum's "Art of the Computer Game" exhibit shortlist; *Fallout 3* was featured in the "Art of the Computer Game" exhibit; and *Fallout 4* won multiple Interactive Achievement Awards and a BAFTA Games Award for Best Game in 2016.
2 *Fallout* also has several spin-off games such as *Fallout: Brotherhood of Steel* (Interplay Entertainment 2004), and *Fallout Shelter* (Bethesda Game Studios 2015).
3 In 2015, the year *Fallout 4* was released, the Entertainment Software Association (2016) reported US digital game sales reached $16.5 billion USD (p. 12). Twenty-five to 35 percent of these games were roleplaying and shooter, which commonly depict post-apocalyptic worlds. In fact, *Fallout 4* ranked in the top three best-selling games that year (pp. 10–11).
4 See Video games and embodiment. *Games and Culture*. 3(3–4), pp. 253–263.

5 See *My Life as a Night Elf Priest*, University of Michigan Press.
6 See *Communities of Play*, MIT Press.
7 See *Video Games and Storytelling*, Palgrave Macmillan.
8 See Moral decision making in *Fallout*, *Games Studies*. 9(2).
9 See Wicked games: On the design of ethical gameplay, *Desire' 10 Proceedings*, pp. 101–111.
10 See The presence of the past in *Fallout 3, Play the Past*.
11 See Playing with sustainability, *First Monday*. 19(5).
12 See Clarifying sustainable development through roleplay, *Simulation & Gaming*. 46(6), pp. 697–712.
13 See Ethical thinking and sustainability in role-play participants, *Simulation & Gaming*. 46(6), pp. 643–696.
14 I purposefully use "envirotechnical" not "biotechnical" for these systems because they don't require biological, chemical, or genetic engineering; instead, they rely on environmental factors such as radioactive elements, water, and air as well as human bodily interventions (Pritchard 2012).
15 See Raw sewage contaminating waters in Puerto Rico after Maria, www.washingtonpost.com/
16 For other related definitions see Costanza, et al. (2007); Steffen, et al. (2011); and Butzer (2012).

References

Batti, B., 2015. High and low culture: Video games, narrative potential, and the literature department. *Not Your Mama's Gamer*. [Online]. [Accessed 10 August 2016]. Available from: www.nymgamer.com/

Berger, P., 2008. There and back again: Reuse, signifiers and consistency in created game spaces. In: Jahn-Sudmann, A. and Stockmann, R. eds. *Computer games as a sociocultural phenomenon: Games without frontiers, wars without tears*. New York: Palgrave Macmillan, 47–55.

Blanchard, O. and Buchs, A., 2015. Clarifying sustainable development through roleplay. *Simulation & Gaming*. 46(6), 697–712.

Butzer, K. W., 2012. Collapse, environment, and society. *PNAS*. 109(10), 3632–3639.

Cavalcanti, S., 2008. Preconscious apocalypse: The failure of capitalism in computer games. In: Jahn-Sudmann, A. and Stockmann, R. eds. *Computer games as a sociocultural phenomenon: Games without frontiers, wars without tears*. New York: Palgrave Macmillan, 131–138.

CNN Library., 2017. Flint water crisis fast facts. [Online]. [Accessed 14 September 2017]. Available from: www.cnn.com/

Costanza, R., Graumlich, L., Steffen, W., Crumley, C., Dearing, J., Hibbard, K., Leemans, R., Redman, C. and Schimel, D., 2007. Sustainability or collapse: What can we learn from integrating the history of humans and the rest of nature? *Ambio*. 36(7), 522–527.

Diamond, J., 2005. *Collapse: How societies choose to fail or succeed*. New York: Viking Press.

Entertainment Software Association., 2016. *Essential facts about the computer and video game industry*. [Online]. [Accessed 3 July 2016]. Available from: http://essentialfacts.theesa.com/

Falero, M., 2015. *A brief history of post-apocalyptic video games*. [Online]. [Accessed 9 August 2016]. Available from: www.gameskinny.com

Fallout Wiki., n.d.a. *Project purity*. [Online]. [Accessed 16 October 2016]. Available from: http://fallout.wikia.com/

Fallout Wiki., n.d.b. *Vault*. [Online]. [Accessed 16 October 2016]. Available from: http://fallout.wikia.com/

Gamepedia., n.d.a., *Desert rangers*. [Online]. [Accessed 14 July 2016]. Available from: http://wasteland.gamepedia.com/

Gamepedia., n.d.b., *Highpool*. [Online]. [Accessed 16 October 2016]. Available from: http://wasteland.gamepedia.com/

Gee, J. P., 2007. *Good video games + good learning: Collected essays on video games, learning and literacy*. New York: Peter Lang.

Gee, J. P., 2008. Video games and embodiment. *Games and Culture*. 3(3–4), 253–263.

Gee, J. P., n.d. *Why are video games good for learning?* [Online]. [Accessed 6 May 2015]. Available from: www.academiccolab.org/

Hall, C., 2015. The Fallout timeline. *Polygon*. [Online]. [Accessed 14 September 2017]. Available from: www.polygon.com/

Hindmarsh, R., 2013. Nuclear disaster at Fukushima Daiichi: Introducing the terrain. In: Hindmarsh, R. ed. *Nuclear disaster at Fukushima Daiichi: Social, political and environmental issues*. New York: Routledge, 1–21.

Kelly, S. and Nardi, B., 2014. Playing with sustainability: Using video games to simulate futures of scarcity. *First Monday*. 19(5), n.p. [Online]. [Accessed 6 May 2015]. Available from: http://firstmonday.org/

Kickstarter., n.d. *Wasteland 2*. [Online]. [Accessed 15 January 2017]. Available from: www.kickstarter.com/

Lifton, R. J., 2017. Robert Jay Lifton on the apocalyptic twins of nuclear and climate threats & reflections on survival. *Democracy Now!* [Online]. [Accessed 16 October 2017]. Available from: www.democracynow.org/

Määttä, J., 2015. Keeping count of the end of the world: A statistical analysis of the historiography, canonisation, and historical fluctuations of Anglophone apocalyptic and post-apocalyptic disaster narratives. *Culture Unbound*. 7, 411–432.

Messner, S., 2015. Just how realistic is *Fallout 4*'s post-apocalypse anyway? *Motherboard*. [Online]. [Accessed 16 August 2016]. Available from: https://motherboard.vice.com/

Michigan Civil Rights Commission., 2017. The Flint water crisis: Systemic racism through the lens of Flint. [Online]. [Accessed 14 September 2017]. Available from: www.michigan.gov/

Middleton, G. D., 2012. Nothing lasts forever: Environmental discourses on the collapse of past societies. *Journal of Archaeological Research*. 20, 257–307.

Mukherjee, S., 2015. *Video games and storytelling: Reading games and playing books*. London: Palgrave Macmillan.

Narayan, C., 2017. "Apocalyptic" devastation in Puerto Rico, and little help in sight. *CNN*. [Online]. [Accessed 16 October 2017]. Available from: www.cnn.com/

Nardi, B., 2009. *My life as a night elf priest: An anthropological account of world of warcraft*. Ann Arbor: University of Michigan Press.

Owens, T., 2010. The presence of the past in *Fallout 3*. [Online]. [Accessed 16 August 2016]. Available from: www.playthepast.org/

Pearce, C., 2011. *Communities of play: Emergent cultures in multiplayer games and virtual worlds*. Cambridge: The MIT Press.

Plunkett, L., 2012. Why people give a shit about a 1988 PC roleplaying game. *Kotaku*. [Online]. [Accessed 18 March 2016]. Available from: http://kotaku.com/

Pritchard, S. B., 2012. An envirotechnical disaster: Nature, technology, and politics at Fukushima. *Environmental History*. 17, 219–243.

Schrier, K., 2015. Ethical thinking and sustainability in role-play participants. *Simulation & Gaming*. 46(6), 643–696.

Schulzke, M., 2009. Moral decision making in *Fallout*. *Game Studies: The International Journal of Computer Game Research*. 9(2), n.p. [Online]. [Accessed 16 August 2016]. Available from: http://gamestudies.org/

Sicart, M., 2010. Wicked games: On the design of ethical game play. *Desire Network Conference on Creativity and Innovation in Design, 16–17 August 2010, Aarhus*. Lancaster: Desire Network, 101–111.

Steffen, W., Persson, A., Deutsch, L., Zalasiewicz, J., Williams, M., Richardson, K., Crumely, C., Crutzen, P., Folke, C., Gordon, L., Molina, M., Ramanathan, V., Rockström, J., Scheffer, M., Schellnhuber, H. J. and Svedin, U., 2011. The anthropocene: From global change to planetary stewardship. *Ambio*. 40(7), 739–761.

Sturgeon, N., 2009. *Environmentalism in popular culture: Gender, race, sexuality, and the politics of the natural*. Tucson: University of Arizona Press.

Taylor, B. C. and Kinsella, W. J., 2007. Introduction: Linking nuclear legacies and communication studies. In: Taylor, B. C., Kinsella, W. J., Depoe, S. P. and Metzler, M. S. eds. *Nuclear legacies: Communication, controversy, and the U. S. nuclear weapons complex*. Lanham: Lexington Books, 1–38.

Tyler, T., 2009. The test of time: McLuhan, space, and the rise of *Civilization*. In: Dobrin, S. I. and Morey, S. eds. *Ecosee: Image, rhetoric, nature*. Albany: SUNY Press, 257–277.

Wasteland Wiki., n.d. *Wasteland 2 vision document*. [Online]. [Accessed 13 September 2017]. Available from: http://wasteland.wikia.com/

Wood, S. D., 2011. Ecocide law would be "game changer" for environment. *Positive News*. [Online]. [Accessed 24 January 2015]. Available from: www.positive.news/

7 Zooming out, closing in
Ecology at the end of the frontier

Alison E. Vogelaar and Brack W. Hale

The final sequence of the 2013 sci-fi space thriller *Gravity* finds protagonist Dr. Ryan Stone hurtling through space in an emergency evacuation attempt after satellite debris struck the space station on which her NASA shuttle was docked. Upon reentering the atmosphere, her cramped space capsule erupts in flames and is pulled forcefully toward Earth's surface. Stone's body is sweat-drenched and vigorously shaking under the physical force of re-entry. It is not clear whether the capsule, or her own body, will survive the journey or the impact. Spoiler alert: the capsule's chute releases in the nick of time, and the capsule conveniently settles in a wilderness lake. Once it has landed on the lake bottom, Stone evacuates, disrobes, and comes up for air for the film's first Earthly scene – a scene that starkly contrasts the metallic, ethereal, fragile environment of the space capsule in which we have spent much of the past 90 minutes. The remaining few seconds of the film plant Stone in this gorgeously oppositional scene where we find her floating on her back, gazing at the crystal blue sky and the lush foliage, and swimming up to the shore where, grasping the red-brown earth, she tries to stand for the first time in many weeks and is clumsily reminded of the *gravity* keeping her, indeed all of us, firmly rooted on this planet.

This chapter reads this cinematic *rebirth* as symbolic of the larger cultural shift from one prominent environmental discourse,[1] for which we shall borrow the term "spaceship ecology," toward a new but as yet nebulous discourse. While recent decades have seen the construction and circulation of several new approaches in ecology and the environmental sciences – including sustainability, resilience, novel ecosystems, and the Anthropocene – the shape and boundaries of this new environmental imaginary are as yet obscure. At once a celebration of the ideas central to spaceship ecology *and* a sobering acknowledgment of its inherent limitations for grappling with, and responding to, the gravity of our current environmental epoch, *Gravity* is a befitting text with which to begin an exploration of both where we have been and where we might be headed as regards environmental imaginaries. This chapter takes up residence in the liminal space provided by the film, exploring the key features, legacies, and limitations of "spaceship ecology" as it has influenced popular understandings of our collapsing planet Earth and then tracing the discursive features of what might come next.

Consistent with the theme of this volume, we believe that our present environmental crisis is rooted in part in our discourses, narratives, and imaginaries. We are living in a moment of collapse in both real *and* symbolic terms; Earth and our modes of articulation are each collapsing under the pressure of our times and our society. As such, successful interventions will heed as much the role of language in environmental collapse as they do the material evidence of it. This chapter builds upon a rich set of interdisciplinary literatures that explore the environmental movement and its related discourses. The areas of ecocriticism, environmental rhetoric, the rhetoric of science, environmental discourses, science and technology studies, and environmental history have since the 1980s produced a wealth of insights on the construction and negotiation of nature, the environment, and environmental problems in diverse texts and discursive communities.[2] Our study builds in particular upon the extensive histories of this eco-cultural period provided by environmental historians and humanists Peder Anker (2005), Michael Egan (2015), Fernando Elichirigoity (1999), Ursula Heise (2008, 2011), and Sabine Höhler (2014), who variously explore the technical and cultural manifestations and implications of ecological thinking in the period from 1960–1990.

This chapter also partakes in a larger project exploring the rich and varied discursive features of environmental thinking associated with the field of ecology. The term "ecology," coined in the late nineteenth century by German biologist Ernst Haeckel is a combination of the Greek terms *oikos* and *logos*, which roughly translates to "the knowledge or study of the (natural) household" (Colinvaux 1986; Odum and Barrett 2005). The field of ecology broadly explores the functions of, and relationships within, the natural world, including: how species interact with each other; how they interact with the environment around them; and how the landscape influences the ecological communities that inhabit it. While ecology began as a sub-field of biology, research into ecological communities (e.g., Clements), food chains and material cycling (e.g., Lindeman and Hutchison), and whole lake studies (e.g., Birge and Juday) saw ecology emerge as a discipline in its own right in the latter part of the twentieth century (Odum and Barrett 2005). Ecology's focus on ecosystems' and environments' *functionality* have put it in the center of the conversation on anthropogenic influences and interventions upon our planet. Ecologists have published widely on the impacts of human activities, including hunting, farming, resource extraction, pollution, and climate change. As with all forms of knowledge production, ecology is constituted with formed by a wide variety of approaches and constituents; it is also constitutive of the wider society in which it operates. The past 25 years have witnessed increasing interest within the field of ecology in the linguistic and symbolic commitments and implications of the field. We recommend in particular, Joel B. Hagen's (1992) *An entangled bank: The origins of ecosystem ecology*, Mark A. Davis's (2009), *Invasion biology*, Brendon Larson's (2011) *Metaphors for environmental sustainability: Redefining our relationship with nature*, and William Mark Adams and Martin Mulligan's (2015) *De-colonizing conservation: Strategies for conservation in a postcolonial era* as particularly rich critical examinations of the conceptual and discursive commitments and conundrums at the core of ecological inquiry.

Since the 1960s, ecological ideas, terminologies, and theories have become the central force in many societies' understandings of the natural world, its inhabitants, functions, and relationships. As a rich area of knowledge production, ecology is an important vector for exploring the deep commitments, concerns, and controversies that constitute our environmental moment. What is more, ecology has, in the same time period, had an intimate relationship with popular culture and fiction. Ecologists and environmental scientists have increasingly turned to popular media and channels to communicate directly with publics about the imminent crises revealed by ecological and environment research. Alternately, ecological ideas and concerns have inspired and/or lent themselves naturally to genres of popular fiction including most prominently scifi (sf) and dystopian fiction. As such, this exploration of the transition from "spaceship ecology" to new environmental imaginaries turns to the realms of both scientific and popular culture.

Stage I: zooming out, closing in

The term "spaceship ecology" was popularized by the ecologist and science writer Garrett Hardin in his 1993 book, *Living within limits: Ecology, economics, and population taboos*. It was used to retrospectively describe the cultural and intellectual transition in the 1970s from the four centuries long "age of exuberance" to a more sober period based in a growing recognition of ecological and economic "limits" represented by the form and functionality of the "spaceship." According to Hardin, and economist Kenneth Boulding before him, the environmental crisis that manifested in the 1960s was deeply rooted in the practices and logics of European colonization. The "discovery" of the "New" World, and subsequent dispersal of Europeans from the then densely populated Europe to the less densely populated Americas, led to practices of production and consumption that ignored both the resources involved in such production and the wastes generated by it. Indeed, early expansion into the American 'frontier' was marked by the rampant plundering of resources and subsequent production of waste. The idea of a seemingly endless frontier also influenced the budding field of economics which had, by the late nineteenth century, abandoned an economics centered in "the commons" and begun to espouse a form of "cowboy economics" (Boulding 1966) that was, according to Hardin and others, "sedated by delusion of limitlessness" (1993, p. 6). The ecological thinking that emerged after this "cowboy" period, which we, echoing Hardin, call spaceship ecology, is thus characterized by its reactionary stance toward, and inevitable embeddedness in, the paradigms, practices, and technologies of (terrestrial and extraterrestrial) frontierism.

Spaceship ecology is embedded in the complex period of Western culture between 1960 and 1990,[3] retrospectively dubbed *both* "The Space Age" and "The Environmental Age."[4] This brief period saw Earthlings engage in two epic quests: one to colonize space and the other to save planet Earth. Space colonization and saving the planet were fundamentally different projects, informed by alternative ideologies, preoccupations, stakeholders, and approaches. Even so, both quests were culturally pervasive – produced by and embedded in all spheres of human activity from knowledge production, to political activity, to popular culture – and each quest informed the other, manifesting ultimately in pervasive ways of thinking about the environment and environmental degradation. French cultural historian and philosopher Michel Foucault (1986) has described the twentieth century as the "epoch of space" – a period during which, as Sabine Höhler states, humans became both cognizant of, and preoccupied with, limitations to both *geospace* (territory) and *biospace* (livable habitats) (2014). Höhler more specifically positions the "historical process of spatial confinement and control" associated with this period in relationship with the end of European imperial expansion when the "seemingly endless process of global expansion came to a close" (2014, p. 1).

In concert with (and indeed related to) such spatial and psychological transformations, this period also saw the development of technologies of globalism (most notably the satellite and computer) that allowed humans to see and compute on scales never before imagined, let alone possible. This resulted in radical transformations in collective conceptions of the natural world and our place within it (Heise 2008, Gee and Vogelaar 2018). These shifts were signaled in large part by the emergence, following World War II, of a number of political and scientific practices that began to imagine the planet as a whole, key among them satellite imaging and computer simulation (Elichirigoity 1999). While these technologies were largely inspired by military pursuits (first World War II and then the Cold War and its related space race), they were quickly adapted to alternative uses including the budding environmental movement and its related academic field, the ecological sciences.[5] While ecologists had long thought in terms of interconnected systems, these technological developments allowed them to collect, process, and visualize ecological systems at a scale and rate heretofore unimaginable. This toolset was particularly salient for scientists interested in the emergent area of anthropogenic environmental impacts; an area popularized both by the environmental movement and by scientists like Rachel Carson (*Silent spring* 1962), Garrett Hardin (*Tragedy of the commons* 1968), and Paul and Anne Ehrlich (*The population bomb* 1968), who provided provocative accounts of bleak futures caused by the perpetuation of present environmental abuses including the rampant use of pesticides, economic overproduction, and population growth.

In spite of these new, apparently expansive ways of seeing, ecological thinking at the end of Earth's frontier was preoccupied with imagining, and subsequently managing, an Earth defined not by abundance but by limits. Indeed, philosopher Peter Sloterdijk has suggested that an "ontology of enclosed spaces" was the dominant framework for understanding the planet at this time. According to Sabine Höhler, this ontology saw the evocation of persistent "themes of enclosure" prominent in Western cultural history that manifested specifically in the "spaceship" metaphor (2010, p. 15). Guided by the new insights, imaginaries, and ontologies provided by satellite imaging and computer simulations, as well as pervasive fears (grounded in mounting scientific evidence) of human-induced environmental collapse, a whole new set of vocabularies, constructs, and assumptions emerged. Key among them was the idea of a "spaceship Earth" whose carrying capacity had been exceeded and overshot because of exponential population growth and the related mismanagement of the commons. In this scenario, total environmental collapse was avoidable only if we submitted to radical and immediate global environmental policies managed by scientific and political experts. There is no underestimating the power of the 1968 image, *Earthrise*,[6] in helping to produce the simultaneous "zooming out and closing in" characteristic of this period. *Earthrise*, as it became known, was an impromptu by-product of the Apollo 8 mission; the first manned spacecraft to leave the Earth's orbit. Upon its fourth orbit around the darkside of the moon, Apollo 8's William Anders caught a brief glimpse of Earth 'rising' over the horizon, and immediately decided to capture in photographic form. Ander's existential awe ("Oh my God!" he is recorded as saying, "Look at that picture over there! There's the Earth coming up. Wow, is that pretty.") did not remain his own and the image struck an immediate chord with a global audience. It's little wonder why: *Earthrise* offered for the first time an impossible view of Earth that allowed us to observe it from a distance and as a whole. This was not Earth the home or the land, this was Earth the place, the phenomenon, the photograph (Vogelaar 2011). This was spaceship Earth.

The 1972 report, *The limits to growth (LTG)*, is evocative of, indeed, fundamental to, this new way of thinking about the planet Earth generally and ecosystems more specifically as contained spaces. *LTG* was a study produced by the Club of Rome (an international group of industrialists, politicians, and scientists) that combined systems dynamics,[7] newly evolved computing technology, and existing data on human and environmental variables to develop a "world model" with which the researchers could "experiment" and in turn model possible environmental futures (Meadows et al. 1972). The model, called World3,[8] computed the cumulative effect of five key problems facing global society in the early 1970s: rapid industrial growth, exponential population growth, the lack of adequate nutrition, the growing use of natural resources, and destruction of the environment. Using a *scenarios* approach, which draws upon experts' knowledge about a system, its possible futures and quantitative models (Bennett et al. 2003), the authors examined

12 possible futures, ranging from a "business as usual (BAU)" scenario to those imagining different mixes of increased supplies of natural resources, increases in food production, implementation of controls on population and on pollution, as well as different timelines for the initiation of these policies: 1975 and 2000. The authors of *The limits to growth* ultimately sought to model a world system that was "sustainable without sudden and uncontrollable collapse . . . capable of satisfying the basic material requirements of all its people" (Meadows et al. 1972, p. 158).

The outcomes of the *LTG* modelling scenarios were alarming. The Business as Usual scenario led to system (Earth) collapse within one hundred years (defined by dramatic and sudden decreases in both human population and industrial output). Despite the modifications built into the nine other models to control factors that led to collapse in the BAU model, the interconnections between system elements drove these model systems to collapse within one hundred years (i.e., by circa 2070). Only two of the twelve models did not end in collapse; and these avoided collapse by introducing aggressive global policies and regulations meant to stabilize population growth and industrial production, decrease consumption, reduce pollution, shift global society's output to services and food production, and increase the efficiency and lifetime of industrial materials. In making visible the potential outcomes of a global system characterized by embedded positive feedback loops and exponential population growth, the World3 scenarios and subsequent *LTG* report revealed the inevitability and imminence of collapse without immediate[9] international policy and regulation.

Like other forms of "enclosed" ecology (e.g., conservation, island, restoration, and invasion ecology), spaceship ecology was based in notions of ecosystems as ecologists understood them in the middle of the twentieth century – as "steady states" that could be known, created, contained, and/or restored. Like other forms of cultural production in this period, spaceship ecology was characterized by a persistent and nostalgic desire to return to some imagined, idealized, and stable past (ecological) state. This resulted in an impulse to codify, contain, and control ideal ecosystems. Modelling and simulation were central in this pursuit as they helped to organize and visualize complex systems and overcome the problems of grand (often global) scales and unknown futures.

While much good has come from this line of ecological research and thinking, most significantly our ability to understand environmental issues as planetary issues, it also has limitations. In an effort to explore these issues, we conclude this section with a brief account of Biosphere 2, an inevitably flawed yet nonetheless marvelous ecological experiment that is illustrative of what happens when you push a discourse to its teleological end. Biosphere 2 was the penultimate manifestation of spaceship ecology. The collaborative dream of a group of scientists and engineers primarily from the private sector, the goal of Biosphere 2 was to reproduce in miniature a self-contained and totally self-sufficient reproduction of Biosphere 1 (planet Earth); a designation that tellingly suggests that the planet Earth could in fact be replicated. Set in a series of interconnected, greenhouse-like modules in the Arizona desert, the 12,500-square-meter facility housed a self-contained set of subtropical and tropical biomes (e.g., rainforests, savannahs, marshes, oceans, deserts) combined with a human habitat for eight people and an agricultural area (Nelson et al. 1993; Allen and Nelson 1999). The project began in 1984 as a collaboration between private companies and went through years of pilot research, before starting the now famous first experiment in 1991, when eight researchers were sealed into the domes to test the ability of the system to support itself and the humans with no outside support. Even though the goal of the project was to both create self-organizing ecosystems and, at the same time, sustain the eight humans for two years with appropriate levels of nutrition and a safe atmosphere, as well as proper recycling of water and wastes and minimal (< 10%) leakage of air, the designers recognized that a host of things could go wrong (e.g., loss of major plant species, build-up of undesirable gases, crop diseases). And, indeed, things went wrong: carbon dioxide and oxygen levels proved difficult to control and ultimately required external manipulations to keep them at healthy levels, extinctions were more prevalent than expected, including the majority of vertebrate species and all the pollinators, and vines and ants became dominant species (Cohen and Tilman 1996). The simulation encountered problems to such an extent that the initial "mission" was cut short and rebooted (several months later). Despite such challenges, the simulation was not a complete failure. The waste recycling system was very effective, and the first mission met 81% of the crew's food needs. The second mission succeeded in reaching "food sufficiency" (referring to a diet that was nutritionally dense and calorically restricted) with the crew demonstrating many improved health factors, including lower cholesterol and blood pressure (Allen and Nelson 1999, p. 19; Nelson et al. 1993).

Although Biosphere 2's two "missions" failed to recreate Earth's complex ecosystems in a way that suggested long-term sustainability, they nevertheless taught us a lot about the problem of thinking of Earth as a containable, closed system that can exist in a perpetual steady state and can be easily maintained with the optimal "crew," specializations, and species. The Earth is not one big experiment that can be contained and controlled by experts, it is rather complex, dynamic, adaptive, and most importantly, much larger than us. As Aldo Leopold wrote in 1938,

> the outstanding scientific discovery of the twentieth century is . . . the complexity of the land organism. Only those who know the most about it can appreciate how little is known about it . . . who but a fool would discard seemingly useless parts? To keep every cog and wheel is the first precaution of intelligent tinkering.
>
> (1970, p. 190)

Biosphere 2 demonstrated that we still do not fully understand the intricate functioning of our planet and that the danger of rapid and rampant extinction (now happening on Biosphere 1 as we enter the "sixth extinction") is real.

Stage II: sciencing survival

We began with *Gravity*, we turn now to a more recent space thriller, *The Martian*, as it helps us explore spaceship ecology in the wake of *The limits to growth* and Biosphere 2. *The Martian* begins like most of its kind with a mission gone awry. Blasted by a sandstorm on sol[10] six of their 31-sol mission on Mars, the crew of Ares III is forced to emergency evacuate from its research site. During the evacuation, the protagonist, astronaut Mark Watney, is impaled by a communication antenna and presumed dead. The remainder of the story follows Watney's (mostly) solitary quest for survival, a quest that begins with the methodic removal of the antenna lodged in his torso and proceeds over the next two years during which time he uses his wit and "MacGyver"[11] skills to survive on that mysterious red dot that has long consumed earthly imaginaries. Unlike most space thrillers, this story is told predominantly through Watney's diary logs (vlogs in the film) which describe how he uses his two mission specializations, botany and engineering, to "science the sh*t out of" his exile on Mars. His diary entries detail his daily threats, successes, and failures mixing complex mathematical calculations and scientific processes (e.g., "If I want water, I'll have to make it from scratch. Fortunately, I know the recipe: Take hydrogen. Add oxygen. Burn.') with cheeky and self-deprecating comments (e.g., 'So, yeah, I blew myself up"). The Martian (Watney) is also *not* your typical "space hero"; he is on the contrary a "comic geek"; aware of the scientific likelihood of his failure (e.g., "If the oxygenator breaks down, I'll suffocate. If the water reclaimer breaks down, I'll die of thirst. If the Hab[12] breaches, I'll just kind of explode. If none of those things happen, I'll eventually run out of food and starve to death. So yeah. I'm f*cked".) but also playfully delighted ("Yay!," he often emotes) by every hack that prolongs his extraterrestrial existence one more sol. Consistent with the genre, *The Martian*, is a celebration of aerospace science and technology and its related protagonists and pursuits, *but* this is an ironic, self-aware celebration that draws attention to the complex and fraught relationships between science and colonialism, nationalism, industry, and fiction. Like *Gravity*, *The Martian* is a liminal text that provides a window into the imaginary places we have been and the imaginary places we might (have to) go next.

Imagined societies and life on Mars have a long tradition in myth and fiction that importantly predates scientific interest in Mars as a post-earth destination or testing ground for space colonization. Ursula Heise's (2011) *Martian ecologies and the future of nature* explores this enduring fascination with Mars suggesting that contemporary incantations of the genre evoke

Mars not as an "other" world (as in earlier periods) but rather as a trope for *our* world (Earth) in the Anthropocene. Contemporary "Mars settings," she states, "portray the emergence of new, synthetic ecologies that combine human and nonhuman, animate and inanimate, planetary and extraplanetary, biological and technological elements in such a way that these distinctions themselves gradually cease to perform meaningful cultural work" (p. 468–9). In this sense, "Earth and Mars emerge as mirror images of each other" (p. 466) and "Martian ecologies" serve as a metaphor with which to explore, indeed articulate, "the obsolescence of conventional nature" on our own planet (p. 468). No matter what planet we end up on, says Heise, Martian ecologies are our future.

The Martian is an evocative contribution to this canon, and is demonstrative of the tensions associated with the discourse of spaceship ecology in this period of transition. Prose mirroring project, *The Martian* dispenses largely with narrative and character development and is pure plot-problem-solution, problem-solution and again. It is an exciting, exhausting 560-sol survivalist adventure spoken from the cynical, asocial and, yet somehow, optimistic hacker perspective.[13] A literary evocation of "survival science," *The Martian* is illustrative of the evolution of the discourse of spaceship ecology in what has been termed the Anthropocene – the new geological epoch in which we now live whose name highlights the visible human footprint on the Earth's geologic record (Egan 2015). Staging this drama 54.6 million kilometers away from planet Earth, the Martian allows us to view in miniature three key themes of late-spaceship ecology, namely, the foregrounding of envirotechnical systems,[14] the rejection of both nostalgia and futurism (and the privileging of "presentism"), and the related abandonment of *flourishing* as a possibility or aspiration. This is a story of survival.

The potentiality of systemic, global collapse made known during the period of spaceship ecology, and the subsequent recognition that the extreme measures recommended by experts in the field (e.g., *LTG*) were not being met in the timeframe indicated by the models, gave rise to what Dryzek has described as a mood of "survivalism" in environmental discourses (2005, p. 30). Unlike early collapse scholarship, which studied collapse in the *hope* of finding ways to avoid it, survivalism dispatched with that hope concerning itself with how humans might adapt to, survive, and rebuild after the collapse. Extending Soulé's (1985) designation of conservation biology as a "crisis discipline," environmental historian Michael Egan offers "survival science" as an "organizing tool for understanding the working worlds in which various sciences functioned during [this] period of intense environmental disruption" and which stressed "the social significance of survival as a new environmental imperative" (2015, p. 37). Rather than being the product of "a singular disciplinary practice," Egan asserts that

> survival science constituted synthetic, multidisciplinary sciences in which the boundaries between "basic" and "applied" research were blurred

or non-existent. It also demanded new approaches to environmental problems, and placed scientists in a novel socio-political dynamic where scientific evidence ran up against economic and regulatory imperatives, local and industrial interests, and a newfound urgency provoked by fears of imminent environmental collapse on local and global scales. Survival sciences were reactionary, invariably responding to a newly-discovered but extant problem.

(2015, p. 37)

The Martian is set in this survivalist context and *th*e Martian is a survival scientist par excellence – botanist, engineer, systems hacker. Watney's struggle for survival on Mars serves as a metaphor for earthly survival in this period. The lone protagonist exists in a wholly envirotechnical system that requires constant hacking and adaptation and where *thrival* was never a possibility. Luckily for Watney, the Martian, (and the scientists who entered Biosphere 2) there was the possibility of escape back to planet Earth. Unluckily for us Earthlings, there is none. So what can we learn from this discursive and material extension of spaceship ecology? For us, it reveals the necessary evolution of this discourse in the 1980s–1990s to a discourse that recognized and came to terms with our world as one that was forever altered. From that perspective we can then take stock of what we have to work with (materially, intellectually, symbolically), and craft a world from there, guided not by hope or despair but by a keen desire to "die another day." Perhaps, this also suggests that rather than reading *The Martian* as a sci-fi epic we should read it as a realistic, prosaic lesson about how to get on with it here on this one and only biosphere.

Of course spaceship ecology as a way of thinking about the planet and its resources, has not disappeared. It lives on in collapse science, resilience thinking, the language and science of planetary boundaries, invasion ecology, and most recently the idea/science of rewilding. It has been an important discursive contribution to our growing understanding of our planet's systems, functions, and thresholds. It has, however, in recent years, given way, via survivalism, to emergent and novel ways of thinking about what we can do with an already tainted Earth. Research into hybrid and novel ecosystems, the Anthropocene and adaptation, for example, take as their starting point the fact that we cannot recreate what we have lost and instead focus on *hacking* together a survival based in an understanding of the limits of our systems and knowledge. What comes of these emergent threads, we know not yet, but we openly hope that they begin to remember not ecosystems past but that beautiful experience called thriving.

Notes

1 It is difficult to locate this discourse in any meaningful way, except to say that it is both firmly rooted in Western/Enlightenment science, economics, industry,

and culture and also, given the global nature of much of this planet, embedded in geographies and cultures around the world.

2 Deluca's (2005) *Image events: The new rhetoric of environmental activism*; Dryzek's (2005). *The politics of the earth: Environmental discourses*; Garrard's (2011) *Ecocriticism*, Routledge; Gross's (1990) *The rhetoric of science*; Killingsworth and Palmer's (2012) *Ecospeak: Rhetoric and environmental politics in America*; and Latour and Woolgar's (1986) *Laboratory life: The construction of scientific facts.*

3 The book was self-published in 2011 and then re-released in 2014 by Crown. The film was released in 2015 by 20th Century Fox.

4 The Space Age technically began in the mid-1950s with the Russian-US "space race."

5 We use "ecology" as an umbrella term to describe the work being done in a variety of related disciplines including but not limited to conservation biology, population biology, community ecology, and island biogeography.

6 NASA and Anders, B. (1968). Earthrise (image AS8–14–2383). Retrieved on October 20, 2017 from www.hq.nasa.gov/office/pao/History/alsj/a410/AS8-14-2383HR.jpg

7 Systems dynamics is a methodology to analyze how systems function (Little et al. 2016) and the term can be used synonymously with "systems theory" and "systems analysis" (De Vries 2013). The development of computing technology was a crucial part to the development of this field, as it enabled a much higher level of modeling complex systems.

8 World1 and World2 were previous versions of the model developed by Forrester; World2 was the basis of Forrester's 1971 book, *World Dynamics*. Forrester's initial work was primarily in the management field, but in the late 1960s shifted to examining social systems first examining urban systems and then global systems under the guise of the Club of Rome (Forrester 1989).

9 A model with policies introduced by 1975 achieved stability; the same model with a delay of policy introduction until 2000 still led to collapse.

10 A "sol" is a Martian day.

11 *MacGyver* was a popular American television show that ran from 1985 to 1992 that followed the pursuits of secret agent Angus MacGyver, who used low tech tools and his wit to hack into and out of any problem he encountered.

12 Short for "habitat," the sealed structure in which he lives.

13 Significantly, the author, Andy Weir, is a computer programmer and the son of a physicist and an engineer.

14 See England in this volume for more on this concept.

References

Adams, W. M. and Mulligan, M., 2015. *De-colonizing nature: Strategies for conservation in postcolonial era*. London: Earthscan.

Allen, J. and Nelson, M., 1999. Overview and design biospherics and biosphere 2, mission one (1991–1993). *Ecological Engineering*, 13, 15–29.

Anker, P., 2005. The ecological colonization of space. *Environmental History*, 10(2), 239–268.

Boulding, K. E. 1966. The economics of the coming spaceship Earth. In H. Jarrett (ed.), *Environmental quality in a growing economy*. Baltimore, MD: Johns Hopkins University Press, 3–14.

Bennett, E. M. et al., 2003. Why global scenarios need ecology. *Frontiers in Ecology and the Environment*, 1(6), 322–329.

Cohen, J. E. and Tilman, D., 1996. Biosphere 2 and biodiversity: The lessons so far. *Science (New York, N.Y.)*, 274(5290), 1150–1151.

Colinvaux, P., 1986. *Ecology*. New York: John Wiley & Sons.

Davis, M. A., 2009. *Invasion biology*. Oxford: Oxford University Press.

Deluca, K. M., 2005. *Image events: The new rhetoric of environmental activism*. Abingdon, UK: Routledge.

De Vries, B. J. M., 2013. The systems dynamics perspective. In *Sustainability science*. New York: Cambridge University Press, 14–53.

Dryzek, J. S., 2005. *The politics of the earth: Environmental discourses*. Oxford: Oxford University Press.

Egan, M., 2015. Confronting collapse: Environmental science at the end of the world. *Intervalla*, 3, 35–43. Available at: www.fus.edu/intervalla/volume-3-environmental-justice-collapse-and-the-question-of-evidence [Accessed September 10, 2017].

Elichirigoity, F., 1999. *Plant management: The limits to growth, computer simulation, and the emergence of global spaces*. Evanston, IL: Northwestern University Press.

Forrester, J. W., 1989. The beginning of system dynamics. In *Banquet talk at the international meeting of the system dynamics society*. Stuttgart. Available at: http://static.clexchange.org/ftp/documents/system-dynamics/SD1989-07BeginningofSD.pdf [Accessed June 9, 2017].

Foucault, M., 1986. Of other spaces. *Diacritics* 16.1, 22–27.

Garrard, G., 2011. *Ecocriticism*. Abingdon, UK: Routledge.

Gee, G. and Vogelaar, A. E., 2018. *Changing representations of nature and the city: Legacies of the 1960s–1970s*. Abingdon, UK: Routledge.

Gross, A. G., 1990. *The rhetoric of science*. Cambridge, MA: Harvard University Press.

Hagen, J. B., 1992. *An entangled bank: The origins of ecosystem ecology*. New Brunswick, NJ: Rutgers University Press.

Hardin, G., 1993. *Living within limits: Ecology, economics and population taboos*. Oxford: Oxford University Press.

Heise, U. K., 2008. *Sense of place, sense of planet: The environmental imagination of the global*. Oxford: Oxford University Press.

Heise, U. K., 2011. Martian ecologies and the future of nature. *Twentieth-Century Literature*, 57(3) and 57(4), 447–471.

Höhler, S., 2010. The environment as a life support system: The case of biosphere 2. *History and Technology*, 26(1), 39–55.

Höhler, S., 2014. *Spaceship Earth in the environmental age: 1960–-1990*. New York: Routledge.

Killingsworth, M. J. and Palmer, J. S., 2012. *Ecospeak: Rhetoric and environmental politics in America*. Carbondale, IL: Southern University Press.

Larson, B., 2011. *Metaphors for environmental sustainability: Redefining our relationship with nature*. New Haven, CT: Yale University Press.

Latour, B. and Woolgar, S., 1986. *Laboratory life: The construction of scientific facts*. Princeton, NJ: Princeton University Press.

Leopold, A., 1970. *A sand county almanac: With other essays on conservation from round river*. New York: Ballantine Books.

Little, J. C., Hester, E. T. and Carey, C. C., 2016. Assessing and enhancing environmental sustainability: A conceptual review. *Environmental Science & Technology*, 50(13), 6830–6845.

Meadows, D. H., Meadows, D. L., Randers, J. and Behrens III, W. W., 1972. *The limits to growth*. New York: Universe Books.

NASA and Anders, B., 1968. *Earthrise* (image AS8–14–2383). Available at: www.hq.nasa.gov/office/pao/History/alsj/a410/AS8-14-2383HR.jpg [Accessed October 20, 2017].

Nelson, M., Burgess, D. L., Alling, A., Alvarez-Romo, N. F., Walford, R. L., Dempster, W. and Allen, J.P., 1993. Using a closed ecological system to study Earth's biosphere. *BioScience*, 43(4), 225–236.

Odum, E. and Barrett, G., 2005. *Fundamentals of ecology*. Belmont, CA: Thomson Brooks/Cole.

Soulé, M. E., 1985. What is conservation biology? *BioScience*, 25(11), 727–734.

Vogelaar, A. E., 2011. Goracle's travels: En-visioning global communities for climate change in *An Inconvenient Truth*. *Culture, Language and Representation*, 9, 225–244.

Part III
Craft collapse

8 Imagining the apocalypse

Valences of collapse in McCarthy, Burtynsky, and Goldsworthy

I. J. MacRae

It is by now common knowledge that our planet's ecology is rapidly changing. The oceans are acidifying, warming, and rising; the ice caps are melting as the atmosphere warms; the world's freshwater supply is degrading and the rate of biodiversity loss increasing; the planet's sixth great ecological die-off is well underway (Kolbert 2015). The climate is changing, of course – "The global warming signal is now louder than the noise of random weather," NASA scientist James Hansen observed in 2012 – but global climate change is in fact only one of nine 'Earth system processes' in rapid transformation (Ehrlich 2013). Such is the profound impact of the human species on the Earth system that climate scientists and geologists have proposed that the planet has left the 12,000-year relative climatic stability of the Holocene period and is now entering a new geological epoch, the Anthropocene (Zalasiewicz 2011). As ecological economist William Rees observes, "humanity is now the single most significant biophysical force impacting the planet" (2009, p. 198). With our species a global force of nature, the distinction between natural and human histories has collapsed (Ghosh 2016). As the artists treated in this chapter recognize, "By bringing the acceleration of industrial society to natural systems, we have forfeited the luxury of imagining that nature is a fixed back-ground for human affairs" (Kelsey, p. 10). The Anthropocene challenges our very sense of what it means to be human, as Roy Scranton (2013) suggests; the concept elides any (imaginary) line between nature and culture, and compels us to seek new ecological relations. It is in this sense that literature and the visual and creative arts are essential in imagining other – emergent, interdisciplinary, ecologically integrated – forms of human being.

This chapter takes up the photographs of Edward Burtynsky, the ephemeral art of Andy Goldsworthy, and the novel *The Road* by Cormac McCarthy in relation to the previous concerns, with particular attention to how these artists interpret and frame notions of collapse, what I refer to here as ecological *apocalypse*. While the media and modes these artists engage with are diverse, their works are inevitably about human relationships with non-human nature. Each responds to what Burtynsky calls "peak everything" – a scale of resource extraction and depletion that is drawing down the world's resources faster than they can be replenished. These artists incorporate an awareness of what Burtynsky calls "the man-made transformations our civilization has imposed upon nature" – in which *our* in this case refers specifically to "western ideals – the hollow promise of fulfillment and happiness through material gain, . . . the mass consumerism these ideals ignite and the resulting degradation of our environment intrinsic to the process of making things" (2005, p. 7). They ask us to worry and wonder about what might happen when human relationships with a sustaining ecology are shorn.

In other words, in different yet related ways, these three artists address the politics and poetics of ecological collapse in the early twenty-first century. And yet the ethics of their engagement, the attitude and approach they take, is different. Their works draw us into the beauty of the natural world as it is, asserting a living ecology's flux, stability, strength, fragility, and impermanence, while making us aware of Western alienation from natural processes. Each draws our attention to the complexities, ambiguities, nuances, and contradictions of human relationships with nature. And each responds to the need to analyze, understand, imagine, and animate the relationship between Western traditions and ecological processes. The wager of this chapter is that bringing their works together in dialogue as three versions or variants of possible creative and critical responses to a related set problems might, in its own way – and in keeping with the themes taken up here – be *revelatory*. These artists call us to return some agency to nature, and to engage in some collaboration with the ecological world (of which we are necessarily a part). I start here by considering apocalypse as a long-standing, plastic, and prestigious genre, and then take up the work of McCarthy, Burtynsky, and Goldsworthy in turn.

Burtynsky's photographs show the results of extraction processes, the after-effects of production and consumption; McCarthy's postapocalyptic novel offers a vision of almost total ecological collapse, in something very much like a "nuclear winter" scenario (Robock et al. 2007); while Goldsworthy's work, as I argue here, interacts with the landscape in the knowledge that collapse is indeed possible, perhaps imminent, and that new ecological relationships must be found. These artists produce work, we might say, after the "end" – with the knowledge that ecological collapse is ongoing and accelerating. As the father in *The Road* says, "There is no later. This is later" (2006, p. 54). To say that these works are produced with ecological apocalypse as their organizing principle and figurative center is to say that these are end-directed texts, that the shadow or ecological crisis of the end is *immanent*. While Apocalypse might seem a hoary term dusted off from the archives, it is in fact an ancient and very much still living, contemporary image of temporality, a way we continue to make sense of the world and of time, and one that is inseparable from – whether we know it or not – our thinking about the unfolding crises of climate change and ecological collapse.

The word *apocalypse* itself derives from the Greek *apokalupsis*, to uncover or reveal (the root is *kalupto*, to cover or conceal). Apocalypse, as the title of its well-known classical manifestation – the Book of Revelation – makes clear, is an uncovering, a *revelation*. More than this, apocalypse signifies transformation, a new beginning, a second coming: a new earthly justice for the chosen elect. The apocalyptic genre is eschatological in nature (*eschatos*, furthest, or uttermost), and is concerned with final things, the end of the present age, the Day of Judgment, and the age to follow. But Apocalypse does not signal an ultimate end or 'Armageddon,' as in its popular and cinematic versions; rather, it entails a review of the past so as to bring one historical period to a close, thereby ushering in a new beginning.

As historian Eugen Weber has observed:

> Apocalyptic prophecies are attempts to interpret their times, to console and guide, to suggest the meaning of the present and the future. Typically, they relate fear to hope: tribulation and horror will usher in public and private bliss, free of pain or evil.
>
> (1999, p. 31)

The valence of apocalypse is not then strictly negative, as in "destruction" or "catastrophe"; it can and does oscillate between negative and positive poles. Following the Last Judgment there appears "the holy city, the new Jerusalem, coming down from God out of heaven, prepared as a bride for her husband" (Rev. 21:2). Patriarchal imagery and imagination notwithstanding, in Revelation

> catastrophe is balanced against millennium, desolation against fecundity, God's wrath against his mercy. . . . Thus, apocalypse is not merely a vision of doom: For its original audience it was, on the contrary, a luminous vision of the fulfillment of God's promise of justice and communal salvation.
>
> (Parkinson Zamora 1989, p. 2)

Most scholarship has Revelation written by the itinerant Christian prophet of Asia Minor, John of Patmos, in the last decade of the first century. This is the poetic work of an inspired, exquisitely arcane writer. The text itself is dense, transformative, opaque, and seething with energy. There are plagues of lightning, falling stars and fire, as is well known. But what is important is that this torrential imagery is open-ended, inconclusive, and "full of secret allegories at whose original reference we can only guess. . . . Consequently the meaning of the book is, almost uniquely, identical with its various applications" (McGinn, 1987, p. 523). This is crucial in interpreting today's visions of ecological collapse, in that the genre of apocalypse is capacious, variegated, riven with difference, deliberately vague and esoteric, and thus is "ultimately capable of accommodating all human desire" (Davis, 2000, p. 95). It is this convergence or ambiguous play between history and myth that animates any rendering of ecological apocalypse. And it is this transformative potential that makes apocalypse a useful frame for contemporary artists working in ecological contexts. It's a way of casting judgment and of rendering visible the patterns of time, of indicting contemporary practices while calling forth, in whatever guise, a more just, equitable new beginning (as in McCarthy, with the father and son). In the biblical sense – and contemporary meanings of apocalypse cannot be severed from their biblical roots (Bergoffen 1987, p. 11) – the apocalyptic narrator stands outside of time, recounting the past, present, and future from an atemporal point of view beyond the end of time. For the reader of the text, the viewer of the film, the audience of the photograph, as Frank Kermode has most astutely analyzed:

> we are placed, as no one ever was before, at precisely the moment in time when the past may be seen as a pattern and the future, amply predicted in the numerals and images of the text, begins to take exact shape.
>
> (1987, p. 385)

This, I mean to suggest, is the position Burtynsky adopts in his photographs, as does McCarthy's narrator in *The Road*, but which Goldsworthy seeks to incorporate and move beyond in his art of embodied ecological praxis. Apocalypse signifies an uncovering, a revelation; what then do these works of ecological apocalypse *reveal*?

McCarthy's novel *The Road* imagines what more or less total ecological collapse might look like, and reveals the effects of this apocalypse on human and natural histories. The 'landscape' of this novel, in Orhan Pamuk's (2011) sense of the values he imbues and the sentiments he creates in the world of his book, is overwhelmingly grim. An unspecified catastrophic event has triggered ecological collapse, the land is scourged and ashen and relentlessly cold, food is scarce and then has essentially vanished, and "bloodcults" – rogue bands of cannibals and their consorts and catamites – ravage the land. Like "pilgrims in a fable," as we are told on the novel's first page, a boy and his father travel south across this ruined landscape in search of warmth and the sea (3). It is a chimeric goal, motive without meaning (except for the meaning they imbue it with). The novel follows a chronologically linear, generic, road movie structure. It is a lean, pared-down, tightly woven tale in which episodes of violent and dramatic action spool out as knots on the thread of a propulsive, forward-seeking narrative, with a clear, unwavering goal always firmly in the characters' minds. (This too is the reader's experience, of a text lacking in chapter breaks or other signs of suspiration.) These harrowing encounters are interspersed, in turn, with periods of rest, reflection and sleep – even the bounty of a discovered bomb shelter – and with flashbacks in dream and memory (particularly the father's) as they move through the high country around Lookout Mountain, Georgia, and down again into the coastal plain. The unnamed man and child – these are representative 'everymen' whose values, skills, endurance, and endeavor will be harshly tested – must evade human predators, find food and shelter, and keep alive "the fire" which they hold between them. This fire they carry is a metaphor for the kindness, compassion, and love that motivates their journey and keeps them from cannibalism and violence. It is imaginary but not unreal, a fragile, flickering flame, and the light that *reveals* the depravities of a human society shorn of the sustaining envelope of a living ecology.

The narrative picks up some ten years after collapse, as the man and boy are shot at by arrows, stolen from, and stumble upon the remains of "a charred human infant headless and gutted and blackening on the spit" (p. 198). They find people locked in a cellar, stumps charred to prolong their lives – human beings harvested and eaten alive by other humans:

> Huddled against the back wall were naked people, male and female, all trying to hide, shielding their faces with their hands. On the mattress lay a man with his legs gone to the hip and the stumps of them blackened and burnt. The smell was hideous.
>
> (p. 110)

This is a genuinely terrifying episode, in which what the characters actually find in the cellar – a trope of the horror genre – is exceeded, as Benjamin Percy (2013) suggests, by what the reader has imagined will be found. *The Road*, in other words, is a quintessential text of ecological *apocalypse*, one in which we contemplate human and ecological death on a profound scale. McCarthy makes this theme readily apparent as the mother contemplates taking her own life (she was pregnant with the boy at the moment of collapse), and she and her husband for a "hundred nights" sit up "debating the pros and cons of self destruction with the earnestness of philosophers chained to a madhouse wall" (p. 58). This is what Scranton – and surely Cormac McCarthy – consider the philosophical questions par excellence:

> In the epoch of the Anthropocene, the question of individual mortality – "What does my life mean in the face of death?" – is universalized and framed in scales that boggle the imagination. What does human existence mean against 100,000 years of climate change? What does one life mean in the face of species death or the collapse of global civilization? How do we make meaningful choices in the shadow of our inevitable end?
>
> (Scranton 2013)

What ecological apocalypse in McCarthy reveals is a number of possible responses to these questions. There are no cows left, presumably, and no deer, and no birds; the sea itself, when they reach it, looks "Like the desolation of some alien sea breaking on the shores of a world unheard of" (p. 215). What *does* it mean to be confronted with such death? The mother's mature, reasoned, surely gendered response to this absurd world aligns with the vision outlined by Camus in *The Myth of Sisyphus*, in which suicide is the only reasonable reaction to a world gone mad. "Deciding whether or not

life is worth living is to answer the fundamental question in philosophy,"
wrote Camus. "All other questions follow from that" (1955). McCarthy's
mother makes her decision, while father and son walk on into "that ashen
scabland" (16).

The Road, as signaled early on, *is* a fable, a stark and simple tale with a
simple moral, and what ecological collapse reveals in this case is the artifice
of all human creeds, the falsity of extant gods, and the illusion of ethical systems, an agnosticism that underlies much of McCarthy's work. McCarthy's
novel peers into nothingness, an essential absence of human morality and
ethical systems, finding "The frailty of everything revealed at last. Old and
troubling issues resolved into nothingness and night" (28). The father senses
"The world shrinking down about a raw core of parsible entities. The sacred
idiom shorn of its referent and so of its reality" (88–9).

It is this vertiginous, apocalyptic absence against which the reader may
gauge the bond between father and son. The son knows nothing about the
prelapsarian world, and is an amazement to the few travelers they come
across, most of whom have never seen such a young person, who have largely
been killed off and presumably eaten. This absence of memory or experience
before ecological collapse, the lack of any trace of a world prior to the end
is, paradoxically enough, the boy's greatest strength and determining feature,
the epitome of his revelation. He is goodness and compassion incarnate, car-
ing for old men whom they meet on the road (in sharing food), troubled by
the father's protective slippages in honesty and fact, worried even for people
who have stolen their food and clothes. Often terrified in the face of the
collapsed world, the boy is invariably governed by principles of community,
justice, and truth; he wonders whether they are still "good guys" after his
father kills a road agent who would rape, kill, and eat them. The boy remains
somehow intrinsically good throughout, and is filled with generosity and
compassion, an ethic of care and a will to honesty and truth; he works hard
to kindle the compassion, empathy, and love he and his father share.

McCarthy's stark vision is consolidated and even redeemed in the basic
necessity and apparent human need for some artifice and narrative to anchor
and guide belief and experience, the desire of father and son to breathe life
into new gods (beliefs, faith, hope) out of the abdication of the old. "Evoke
the forms," the father hymns to himself while tousling the boy's hair. "Where
you've nothing else construct ceremonies out of the air and breathe upon
them" (74). With this discourse of theodicy McCarthy transcends simple
and familiar generic concerns of the Apocalypse and takes up fundamental
questions of philosophy, mortality, spirituality, and ecology. On the book's
second page the man "squatted and studied the country to the south. Barren,
silent, godless" (4). Raging at a world "all but unaccountable" (48) recognizing the abundant evidence of a godless world, he damns God himself.
These theological concerns constitute a counter-narrative that illuminates
McCarthy's vision of ecological apocalypse, and ultimately exfoliates into
full revelation at text's end. The novel's third page establishes the book's

governing and necessary paradox: of his son the man knows, "If he is not the word of God God never spoke" (5). In this harrowed land the mother's final words to her husband before she goes off to take her own life become words the man and boy live by:

> The one thing I can tell you is that you wont survive for yourself. I know because I would never have come this far. A person who had no one would be well advised to cobble together some passable ghost. Breathe it into being and coax it along with words of love. Offer it each phantom crumb and shield it from harm with your body.
>
> (p. 57)

And so they do, breathing life into new gods – the boy, his compassion incarnate and somehow imbued in flesh and spirit. In so doing they restore the human, the intimate, the local, and answer precisely the question Scranton asks, "How do we make meaningful choices in the shadow of our inevitable end?"

As we have seen, apocalypse as a narrative genre casts a retrospective, ordering glance over all of creation, rendering visible the 'final' fulfillment of time, and imposing an absolute, teleological order and meaning over all that has gone before. Northrop Frye defined the apocalyptic principle in a narrative genre as a "world already explained, a world of total metaphor, in which everything is potentially identical with everything else, as though it were all inside a single infinite body" (1957, p. 136) What this means is that tales of ecological apocalypse (all forms of apocalypse, in fact – as both biblical exegesis and popular cinema reveal) are, paradoxically enough, simplifying, and mythic; they are reductive metanarratives or "total metaphors" that work to project their own neat and totalizing fantasies back onto all of human society, history, and creation – that is, over all that has gone before. This too is what McCarthy's play with genre reveals. His fable is simplifying, reductive, and mythic; it is certainly not history. Himself an aging author with a young son, McCarthy is mediating the concerns of ecological collapse through the filter of personal biography. In a simple sense, the future will never turn out quite this way. Stephen Jay Gould (1987) taught us the importance of time's arrow and of time's cycle; the linear component of time implies, in the longer term and at the very least, ceaseless transformation. It seems almost impertinent to remind the reader of this collection, in the face of very real and on-going ecological degradation, that cod are returning to the Grand Banks, if slowly and fitfully, having collapsed after centuries of intensive fishing; that islands and atolls in the South Pacific, demolished and toxified by nuclear testing in the 1950s, now teem with life; that the scarified plains around Sudbury, sundered by decades of mining and smeltering, and site of some of Burtynsky's iconic imagery and formative experience, is now a reforested pastoral scene. In other words, well-known, historical sites of ecological collapse are showing concrete, indubitable signs of renewal, in our own lifetimes. Such is the possibility of ecological renewal – strong, plastic, pervasive – that apocalyptic thinking tends to overlook. As Rebecca Solnit has suggested, "People have always been good at imagining the end of the world, which is much easier to picture than the strange sidelong paths of change in a world without end" (2016). So what other strange paths might we tread?

We find one such strange path in Edward Burtynsky's photographs. As the apocalyptic narrator, in the biblical sense, stands after the end, at the cusp of a new beginning, able to survey all that has gone before, so too do Edward Burtynsky's photographs appear to 'stand' equidistant from all points in space, and after the apocalypse of resource extraction has ended. Often shot from drones, cranes, ladders, or other high vantage points, even the near-field foreground is distant in these images. These bird's eye views of large-scale human-impacted landscapes tend to be startling in their scope, scale, and attention to particular detail – detail that is balanced and in tension within the larger formal abstraction of a classically composed, often masterfully framed composition. It has often been commented that Burtynsky's photographs offer a strange, seductive beauty, and a terrible portrait of destruction and impending collapse, at one and the same time, inextricably bound. Part of their revelation is that the form, color, light and space of our terraformed earth can also be beautiful, symmetrical, clarifying, and emotionally impactful. These images function as exercises in awareness, a means of paying attention to the scope of extractivist regimes, and to the beauty that lingers still and always in the inalienable world. In toggling between aesthetics and ecology, between beauty and politics, these pictures generate significant emotional and intellectual force. Borrowing from Barry Lopez, a writer who early in his career was also a photographer, Burtytnksy's images can be productively read as "a manifestation of the perversions in our age, our Kafkaesque predicaments" (1998).

As curator Paul Roth explains, Burtynsky's photographs of "the human ecosystem, what we have made of the earth," constitute "a critique of civilization and a foretelling of human ends"; in the tea leaves of these tailings ponds Roth deciphers "littoral zones of the apocalypse" (2009, p. 167). These revelations of *our* (Western) sites of consumption and production make abundantly clear the plunder and toxicity that fuel capitalist regimes. In working to record the after effects of resource extraction economies, Burtynsky also subjects his images to extensive digital post-production, working to reduce differences, in contrast and distribution of light, across the pictorial plane. He prefers to work under a soft and consistent cloud cover, a high cloud that results in a world without shadow but still suffused with light, such that everything in his field of interest is equally illuminated. As he says, "When the light is soft, you sense the volume of a place" (Khatchadourian 2016). In display on a gallery wall the size of these images tends to dwarf the viewer, making her single subjectivity feel insignificant, drawing our attention to the resolution of line and the abstraction of pattern – not to any human individual within the frame (who are rarely Burtynsky's subjects). These large-scale prints seem to imply that any single human life or death is meaningless when set against the monumental scope of any specific extractionist endeavor. In sum then, Burtynsky's preferred methods – favored light conditions, post-production techniques, scale of subject, size of image, and distant, high point of view – combine to reduce or downplay differences within the frame of the photograph, such that the 'true' meaning of these pictures, to borrow a phrase from John Berger, becomes the magnitude of the subject itself, which is generally a vast world transformed through human ingenuity and endeavor. These are indeed *manufactured landscapes* – as the title of his first large-scale book of photographs attests (2003) – images of "human-made feats of engineering of such tremendous proportions that they have taken on the scale of geological forces" (Schuster, p. 194).

A well-established Canadian artist and entrepreneur from St. Catharines, Ontario, who now lives in Toronto, Burtynsky has produced major bodies of work on the oil (2009) and mining industries, the quarrying of granite and marble (2003), and water (2013), and has expanded his work to include producing and co-directing the documentary films *Manufactured Landscapes* (2006) and *Watermark* (2013). He has become more overtly political and ideological as his career has proceeded, less enamored with the aesthetic and more direct, perhaps even documentary in his framing and composition – as in the *China* project (2005), for example. His current subject is the Anthropocene, as imaged in his most recent collection, *Essential Elements* (2016). For Burtynsky,

> We're at a critical moment in history where we're starting to hit the thresholds of human expansion and the limits of what this planet can sustain. We're reaching peak oil, peak fish, peak beef – and the evidence is all there to see in the landscape.
>
> (Wainwright 2016)

To *reveal* these themes, and for his audience to reflect upon them, has become his principal work.

Burtynsky images are motivated by his "profound relationship" with the natural world, without which, as he explains in *Watermark*, he could not do this work. His images contemplate what nature was before capital transformed the world; his work "is a lament for that loss." It is a site of mourning, an expression of grief and sorrow. This aesthetic of lament, loss, and collapse, combined with masterful attention to composition and form, creates what Jennifer Peeples (2011) calls Burtynsky's aesthetic of the "toxic sublime," which she defines as "tensions that arise from recognizing the toxicity of a place, object or situation, while simultaneously appreciating its mystery, magnificence and ability to inspire awe." This has become something of an orthodoxy in the interpretation of Burtynsky's work: to see these photographs as inducing feelings of awe at the scale and scope of impacted landscapes, and to render a sense of human inconsequentiality, thereby muting an activist's response or a call to political action (e.g., Bordo 2006). These are landscapes made by machines and shaped by human hand, representations of the interface between nature and technology, capital, industry, and consumption. As Schuster (2013) and others have shown, the images document sites of labor and production, places where consumer goods begin their journeys into our factories, stores, and homes, even as the specific actions of individual laborers are largely occluded. This is where 'raw' nature is first commodified – extracted, mined, piped, refined, dammed. This is where natural elements enter human supply chains and are converted to resources, where nature has been used to generate wealth, but also the commodity dependencies that enable modern life. The ideal Western consumerism begins its product life cycle here, in places little seen and rarely imagined. Burtynksy's images of mines and quarries imagine absence as well as presence; they register the absence of materials that have been extracted, and record what is left behind, after the use-value of these sites has been exhausted, which is often brooding, hulking, and maleficent – tailings, tires, refineries, quarries. Increasingly also he documents places where we live – floating aquacultural villages in the South China Sea, towers rapidly erected in Shanghai, terraformed communities in California and Florida. His framing and composition techniques rely on familiar conventions of landscape photography and classical landscape painting, as he freely admits. And yet he claims to be one hundred years too late to document the natural beauty of the land. It is his subject matter that is different.

In some ways, of the three artists considered in this chapter, Burtynsky's work is the most ambiguous and difficult to assess. This ambiguity and discretion is precisely their value and meaning: they spur us to interpretation. The images themselves are apocalyptic, capturing and revealing a trace of light and time. They indubitably record what was in front of the lens: we know this event happened, that this place exists and this moment transpired – though what exactly it might mean is less immediately clear. As we contemplate the image we observe a pronounced discontinuity between *now* and *then*, here and there, our consumption and this site of production– between the time and space of the photograph, and what this image might mean to us here, today. Every photograph in this sense presents us with a double image of an event and our reaction to it. It is this gap in space and time that interpretation is meant to fill, to connect our space of viewing with the site of the image.

In this reading, the question of the images' apocalyptic perspective involves the scope and scale of the work, as well as their relation to a single human subjectivity. Do they call us to direct action, or to contemplation and awe? Does their aesthetic move us away from the particularities of lived human experience, as many of Burtynsky's critics attest? These images shock us into registering scale, they implicate us in our gaze (we are their subject), they tie us into the commodity chains which they register and record. But their scale exceeds us; they move us to terror, anxiety, and awe and not toward politics, individual action, freedom. Or so the theory goes. As Lance Duerfahrd suggests, the beauty of these images recuperates their toxicity, and "the viewer is placated through an appreciation for the artist's control of his medium and its iconic language" (p. 1).

Photographs work to collapse diachronic time into a single moment, recording an instant or 'slice' of time; they leave so much out. This is why they are useful in advertising and propaganda; everything beyond the frame is excluded. We see them (naively) as exhibiting truth, incontrovertible presence, the 'real' – what Alice Munro (1978, p. 166) calls their "true lies." The narratives with which we lend them meaning are supplied by that which is outside the frame. The reticence of Burtynsky's photographs reveals something fundamental to the medium itself. As Mark Kingwell observes, "The final truth of the responsible image – the specific rather than the generic real – is that it can serve no purpose other than being. After that, it's up to us" (p. 19). The photographic medium, at least in Burtynsky's work, is itself apocalyptic – simplifying, reductive, mythic, working to project neat and totalizing fantasies back onto all of human history – or at least the subset (Western) with which they are concerned. It is unethical to ask more of these images than they can deliver, however. Interpretation, in the end, is in the hands of the audience; the images themselves refuse to tell us what to think. Rebecca Solnit observed this crucial point a decade ago, "That he [Burtynsky] chooses to pay attention to these places is already a form of engagement, and the questions a photographer raises may be more profound than the answers the medium permits" (2003). While his work frames fragments of ecological apocalypse, raising awareness and important questions, Andy Goldsworthy's imaginative ecological praxis helps formulate a suite of responses to these concerns.

If Burtynsky is akin to a great painter who uses photography (light) to document the scars of our (over-)consumption upon the earth, generally from such distance that the localized, intimate habitus of a single human life is subsumed by the awesome tableau of a transformed planet, Andy Goldsworthy's work interacts with the earth directly as collaborator and co-conspirator. Goldsworthy is an English sculptor who has lived in Scotland for many years. He works as both a sculptor and photographer, crafting site-specific installations out of natural materials. He goes out to work every day he can, in rain or shine, whether on location or at home, and makes and photographs what has come to be called 'ephemeral art,' impermanent pieces made of endemic materials (water, plants, stone) and left there in place, to change in time (Goldsworthy 2004). Short sketches are produced after a successful work, more to document the piece than to further the art of drawing. For Goldsworthy (1990), "Process and decay are implicit" in life, art, and ecology; time is embedded in his art, as it is in nature. Even if a work vanishes due to natural decay, as he observes, it will still be present, its trace part of the record of all events that have transpired in that place over time.

Goldsworthy's creative practice responds directly to place, to be sure. He gets dirty and cold, with split nails and chapped knuckles, in the knowledge that the fine-grained ecology of any given bioregion in which he is working will change, is constantly changing, and that we humans have a necessary and unavoidable role to play in sensitively working with the earth in flux over time. In Andy Goldsworthy's work we encounter an embodied, materialized ethics that moves beyond ethical principles (only), and beyond the articulation of a (simplified, reductive, mythic) apocalyptic perspective, to put into place what Vera Coleman calls "embodied ethical practices" (2016, p. 87). It is the performance of his work in a landscape, not in a studio, that comes to define his contributions to contemporary artistic and ecological discourse. Goldsworthy's work refuses to consider nature and culture as separate categories, or nature as an abstract and mute background against which culture may unfold. His close observation, attention to detail, and sense of pragmatic contemplation produces an embodied and emplaced knowledge that is not strictly verbal, rational, or intellectual but that combines craft, compassion, and sustained practical knowledge of situated and specific ecological processes. In the dialogue between artists I am articulating in this chapter, his work can be said to build on insights in McCarthy and Burtynsky's *oeuvres* to articulate a form of ecological praxis that productively integrates human and natural cultures, moving beyond the specter of apocalypse.

Goldsworthy's photographs of works and accompanying sketches sell for considerable sums in reputable galleries around the globe. His work takes failure as an inevitable part of the creative process, as something element that is indispensable to learning about a specific material and the form he is working to shape. Failure is an opportunity for further learning, and may lead to another path, and another work, which may be more interesting than the original idea. This is to say chance, failure, and variability of local conditions (rain, shine, ice, color of leaf, species of flowers in bloom) are important elements in his relation to place. In some cases, a finished work might seem 'obvious' – but so too is it obvious that no one has done this in quite this way before. Goldsworthy's work is innovative, not obvious. As he puts it:

> I enjoy establishing an order that forces me to look hard to make it complete. When finished the colours flow and weld one stone to another. The same can be said of ideas. The aim is to understand the nature of nature – not isolated materials.
>
> (1994, p. 64)

To "understand the nature of nature": this is Goldsworthy's apocalypse. In the face of collapse, what greater revelation could there be? Sometimes simple, direct ideas are the most far-reaching and complex. That these ideas may be simple to grasp does not mean they are easy to practice. It is in practice that Goldsworthy's work becomes revelatory. What is revealed in his art, in the words of lyric philosopher Robert Bringhurst, is that the natural world is,

> For one thing, simultaneously ancient and brand new stable and ever-changing. For another, it is the very essence of wealth: rich and varied and extensive and complex and intertwined with itself beyond our wildest dreams. Third, it's astoundingly beautiful: delicate, fragile, adaptable, strong and immensely intelligent, attentive and responsive.
>
> (2006, p. 268)

Goldsworthy's work is a site where we might encounter methods, structures, and strategies that can be used to forestall the ecological apocalypse, and those specters of collapse that dominate readings of McCarthy's novel and of Burtynsky's photographs.

Goldsworthy's practice is defined by close observation of and participation in the life-cycles of specific places, and in their integrated ecological relationships; his attention to, and courtesy and care with natural materials, processes, structures, and forms, is exemplary. His creative praxis is marked by an engagement with active work, the performance of physical labor, coupled to a clear thinking in moments of confusion, when the movements and meanings of local materials may not yet be clear or known. His is an embodied ecological knowledge, one that is not strictly verbal, rational, or intellectual, and which combines love, compassion, spiritual awareness, empathy and understanding of specific ecological processes. It is a practice that is antithetical to treating the land as a commodity. In other words, Goldsworthy's work makes visible, and hence available for understanding and criticism, forms of ecological praxis that productively integrate human and natural cultures. An attention to the local, intimate, and specific grounds the work and allows individual pieces to avoid generality, reduction, simplification, myth. Goldsworthy knows full well the dynamics of collapse, of course. Rather than re-diagnosing them, however, or animating an apocalyptic worldview that offers visions of destruction and human greed, violence, selfishness and intolerance, he presents us with another path, one that incorporates the insights of other artists, genres, and forms, and moves them in other, productive directions. It is a human-scaled art: intimate, local, carrying almost the *terroir* of an integrated set of ecological relations, at a specific moment in the landscape's annual round. Goldsworthy's work carries an awareness of the thorns that can stitch a leaf together, and of plant stalks that change color in time; it is an expression of the flexible strength that resonates within natural relations. In his own view, "My art is unmistakably the work of a person – I would not want it otherwise – it celebrates my human nature and a need to be physically and spiritually bound to the earth" (1994, p. 50).

For Goldsworthy then, "A good work is a moment of intense clarity, not mystery" (1994, p. 49). It seeks to clarify a series of ecological relations (properties, values, and the networks that link elements in an ensemble), and is clear that these relations include the living artist, as well as the viewer or audience. His intimate knowledge wants to be communicated, shared, and widely known. It is this move to clarify ecological process, to understand nature and enter into relation with its strength and impermanence, that is more or less absent from Burtynsky's images. It is the memory of perfection the father clings to in McCarthy's prose, the image of the brook trout with which *The Road* ends, the "perfect shadow" of the trout that haunts the book, "Polished and muscular and torsional. On their backs were vermiculate patterns that were maps of the world in its becoming. Maps and mazes" (286–7). As Goldsworthy makes clear, "My intention is not to improve upon nature but to know it – not as a spectator but as a participant" (1994, p. 50). Over his shoulder, leafing through his books of photographs, interacting with his installations in a museum, screening his films and contemplating his work and vision, we may ourselves come into this hard-won knowledge, that the natural world can take on a human-imagined order, and is capable of accommodating the revelation of human desire.

In bringing these three artists together in dialogue around the concept apocalypse, I seek not to tie up each of their complex projects in a single neat bow. These are diverse, accomplished artists, celebrated in their fields. The historical metaphor of apocalypse is meant to be suggestive, not coercive. The connections are lighter and more allusive, and owe much to the method of juxtaposition. By holding each of these artists up against the other, as specific instances of the ecological imagination in action, and with the interpretive frame of apocalypse in mind, it is hoped that the coincidences might fruitful, helping us to think and see again.

I return in closing to my opening gambit, which reads as something of an understatement, that Western society is more or less aware of the ongoing and accelerating ecological apocalypse, that this revelation indicts our attitudes, lifeways, ideology, and culture, and that rather than merely documenting or lamenting our biosphere's rapid transformation – however necessary and important this work may be – we need urgently to explore new, strange paths beyond and through the labyrinth of collapse. It is a tall order, certainly. But part of the meaning and value of Goldsworthy's creative praxis is that it is scalable, finite, and local. It works well in primary schools, in high schools and other places of learning, for example; it is being adopted by communities of retirees, and 'everyday people' are making it part of their daily routine. I have pulled up photos of Goldsworthy's work in haste at a gathering and had friends with their children take up the practice the following day. Dear reader, why not give it a try? It is simple, and fun, and children – indeed, boys and girls of all ages, including adult – respond to its practicality and potentials. The process makes practitioners more aware of natural materials, of the properties of quotidian things they encounter daily, yet may have never fully considered (at least not in this way). It renders the individual a creative subject, interacting with the natural habitus, enabling her to become emplaced and part of a specific landscape – to have local relations, to explore grounded linkages, to belong. If we take seriously Goldsworthy's idea that the trace of any work will remain forever in place, these relations of a specific human to a specific place extend for all of time. The spiritual component of this work does not breathe life into a singular god to replace one dearly departed, but envisions a more personal, intimate relation with spirits that might dwell within these relationships *between* essential elements – rocks, leaves, flowers, soil, trees. We need patience, time, the willingness to be made vulnerable and to experience failure, to be willing to try again and fail better, in order to understand and interweave ourselves within a network of living relations.

It may seem simple enough, but there it is. It is not everything, and to some readers it might not even be much. But it is a place to start, and for a western 'ideal' so profoundly out of ecological balance, so animated by consumerism and fueled by petroleum, practicing an ideology that appears to be careening toward an ecological end, Andy Goldsworthy's practice of ephemeral art can serve as a path into ecological relation, and as an important corrective, missive, and guide.

References

Baichwal, J. (dir.). 2006. *Manufactured Landscapes*. Canada: Foundry Films, National Film Board of Canada. DVD.

Bergoffen, D. 1987. The Meaning of the Apocalyptic Sense of Time. *Apocalyptic Visions in America*. L.P. Zamora, ed. Bowling Green: Popular Culture Press, 11–36.

Bordo, J. 2006. The Wasteland: An essay on *Manufactured Landscapes*. *Material Culture Review* 63: 89–95.

Bringhurst, R. 2006. Wild Language. *The Tree of Meaning*. Kentville, NS: Gaspereau Press, 257–276.

Burtynsky, E. 2003. *Manufactured Landscapes: The Photographs of Edward Burtynsky*. Ottawa: National Gallery of Canada.

Burtynsky, E. 2005. *China: The Photographs of Edward Burtynsky*, With essay by M. Mayer, T. Fishman and M. Kingwell. Göttingen: Steidl.

Burtynsky, E. 2009. *Oil*. Göttingen: Steidl/Corcoran.

Burtynsky, E. 2013. *Water*. Göttingen: Steidl.

Burtynsky, E. 2016. *Essential Elements*. New York: Thames & Hudson.

Burtynsky, E. and Baichwal, J. (dirs.). 2013. *Watermark*. Toronto: Mongrel Media.

Camus, A. 1955. *The Myth of Sisyphus and Other Essays*. New York: Alfred A. Knopf, 3.

Coleman, V. 2016. Emergent Rhizomes: Posthumanist Environmental Ethics in the Participatory Art of Ala Plástica. *Confluencia* 31.2: 85–98.

Davis, J.C. 2000. Utopia and the New World, 1500–1700. *Utopia: The Search for the Ideal Society in the New World*. R. Schaer, G. Claey and L.T. Sargent, eds. New York: Oxford University Press, 95–118.

Duerfahrd, L. 2012. A Scale That Exceeds Us: The BP Gulf Spill Footage and Photographs of Edward Burtynsky. *Imaginations* 3.2. http://dx.doi.org/10.17742/IMAGE.sightoil.3-2.15

158   *I. J. MacRae*

Ehrlich, P.R. and Ehrlich, A.H. 2013. Can a Collapse of Global Civilization Be Avoided? *Proceedings of the Royal Society of Biological Sciences*, January. http://rspb.royalsocietypublishing.org/content/280/1754/20122845

Frye, N., 1957. *Anatomy of Criticism*. Princeton: Princeton UP.

Ghosh, A. 2016. *The Great Derangement: Climate Change and the Unthinkable*. Chicago: University of Chicago Press.

Goldsworthy, A. 1990. *Andy Goldsworthy: A Collaboration with Nature*. New York: H.N. Abrams.

Goldsworthy, A. 1994. *Stone*. London: Viking.

Goldsworthy, A. 2004. *Rivers and Tides: Working with Time*, dir. T. Riedelsheimer. San Francisco: Microcinema International.

Gould, S.J. 1987. *Time's Arrow, Time's Cycle: Myth and Metaphor in the Discovery of Geological Time*. Cambridge: Harvard University Press.

Hansen, J. 2012, May 9. Game Over for the Climate. *The New York Times*. www.nytimes.com/2012/05/10/opinion/game-over-for-the-climate.html?_r=1&=undefined

Kermode, F. 1987. Introduction (To the New Testament). *The Literary Guide to the Bible*. R. Alter and F. Kermode, eds. Cambridge, MA: Belknap Press of Harvard University Press, 375–386.

Khatchadourian, R. 2016, December 19 & 26. The Long View: Edward Burtynsky's Quest to Photograph a Changing Planet. *The New Yorker*. www.newyorker.com/magazine/2016/12/19/edward-burtynskys-epic-landscapes

Kingwell, M. 2005. *China: The Photographs of Edward Burtynsky*. Göttingen: Steidl, pp. 16–19.

Kolbert, E. 2015. *The Sixth Extinction: An Unnatural History*. London: Bloomsbury.

Lopez, B. 1998. Learning to See. *About This Life: Journeys on the Threshold of Memory*. Toronto: Random House, 223–239.

McCarthy, C. 2006. *The Road*. New York: Alfred A. Knopf.

McGinn, B. 1987. Revelation. *The Literary Guide to the Bible*. R. Alter and F. Kermode, eds. Cambridge, MA: Belknap Press of Harvard University Press, 523–541.

Munro, A. 1978. *Who Do You Think You Are?* Toronto: Macmillan.

Pamuk, O. 2011. *The Naive and the Sentimental Novelist: Understanding What Happens When We Write and Read Novels*. London: Faber & Faber.

Parkinson, Z.L. 1989. *Writing the Apocalypse: Historical Vision in Contemporary U.S. and Latin American Fiction*. Cambridge: Cambridge University Press.

Peeples, J. 2011. Toxic Sublime: Imaging Contaminated Landscapes. *Environmental Communication: A Journal of Nature and Culture* 5.4: 373–392.

Percy, B. 2013, May 14. Cormac McCarthy's *The Road* May Have the Scariest Passage in All of Literature. *The Atlantic*. Interview with Joe Fassler. www.theatlantic.com/entertainment/archive/2013/05/cormac-mccarthys-i-the-road-i-may-have-the-scariest-passage-in-all-of-literature/275834/

Rees, W. 2009. *Degradation and the Arrow of Time*. Burtynsky, E. Oil, ed. Göttingen: Steidl/Corcoran, pp. 195–200.

Robock, A., Oman, L. and Stenchikov, G.L. 2007. Nuclear Winter Revisited with a Modern Climate Model and Current Nuclear Arsenals: Still Catastrophic Consequences. *Journal of Geophysical Research* 112.

Roth, P. 2009. *The Overlook*. Burtynsky, E. Oil. Göttingen: Steidl/Corcoran, pp. 167–69.

Schuster, J. 2013. Between Manufacturing and Landscapes: Edward Burtynsky and the Photography of Ecology. *Photography and Culture* 6.2: 193–212.

Scranton, R. 2013, November 10. Learning to Die in the Anthropocene. *New York Times*. http://opinionator.blogs.nytimes.com/2013/11/10/learning-how-to-die-in-the-anthropocene/?_r=0

Solnit, R. 2003, August 13. Creative Destruction. *The Nation*. www.thenation.com/article/creative-destruction/

Solnit, R. 2016. *Hope in the Dark: Untold Histories, Wild Possibilities*. Chicago: Haymarket Books, 2nd edition.

Wainwright, O. 2016, September 15. Edward Burtynsky on His Ravaged Earth Shots: 'We've Reached Peak Everything. *The Guardian*. www.theguardian.com/artanddesign/2016/sep/15/edward-burtynsky-photography-interview

Weber, E. 1999. *Apocalypses: Prophecies, Cults, and Millennial Beliefs Throughout the Ages*. Toronto: Vintage Canada.

Zalasiewicz, J., Williams, M., Haywood, A. and Ellis, M. 2011. The Anthropocene: A New Epoch of Geological Time? *Philosophical Transactions of the Royal Society*. http://rsta.royalsocietypublishing.org/content/369/1938/835

9 "Something akin to what's killing bees"

The poetry of colony collapse disorder

Matthew Griffiths

A key problem in composing the literature of collapse is that of representation: what do we convey when we write "collapse"? If the physical sense of bodily exhaustion is where the idea begins, how can this be scaled up into the dramatic decline of societies on a global scale – or indeed, the failure of planetary processes that enable life? However, if we choose to narrate collapse rather than describe it, the problem of representation persists, albeit in a different form: there needs to be a distance between the moment of collapse and the moment of narration because, if we write in the former, can we definitively refer to it as a collapse?

In this chapter, I will examine how this dilemma plays out in writing a particular instance of "collapse," namely the unprecedented decline in honeybee hives over the past ten years or so that is referred to as "colony collapse disorder." The phenomenon occurs at the intersection of the scales I have outlined: a single hive comprises thousands of bees, yet can be "kept" by an individual person; furthermore, as a diagnosed "disorder," it invokes widespread collapse beyond that individual's purview, but it is still defined, and less difficult to conceive than the much broader environmental collapse that we understand to be occurring across many fronts on a planetary scale.

It is these qualities, I suggest, that have prompted a number of contemporary poets to respond to colony collapse disorder, because it enables them to address wider fears of collapse in the formal space of their discourse. As their work is also situated in a much longer tradition of bee poetry, it is instructive to see what that tradition enables contemporary poets to do, as well as considering what other conventions are complicated by colony collapse. The poetry itself occurs at various points of intersection, between image and narrative, between present moment and the literary tradition, between the lyric and the apocalyptic.

Particularity → planetarity

To identify what is particular to the poetry of collapse, we can compare it with more widely known discourses. Jared Diamond for instance confronts the conundrum of scale in defining the term in *Collapse: How Societies*

Choose to Fail or Survive, when he describes the phenomenon as "an extreme form of several milder types of decline, and it becomes arbitrary to decide how drastic the decline of a society must be before it qualifies to be labeled as a collapse" (2005, p. 3). To identify its arbitrariness is to show how slippery the term is, escalating quickly from "milder" declines into something much more "extreme." We may then infer that our understanding depends on an instinctive sense of scale, an ability to distinguish between mild and extreme; but this returns us to the original question around the transition from personal to planetary comprehensions of collapse.

Diamond attempts to make this problem amenable to scientific analysis by adopting the "comparative method" – that is, "to compare natural situations differing with respect to the variable of interest" (p. 17) – examining multiple historic instances in order "to understand societal collapses to which environmental problems contribute" (p. 18).[1] It is with these instances that he gestures at our current moment when, thanks to the extensive influence of humankind, collapse is threatened – or has already begun – on a global scale: "collapses of past civilizations have taken on more meaning than just that of a romantic mystery. Perhaps there are some practical lessons that we could learn from all those past collapses" (pp. 7–8). Diamond's method is cumulative; by collating data from history, he aspires, implicitly, to have a working theoretical model of "collapse." His analysis therefore cycles from particular to abstract and back in a scaled-up version of the relation I have sketched between bodily and environmental understandings: "collapse" remains an object of representation in its various instances, but its definition derives from considering these together.

If we think instead of collapse as a mode rather than object of representation, though, we face similar problems. As a grand narrative, "collapse" should already arouse critical suspicion – why do we use this model for past societies, as Diamond does? Is there a tacit sense of superiority in remarks such as "Why did some past societies fail to see the messes that they were getting into, and that (one would think in retrospect) must have been obvious?" (p. 8); or indeed the titular proposition that these societies must therefore have chosen their fates? Even in the attempt to analogize our present moment in the fall of historic societies, Diamond inserts a distance between them and us. We know what a past collapse looks like because it seems, from our point in time, to have had an identifiable end.

But "collapse" also threatens the very idea of narrative – it is not closure or denouement; neither does it mark a "mild decline," nor the continuation of a cycle. Rather, it necessarily signifies the failure of existing structures to survive through time, and would as such lie outside narration by the cultures that those structures sustained. Narratives that do seem to contain "collapse" tend to reassert the very structures it undermines.[2] Where Diamond is able to collate evidence from a range of societies, their own collapses have to have been more or less discrete because other cultures remained to identify and narrate their ends. Once society becomes global and deepens its dependence on planetary processes, the threat of collapse means there may be no subsequent vantage point from which to narrate it.

The idea of disorder

In colony collapse disorder, or CCD, we can witness at a smaller scale this failure to contain collapse. First diagnosed in late 2006 (Watanabe 2008, p. 384), CCD is a phenomenon in which honeybee populations decline at a seemingly unprecedented rate, observed initially in the USA but later reported in Canada, the UK, Europe and Taiwan (Nimmo 2015a, p. 181). Francis L. W. Ratnieks and Norman L. Carreck note that

> In fall 2006 and spring 2007, many U.S. beekeepers encountered hives without adult bees but with abandoned food and brood. It was widely believed that these were symptoms of a new and highly virulent pathogen. *In the absence of a known cause*, the term "Colony Collapse Disorder" (CCD) was coined.
>
> (2010, p. 152, my italics)

This suggests the generic nature of the term was necessitated by the difficulty scientists have had in singling out a cause for the phenomenon, and Ratnieks and Carreck go on to write that research published by the U.S. Colony Collapse Disorder Steering Committee in 2009 indicated that CCD:

> may be caused by many agents in combination – the interaction between known pests and pathogens, poor weather conditions that diminish foraging, lack of forage, and management factors such as the use of pesticides and stress caused by long-distance transport of hives to nectar sources or pollination locations.
>
> (p. 153)

Still more recently, sociologist and posthumanist thinker Richie Nimmo reports that "Despite ongoing investigations at numerous institutions, none of these [factors] has yet emerged as a convincing candidate for a sole causal explanation of CCD" (2015a, pp. 181–2).

Absent a single explanation, the persistence of the idea of CCD suggests the potency of the concept of collapse itself as an organizing force, a means of bringing the phenomenon within our comprehension. Nevertheless, we should also note that "collapse" is not the head noun in the noun phrase "CCD," a function that falls to "disorder," which not only scales the individual instance up into a broader phenomenon, but at the same time defines it as a bodily experience, "an illness that disrupts normal physical or mental functions" (Oxford). The phenomenon is at once individual and planetary, shuttling between the two scales.

It is this scalar relation that, I propose, both enables and complicates literary engagement with the broader concept of collapse through the phenomenon of CCD. Furthermore, as Catriona Sandilands observes,

> Poetry . . . may create an aesthetic space in which bees not only enter human biopolitics (they are already there), and not only have political lives of their own (they already do), but also pierce the anthropocentric experience of human political subjectivity itself.

(2014, p. 157)

While Sandilands is interested in the ways poetry enables us to imagine shared "space" between ourselves and bees, giving clearer access to the relations Nimmo has described, I am interested here in the way that poetry as a discourse can also talk about what happens when these relations collapse. As a hybrid entity, the hive is an ideal one for expressing the non-viability of a worldview that separates culture and nature. CCD may expose the entanglement of these two terms, along the lines that sociologist Bruno Latour argues in *We Have Never Been Modern* (1993), but they have always been entangled, and poetry offers a distinctive way of relating this. As such, in the time since CCD was identified, several prominent works of poetry have concerned themselves with bees, and Dai George noted as early as 2011 that "Over the last five years or so, the bee has passed from being a fashionable and fertile symbol and turned into a sort of obsession for British poets" (p. 9).

The bee tradition

Poets taking up or taking on the theme of CCD work in a rich tradition of poetry about bees, a tradition in which the hive has always proved fertile for analogies with human society. Claire Preston explores these rich associations in her 2006 survey of the insect's wider cultural significance, *Bee*, noting that it has been "associated with both public *and* private virtues: the bee stands both for the outer-directed life of social benefit as well as the ancient and attractive convention of retirement from public life" (pp. 11–12; author's italics). In touching on the history of bee poetry here, I aim to identify some of the key tendencies in the relationship between bees and humans this work expresses, and with which recent poems concerning CCD engage.[3]

One of the earliest texts in this tradition is Virgil's *Georgics*, a Roman handbook of agricultural best practice in verse, itself attending to and written in a moment of collapse. In C. Day Lewis's wartime translation of the fourth book, which concentrates on apiculture, the poet writes, "life brings to the bees the same bad luck as to humans,/They may suffer severe illness" ([1940] 1983, p. 117); and, in his introduction to the poem, R.O.A.M. Lyne highlights the relationship of this episode with Rome's civil wars of the mid-first century B.C. "Virgil presents the bee society as something which can be *re-created* even after a *plague* has wiped it out," and as such the "allegorical society" of the insects provides a "model for the efficient, immortal state" (1983, pp. xxix, xxx; author's italics). For Virgil, the colony offers a coded and cogent metaphor for writing about the collapse of the Roman Republic and the means of the polity's restoration, "based on traditional Roman views and traditional modes of thinking" (p. xxx).

This analogy is possible because of a separation between countryside and conflict enacted in Virgil's poem, what Terry Gifford describes as the "oppositional potential" of the pastoral mode (1999, p. 36): the poet is able to envisage a process of collapse by finding a separate vantage point, rather than writing from within the collapse itself. "[T]he moral, peaceful, rural life of this poem communicates, subliminally, a reaction to the trauma of war beyond its pages," writes Hattie Ellis (2004, pp. 62–3). The death of one bee colony and the creation of a new one serves Virgil as a microcosm for the difficult transition to the Principate, yet the colony has not collapsed *because of* the fall of the Republic, and there is no whiff of moral culpability in the poem's relation of Aristaeus' beekeeping; this shepherd is simply unfortunate to be working in an area sacred to Orpheus and has fallen foul of the nymphs who honor him. As Gifford writes, "the idealising of country values is made by Virgil explicitly as a criticism of life in the city" (1999, p. 19). This distinction between rural and urban, however, is troubled when cultural practice is complicit in the collapse of beehives, as is the case when CCD emerges.

The analogy of beehive with society became well established in the centuries after Virgil, with a number of instances cited by Preston and other writers. In Shakespeare's *Henry V*, "the honey-bees," are "Creatures that by a rule in nature teach/The act of order to a peopled kingdom" (I.ii.187–189). The eighteenth century subsequently offers a number of variations: in Bernard de Mandeville's *The Grumbling Hive or The Knaves Turn'd Honest* (1705) – in later editions, *The Fable of the Bees or Private Vices, Public Benefits* (1714 and 1729) – the bees are replaced by corrupt humans in ironic inversion; in John Gay's fable *The Degenerate Bees* (1738), the bees themselves signify a corrupt society that has ostracized the poet's friends Swift and Pope; and Jacque Vanière's *The Bees* avers, in Arthur Murphy's translation, that "their [the insects'] ruling passion is the public weal" (Preston, p. 15). However, Laura Steele notes that "neither Mandeville . . . or John Gay in his response . . . use bees in any metaphorical detail at all. The Mandeville poem is remarkable for a lack of them"; so well known is the analogy that "the Hive is a form of lyrical scaling" (2007), with the human subject presumed to be the point of interest.

The trend continues in the nineteenth century, in for instance John Greenleaf Whittier's "The Hive at Gettysburg" (1868), which uses bees as a metaphor for the Union's victory in the US civil war. In Emily Dickinson's bee poems, of which there are a number, the bee tends in contrast to be a solitary image, most often referred to as "he" or "her" and wild rather than part of a hive or colony, acting as a point on to which the poet projects her imagination of liberty or courtship. This negotiation between social and individual persists in the bee poetry of the twentieth century. Reading Osip Mandelstam's poem "Take from my palms," for instance, Preston notes "the melancholy selflessness of the spent bee, whose dead, used-up body reminds us of the cruelly mortal miracle whose evidence is honey" (2006, p. 17). With its focus on the individual insect, we begin to see how the bee depends on its society and that its identity is relational, though the society itself relies rather on the collective of the colony that the individual bees comprise. Preston has already cited the aphorism that "One bee is no bee," because they are only effective at producing honey as a colony, "so almost none of the standard western ideas of individuality and autonomy of self have any purchase" (p. 15). Conversely, in Gertrude Stein's bee poems, roughly contemporary with Mandelstam's, the insect's associations again tend towards the lyrical and romantic: "You are my honey honey suckle./I am your bee" is a phrase rehashed on several occasions in "A Sonatina Followed by Another" ([1921] 1953, p. 8), while "Bee Time Vine" (1913) itself flits cryptically and alyrically from one image, one syntax to another like a solitary insect, pollinating the poem itself.

In the mid-twentieth century, bees occur in a sequence of four poems in Sylvia Plath's posthumous collection *Ariel*, resonating with her personal experience, both as an outsider – an American living in Britain – and as a woman. In the first of these poems, "The Bee Meeting," Plath's narrator is a wary presence among other villagers who are all already clad for beekeeping, and as she is dressed in hat and veil she is taken into their number, "making me one of them" ([1965] 1999, p. 56) – an act implicitly rehearsed by the later capture of the queen bee. "The Arrival of the Bee Box" alludes to Virgil when the narrator describes herself as "not a Caesar" (p. 58) and cautious at the prospect of opening her new acquisition. In the following poem, "Stings" (p. 61), she asserts she is "in control," but by the last of the four poems "Wintering," "it is they who own me" (p. 63). Throughout the poems, as through the book, Plath's tone is confessional and self-dramatizing, her attitude towards the bees ambivalent. Rather than standing for society, their presence signifies a buzzing state of mind, powerful and never wholly under the narrator's control; Tammy Horn writes, for instance, that "The Arrival of the Bee Box" tackles "Plath's inability to put into language the noise of the hive and her mind," which "come together" in the poem (2005, p. 217).

This idea of control, which seems to shift from the insects to Plath and back, is analyzed in more detail by Nimmo. He points out that, unlike conventional livestock farming where animals (usually mammals or poultry) become objects in the network of agricultural production, "beekeeping has tended to be perceived and to be represented . . . as a more hybrid or mutual endeavour involving a form of interspecies collaboration between bee societies and human societies"; this means that we might "grasp apiculture non-anthropocentrically as a hybrid human–non-human assemblage" (2015a, pp. 189–90), informed by the idea of hybridity developed by Latour in *We Have Never Been Modern*.

Plath's poems play with the poles of human control to arrive at an uneasy correspondence between bee and keeper. Nimmo refers to the "deeply historical and hybrid practice," of the kind in which those attending Plath's bee meeting participate, but this understanding "breaks down somewhat when considering very large-scale apiculture and commercial pollination operations, with their ecologically unsustainable monocultures, economies of scale and intensive profit-driven practices" (pp. 193–4). He argues that "CCD is exactly the sort of crisis that we should anticipate facing with increasing frequency" (p. 195) as agricultural practices intensify, and understanding of their interactions and impacts remains limited or under-investigated. The tension between the two understandings of apiculture – domestic and industrial – plays out in the contemporary poetry of colony collapse disorder.

Buzzwords

One particularly prominent example in this vein is Carol Ann Duffy's 2011 collection *The Bees*; as the UK's poet laureate, Duffy performs a public role similar to Virgil's, a responsibility acknowledged in the title of one piece, "Virgil's Bees" (p. 23),[4] while "Ariel" (p. 11) recognizes the significance of Plath in the bee poetry tradition. Bees themselves form a repeated motif in the collection, the subject of several poems – including "Bees," "The Bee Carol," "Snow" and "A Rare Bee" – and also serve as an image in many more. Yet the insects tend to fulfil one of just a few functions across this work.

In "Bees" and "Poetry" (p. 3, p. 16) they are a figure for the arts, such as poetry and music, and in "The Female Husband" (p. 20) they are invoked among livestock to form part of a nostalgic pastoral, lacking the finer distinctions of Nimmo's analysis. But their main function is to serve as an index for contemporary environmental crisis. "Ariel," for instance, mentions the insecticides that are among the anthropogenic factors suspected of contributing to CCD, while in "Telling the Bees" (p. 52), Duffy reverses a folk tradition in which bees would be informed of the death of their keeper by having the narrator find them all dead in their hive, implicitly bringing us the unwelcome news of colony collapse.

Beelife in Duffy's poems signals joy or former glories – "Hive" (p. 31) and "Drone" (p. 78) exemplifying this tendency – such that their death weighs heavily with the environmental collapse that recurs throughout the book, in poems such as "The English Elms" and "Parliament" (p. 40, p. 50). CCD is not itself mentioned, but Duffy's treatment of the theme of collapse is much less subtle than Virgil's. The golden-age visions with which bees are associated lack the complexity of true pastoral and seem – to borrow one of Gifford's analyses – "an escapist pastoral that self-indulgently ignores, or touches too lightly upon, the urgent political issues" (1999, p. 146). Meanwhile, her poems concerning bee death, although lyrical, are tinged with sanctimony – falling foul of the dilemma Dai George identifies when he asserts that

> poetry is dead in the water once it finds itself a settled task – a conundrum that ecological poetry, and all poetry of principle, must continually struggle with. The truth is that bee poetry has become a crowded market. . . . To write a bee poem now, it may be necessary to employ . . . ironies and tonal disturbances.
>
> (2011/12, p. 13)[5]

Without such distinctive qualities, collapse in Duffy's poems reads as a fall from grace of the kind rehearsed in the canon since the Bible. As Raymond Williams writes in *The Country and the City*:

> Is it anything more than a well-known habit of using the past, the 'good old days', as a stick to beat the present? It is clearly something of that, but there are still difficulties. The apparent resting places, the successive Old Englands to which we are confidently referred but which then start to move and recede, have some actual significance, when they are looked at in their own terms. Of course, we notice their location in the childhoods of their authors, and this must be relevant. Nostalgia, it can be said, is universal and persistent.
>
> (1973, p. 12)

Inasmuch as Duffy's poems represent a narrative of collapse, they are already familiar. CCD becomes a new means of expressing constant themes, so that rather than making a distinctive insight they merely express Williams's "universal and persistent" nostalgia. Indeed, a number of poems in *The Bees* allude to narratorial childhoods, in response to the death of the mother: the bees, with their pastoral associations, are being used to evoke a lost idyll, in part Britain's and in part the narrator's own.

One poem in which Duffy complicates this relationship is "The Human Bee," which describes a person tasked with pollinating orchards; this phenomenon has been reported, for instance, in "Sichuan Province in China where," Nimmo observes, "every pear tree has had to be painstakingly pollinated by human workers since all honeybees were wiped out by pesticide misuse more than 20 years ago" (p. 184). The substitution of bees with human workers in Duffy's poem is ultimately incomplete, because the narrator acknowledges their own failure to make honey or fly, suggesting not only that the practice problematizes the historic analogy between human and bee, society and colony, but that they still share, as in Virgil, a sickness: the narrator at the end of the poem is unable to see clearly and has a shaking hand. As such, the poem marks the hybridity – always present but exposed in the moment of crisis – of humankind and bees in apiculture, and especially in industrialized apiculture.

The human–bee continuity is more pronounced in Jo Shapcott's "Six Bee Poems," also 2011. This sequence comprises one thirteen-line piece and five subsequent fourteeners – sonnets that do not follow a strict metre or rhyme scheme – and begins with a personal association between the bee(hive) and the narrator also evident in Duffy's book. In the first piece, "I Tell the Bees" – drawing on the folk tradition like Duffy's similarly named poem – the narrator inherits a hive from a partner who has left her. Through the subsequent poems, the boundaries between human body – human selfhood – and colony are collapsed, with the bees materially taking the place of the narrator's tears and words in the second poem, "The Threshold" ("I spoke bees, I breathed bees") and occupying the narrator's body in the subsequent piece "The Hive" ("The colony grew in my body"). While Duffy makes a similar comparison between language and insects in "Bees" (2011, p. 3), Shapcott moves this beyond correspondence to a material substitution that verges on the grotesque. She thus achieves "tonal disturbances" of the kind George advocates, with the hybridization of human and hive a troubling reminder of collapsing distinctions between the cultural and natural, the personal and the planetary.

There is also a suggestive association in "Going About With The Bees" when the narrator brings the insects into a bank and "we all watched the money dissolve like wax," which resonates with public consciousness of the financial collapse in 2008. The poetic image enables Shapcott to compact a wealth of associations, transacting ecology and economy to show how entangled they are. As Nimmo indicates, CCD "is an agricultural–economic crisis as much as an environmental one, since the Western honeybee is the pollinator of choice for much of the world's commercial agricultural crops" (2015a, p. 183), a connection that poetry is able to communicate with particular immediacy.

It may still be problematic, however, that in Shapcott's poem entitled "CCD," the phenomenon of collapse is profoundly human, with the bees abandoning the "hive" of the narrator – "My body broke when the bees left" – but leaving her reshaped in their own image: "I think my body cells/ may have turned hexagonal/though the bees are long gone." On the one hand, this is a further boundary collapse, beyond the economic institution of the banks to the physical body; on the other, the correspondence becomes so precise as to invoke the unthought parallel between bodily and planetary that Greg Garrard critiques, "the partially concealed normativity of ecological and personal health" (2012, p. 503), itself implicit in the term "disorder" as I have suggested. Apart from its title, there is little sense in Shapcott's "CCD" that the environmental phenomenon itself is in play, that beyond the narrator's presumed heartbreak colonies are at stake;[6] nevertheless, Shapcott's overall conceit means that her poems remain more open, with the division between human and animal less distinct, than Duffy's.

Knowing the bees

In the opening poem of Shapcott's sequence, the narrator's partner takes only *The Cyclopedia of Everything Pertaining to the Care Of the Honey-Bee* with him as he leaves, signaling the absenting of science and technical knowledge that precipitates the eventual collapse of the colony (whether we read that as metaphorical or material). The theme of knowledge in the practice of apiary is taken up by Sean Borodale, whose *Bee Journal* (2012) is, in formal terms, a nonfictional record of his own beekeeping rather than an exploration of the bees as a motif or conceit.

What in the context of CCD is the role of such knowledge? Is it to inform the practice of beekeeping, as a means of ensuring bees' survival? Borodale's project, and the *Journal* in which it results, would seem to be engaging with the resurgence of interest in apiary,[7] and rather than employing collapse as a metaphor it details the establishment and eventual failure of his own hive through the narrative sketches of the poems. As such, CCD hovers in the background of the poems, which become exemplary of, or metonymous for, it. The traditional analogy of colony and society is wittily disavowed in a pun on the brand name for his hive, a National ("5th June: Bee Smoker," p.10), and there is a clear separation between the invocation of collapse in "13th December: Evidence of Cold Snap, a Page of Scattered Bees from the Hive Floor" – in which he finds his own bees dead (p. 30) – and the awareness of mass bee death elsewhere in "29th July: Late Afternoon." It is as though, in response to the threat of collapse, Borodale in his double guise as beekeeper and bookkeeper makes an effort to direct his attention at one time *either* to his own hive *or* to the wider context in order to keep these separate, a distinctively scientific form of learning and knowing.

Borodale's means of attending to the bees is explicitly mechanical in "17th October: Audio Recording" (2012, p. 67), in which microphones are lowered into the hive to record their sound, and there is also the continual process of checking the hive and its components – "16th October: Super Check" (p. 65) and "6th December: Hive Check" (p. 71) – that along with the note-taking form of the poems point to the experimental quality of the knowledge gained. This is complemented by the scientific instruction implicit in "15th January: Herb Tea" (p. 82), where what seems to be a textbook's warning about the dangers to bees in some imported honeys is itself imported directly into the text – a bringing of knowledge into the poems that contrasts with the way it is specifically removed at the beginning of Shapcott's sequence.

Despite the scientific practice enacted here, the boundary between immediate and global remains under threat in these poems, such that in "29th July: Interior" (p. 57), when reference is made to a swarm that has physically collapsed, it so soon follows the mention of bees dying elsewhere on a large scale in the previous poem that Borodale may well be asking whether his own hive has fallen to the disorder. This sense of dissolution even affects the poet when he offers views of himself from two different perspectives in "25th June" (p. 49), as though he cannot separate knowledge and practice, poetry and apiary. While for Virgil verse was the natural form in which the knowledge of beekeeping could be recorded and transmitted, over the course of the subsequent centuries that knowledge was hived off into the science that eventually led to the industrial practices of which Nimmo is critical. For Borodale, verse is a form in which such knowledge has to be reconciled with practice, through narrative at the smaller, domestic scale.

Is it problematic that the book ends with Borodale acquiring a new colony in "3rd July: Gift" (p. 90), months after the textless poem "24th/25th January: Bees Die" (p. 83), as though the first colony, however closely attended and cared for, is so easily replaced? That would bring the collection into alignment with the cycle of the seasons, eschewing collapse to affirm a hesitant continuity, perhaps with an ambition to practice better apiculture in the light of the previous failure. The hopeful tone of this "Gift" satisfies as a conclusion to the narrative of the *Journal*, but as an assertion of closure neglects the very collapse that seems to have prompted the project in the first place.

While this puts Borodale's work into Gifford's category of the post-pastoral in "its recognition of a creative–destructive universe equally in balance in a continuing momentum of birth and death, death and rebirth, growth and decay, ecstasy and dissolution" (1999, p. 153), it remains pastoral in that it is ultimately separate from and unaffected by the world outside it. Despite the rumors of collapse elsewhere, the book contains it by narrating the failure of Borodale's hive alone and keeping that wider threat at bay. As Sandilands remarks, "we become deeply aware of the bees' affective presence in his life," (2014, p. 166), but there is, as in Shapcott's "CCD," little sense of planetary endangerment in this personal grief.

Past prospect

In the sense that CCD affects hives as hybrids of human and natural agency, what Sandilands calls "bee–human relations as a coming together of worlds" (p. 167), the strategy of conservation in and of itself, practiced by Borodale among many others, will be insufficient to safeguard the bees, because it would entail the management of all environmental vectors that may contribute to the disorder. In contrast, taking the hive into poetry may enable the preservation of the bee poem tradition and its re-examination in the light of CCD. Sherman Alexie's comic "In the Matter of *Human v. Bee*," the first poem anthologized by James P. Lenfestey in 2016's *If Bees Are Few*, reflects more openly on the role of the bee poem: "I sing this song/ to bring them back,//Or say goodbye" ([2009] 2016, p. 6). This song is an act of memory that stands in for the bees as it bids them farewell – as when, in Dickinson's "To make a prairie it takes a clover and one bee," "revery alone will do/If bees are few" ([1896] 2016, p. 49), giving Lenfestey the title of his anthology.

In contrast to this retrospective vision that summons the vanishing bee back into being is recent work by a pair of British poets. John Burnside's *Melissographia*, anthologized in *If Bees Are Few* but itself a limited-edition art book in collaboration with Amy Shelton, comprises four poems named for the seasons, in the sequence "Spring" to "Winter." Without explicit reference to CCD or the potential for environmental collapse, Burnside's poems could read as an imposition of a normative seasonal order of a kind that, in the light of the changing climate, may seem problematic. So when, at the end of "I Spring" Burnside writes "as now gives way to now,/ad infinitum" (Burnside and Shelton 2009, n.p; author's italics) and there is a suggestion of perpetual cycles – of a kind that I have discussed elsewhere as depending on the current interglacial, the geologically contingent moment of human existence[8] – the bees are a means of connecting us with it, the sound they make echoing in our bones; as indeed, is their being "tidal" here, or like "cirrus" cloud in the subsequent poem (n.p), themselves a force of nature.

But this supposedly perpetual cycle could itself be read as the resonance of spring in the human experience, a tangential vision from the upward arc of the seasonal turn, so Burnside communicates the sensation of spring rather than an eternal verity. Thus when reference is made in "II Summer" to the "golden aside" that the bees "reserve/for the life to come," we are not only to read the honey stored for future tasting, but pick up on the religious connotations of "the life to come," itself alluding to the folk belief that bees were what Preston describes as "the embodiment of the soul returning to heaven" (2006, p. 17). Similarly, in the final poem of his sequence, "'IV Winter," Burnside writes of the "the loopholes we leave, in case/the bees return," which in the poem-world may refer to a particular colony, but resonates beyond the text with the doubt prompted by awareness of CCD. Burnside's narrative is not poised on the moment of collapse but shows how fragile our conception of seasonal order actually is, in the sense that this, too, is exposed to the depredations of the twenty-first century.

Burnside's own interest in bee death is clear in an interview in *Poetry Wales* reflecting on the composition of *Melissographia*, where he says "when we first started on this project – a few years ago now – there was a good deal of concern about bee mortality, and not much was being written at the time. Now, there are more people getting involved, which is good" (2011/12, p. 15). He goes on to suggest that "a poem that preaches about ecology matters is a mistake, but if a poem draws attention to what is happening to bees . . . and does it well enough, then it might make a small difference in how people think" (ibid.). This does account for his more conventional approach in *Melissographia*, but it still depends, however cautiously, on an ethics of attention that is problematic in ecocriticism.[9]

Less tentatively than Burnside, Lenfestey argues that "Poets do what we can, in our reverie, our observation, our listening, our metaphors, our occasional beekeeping, our outrage, our grief, to keep the sweetness and sting of these poetic companions alive" (2016, p. xxiv). But as in Borodale's *Bee Journal*, the act of attending-to, and indeed tending-to, is insufficient in itself to ensure bees' survival, because the singularity of vision it entails is unable satisfactorily to account for the threat of collapse on a planetary scale, or the industrial apiculture that is more heavily implicated in CCD. A poem about such practices would have to be an affront to the pastoral and lyrical character of the bee tradition, straining even the "ironies" and "tonal disturbances" that George advocates.

When Burnside says of his bees "Their summer ends with ours" (n.p), there is at least a recognition in this fraught commonality, as in Virgil, that not only is a particular season passing, but that the human moment on Earth is at risk of collapse as well. Historically speaking, "The health of ecosystems can be judged partly by the health of bees," writes Preston (2006, p. 15) and this idea is reinforced, explicitly, in Alec Finlay's 2014 work *Global Oracle: a Work of Prophetic Science*; in the first book of this, "Star-Fallen Honey," "Bees are oracular/foretelling the weather" (n.p). Finlay's work, part of a multimedia project that also included art installations on the campus of the University of Warwick, rehearses much of Western bee lore in this vein, emphasizing in his text and images the commonality of bees and humans, with the device of the artificial satellite enabling a scaled view of human society as hive throughout the work.

In the fourth book, "The Spirit of the Hive," the artifice of this process is made explicit, "*as if we were/to be read/as bees*" (n.p., author's italics), and the tradition of the hive's analogy with society is traced in the passage that moves from the scientific separation of humans and bees – "Nowadays we accept/bees do not inhabit/the same world" – to the understanding brought by CCD that no such separation ever obtained, and we "share the bees'/disastrous forecast" (n.p.). This makes good on poetry's promise to recombine techno-scientific and lyrical relations between humans and bees; so, in returning to the classical tradition of bee lore, Finlay also returns us to the Virgilian observation of commonality between human and insect societies.

Collapse as condition

US poet D. A. Powell's 2009 collection *Chronic* touches on a number of themes addressed by the foregoing analysis. His work again makes explicit the process of analogy by which we understand ourselves, when in the title poem he invokes "the delicate, unfixed condition of love, the treacherous body/the unsettling state of creation and how we have damaged," before asking rhetorically "isn't one a suitable lens through which to see another[?]" (2009, p. 35). At first, this might seem to be a kind of pathetic fallacy in which the environment enacts a state of mind or feeling, but Powell's use of the "lens" image allows us to look from either side: heartbreak and ill health are figures for global concerns, as Garrard argues, as much as environmental collapse is a projection of personal suffering. Over the page, this relationship is expressed altogether more playfully: "choose your own adventure: drug failure or organ failure/cataclysmic climate change/or something akin to what's killing bees – colony collapse" (p. 36). The unsettling quality of this list is both its multiple components – we cannot now turn anywhere without seeing evidence of collapse – but also that there is no stable ground on which we can stand to survey the "chronic" condition of self–planet, itself a continuity rather than an opposition.[10]

As a result, Powell's vision contains hybrid entities still more unsettling than those presented by Shapcott: he refers to "the farmers – almost extinct" (p. 7), a reversal of the idea of species endangerment that highlights the complicity of and threat to agribusiness in the prospect of collapse, and also to "the meatbees . . . /gathering to the great banquet of humankind" (p. 51). Finally, in his fourteener entitled "collapse:" there is a doubly physical attention to the planet and the body of a former lover, the poem gleefully punning on the geological terms *"butt cleat," "creep," "parting"* and "slag pile" (author's italics) while lines are shifted off their left-hand margin to evoke "[the slow movement downhill . . . the eroding elements of the planet's core]" in an oscillation between personal and planetary scales that concludes with "terrestrial heave/bottomed your way to the top" (p. 63; author's parentheses).

The recurrence of collapse as a theme throughout the different contexts of Powell's poems in *Chronic* speaks to the way that the bee poem in the time of CCD cannot be an isolated phenomenon, a momentary image for the poet, because the ethical commitment entailed by writing about CCD demands more detailed consideration than a single lyric can offer. It is telling, for instance, that most of the prominent examples I have considered here occur in sequences, or use the bee or colony collapse as a repeated motif throughout a particular collection.

Continuity of collapse

The colony can function in poetry as a microcosm insofar as it is self-contained, because it enables us to map on to its contents those objects or concepts that are too abstract, distributed, or large to envisage. What makes it particularly resonant as an analogy is that a colony also denotes a human settlement, and in the present moment can be scaled up to signify Western civilization, which has economically and imaginatively colonized most of the planet.[11] However, when collapse begins in the hive, the possibility of containing it there is brought into question, because it always implicates human activity – the transport and keeping of bees, the use of pesticides and so on – as thinkers such as Nimmo have identified.

If the hive in the era of CCD allows us to witness in miniature the potential for planetary environmental collapse, the unreflexive adoption of bee poetry conventions – as demonstrated here most clearly by Duffy – does something similar for poetry: it suggests an impulse to reach for affirmative, historic examples of our more sympathetic, or at least less instrumentalized, relations with and in nature. How, then, does the bee poem in the age of CCD engage with the concept of collapse? While it brings into focus the threat to ordered societies, it has difficulty imagining beyond their end, instead looking back to a time in which bees symbolized a nature in literal harmony, the physical and metaphysical resonances of Burnside's poems, perhaps, or the peculiarly English idylls of Duffy's. If the narratives continue, they depend, or at least invoke, an idea of cyclical, seasonal time, as in Borodale and Burnside, that seems problematic. Inasmuch as collapse itself is imagined, it is prospective, and we are positioned on the decline that will lead there; but collapse itself does not come clearly into focus, it is a narrative whose denouement is being forever pushed back, as nostalgia in Williams's model forever positions the golden age as one or two generations previously.

But the idea of the colony has a double significance in these recent poems. First, it inherits this expected metaphorical quality from the tradition of bee poems that I have outlined, to serve as way of containing and representing the idea of collapse, because the bees are manifestly many, working in close, well-defined relationships between one another in a way that seems both to resemble human economies and simplify them into a smaller number of functions; as Sandilands points out: "Bee biopolitics have a long history of entanglement with bee metaphoricity" (2014, p. 161). But even while the number of bees in a single colony is many, they are nonetheless reasonably small, relatively self-contained communities, visible and comprehensible, and when a collapse occurs it is evident within a short period of time.

So the collapse of one colony may seem like a definable occurrence; yet it is complicated both by an awareness of other colony collapses – hence the idea of a disorder – and by the evident dependence of human economies and ultimately societies on there being sufficient numbers of honeybees available for the pollination of crops.[12] The colony is not only a metaphor but is, second, a metonym, a representative part of an ever-widening disorder in which the entanglement of humans and bees examined by Nimmo and Sandilands becomes still knottier, and the separation between hive and society in the bee poem tradition collapses.

The versatility of poetic forms and modes means that the texts I have examined here need not close themselves off from such wider implications; and it is telling that when they do so, either by setting out their stall too explicitly or cleaving too firmly to their vision of tradition, they are both less successful at engaging with the phenomenon and less successful as poems, as both George and Burnside suggest. The best poems of CCD, such as Shapcott's and Powell's, resist such closure not by attempting to narrate collapse, but by enacting it – conscious of the tradition, but also conscious that if their work is to be effective then it must show that this tradition is itself in danger of collapse.

Acknowledgements

The extract from the *Georgics* of Virgil translated by C. Day Lewis is reprinted by permission of Peters Fraser & Dunlop (www.petersfraserdunlop.com) on behalf of the Estate of C. D. Lewis. I would also like to thank Faber & Faber for permission to quote from the work of Sylvia Plath; Jo Shapcott c/o Georgina Capel Associates Ltd for permission to quote from "Six Bee Poems"; United Agents for permission to quote from *Melissographia* by John Burnside; and Alec Finlay for permission to quote from his *Global Oracle*. D. A. Powell excerpts from "chronic," "central valley," "for the coming pandemic," and "collapse:" from *Chronic* copyright © 2009 by D. A. Powell are reprinted with the permission of The Permissions Company, Inc., on behalf of Graywolf Press, Minneapolis, Minnesota (www.graywolfpress.org). Special thanks to Betty Siegenthaler, Polly Atkin and staff at the Saison Poetry Library in London, who provided help, resources and guidance for my research.

Notes

1 Note Diamond's implicit naturalizing of historic collapses by applying a method developed for the analysis of "natural situations" to "societal" ones.
2 Inasmuch, "collapse" would be typical of a number of ways in which the present natural–historical moment is characterized. Compare the way that Martin McQuillan in "Notes Toward a Post-Carbon Philosophy" examines the similarly bandied-about term "crisis", to which he ascribes considerable normative force: "to identify an event as a crisis is always to ontologize it and to submit it to the model of the crisis that would explain it and domesticate it" (2012: 274).
3 Note that more extensive coverage of the tradition of bee writing is given not only in Preston (2006) but also Ellis (2004) and Horn (2005), while Lenfestey (2016) anthologizes a number of examples of both contemporary and historic bee poems, although with an emphasis on the former.
4 Unlike Virgil, however, Duffy exercises greater license to write – openly and critically – about the establishment that has appointed her, explicitly questioning the ruling order in poems such as "Big Ask" (p. 9) and "Politics" (p. 12).
5 George is not here advocating Gifford's concept of the post-pastoral, although his prescription begins as Gifford's does in an awareness that "The danger that green literature becomes didactic in a simplistic way is really a danger that it loses its power as art and becomes reductive propaganda or vague 'right-on' rhetoric" (Gifford 1999, p. 171).
6 Compare this with Polly Atkin's poem "Colony Collapse Disorder" (2017, p. 3), whose speaker may be bee or human and moves from city to country, a transition that disorders sense of self and place: "Taken away from elsewhere I dim".
7 Nimmo for instance remarks on "the context of rapid growth in the uptake and popularity of urban beekeeping in numerous Western cities in recent years", associating it with "the burgeoning public and media interest in bees amidst growing concern about declining honeybee numbers that have been linked to agricultural pesticide usage" (2015b, p. 124).

8 See Griffiths (2017, p. 3).
9 As Timothy Clark has pointed out in *Ecocriticism on the Edge* – a title that puts the discipline itself on the brink of collapse – "What if the . . . transformed imagination . . . this awareness of interconnection, could not be assumed to be an effective agent of change – in other words, *how far does a change in knowledge and imagination entail a change in environmentally destructive modes of life?*" (2015, p. 18; author's italics).
10 Powell seems to revel in what Clark describes as the "derangements" that occur in such juxtapositions, as for example in the following: "One symptom of a now widespread crisis of scale is a derangement of linguistic and intellectual proportion in the way people often talk about the environment, a breakdown of 'decorum' in the strict sense. Thus a sentence about the possible collapse of civilization can end, no less solemnly, with the injunction never to leave a TV on standby or forget to recycle a cardboard box" (2015, p. 37).
11 Note that Horn writes of European settlers in America that, "Just as the English craved order, so too did the colonists, and the beehive image represented efficiency, industry, and, most important, social stability" for them (2005, p. 16). However, "The beehive rhetoric . . . was difficult to comprehend by those people who were not English" (p. 38); that is, Native Americans, who regarded the insect with suspicion, associating it with the colonists' presence.
12 In a quotation attributed to Einstein and used by Alexie as an epigraph to "In the Matter of *Human v. Bee*", "If the bees die, man dies within four years" (Lenfestey 2016, p. 3).

References

Atkin, P., 2017. *Basic nest architecture*. Poetry Wales Press–Seren, Bridgend.
Borodale, S., 2012. *Bee journal*. Random House–Cape Poetry, London.
Burnside, J., 2011/12. Interview by Dai George. *Poetry Wales* 47.3, 15.
Burnside, J. and Shelton, A., 2009. *Melissographia*. University of Plymouth Letterpress Studio, Plymouth. 62 of 100.
Clark, T., 2015. *Ecocriticism on the edge: The Anthropocene as a threshold concept*. Bloomsbury, London.
Diamond, J., 2005. *Collapse: How societies choose to fail or survive*. Penguin–Allen Lane, New York and London.
Duffy, C. A., 2011. *The bees*. Picador–Pan Macmillan, London.
Ellis, H., 2004. *Sweetness & light: The mysterious history of the honeybee*. Harmony, New York.
Finlay, A. and Tuulikki, H., 2014. *Global oracle: A work of prophetic science*. Morning Star and The University of Warwick Art Collection, Warwick.
Garrard, G., 2012. "Nature cures? or How to police analogies of personal and ecological health." *Interdisciplinary Studies in Literature and Environment* 19.3, 494–514.
George, D., 2011/12. "The buzz of the bee through poetry." *Poetry Wales* 47.3, 9–14.
Gifford, T., 1999. *Pastoral*. Routledge, London and New York.
Griffiths, M., 2017. *The new poetics of climate change: Modernist aesthetics for a warming world*. Bloomsbury Academic, London.
Horn, T., 2005. *Bees in America: How the honey bee shaped a nation*. University Press of Kentucky, Lexington.

Latour, B., 1993. *We have never been modern*, trans. C. Porter. Harvard University Press, Cambridge, MA.

Lenfestey, J. P., ed., 2016. *If bees are few: A hive of bee poems*. University of Minnesota Press, Minneapolis.

McQuillan, M., 2012. "Notes toward a post-carbon philosophy: 'It's the economy, stupid'" in Tom Cohen ed., *Telemorphosis: Theory in the era of climate change*, vol. 1. MPublishing–Open Humanities Press, Ann Arbor, MI, 270–92.

Nimmo, R., 2015a. "Apiculture in the Anthropocene: Between posthumanism and critical animal studies" in Human Animal Research Network Editorial Collective eds., *Animals in the anthropocene: Critical perspectives on non-human futures*. Sydney University Press, Sydney, 177–99.

Nimmo, R., 2015b. Review of *Buzz: Urban beekeeping and the power of the bee* by Lisa Jean Moore and Mary Kosut. *Cultural Sociology* 9.1, 124–5.

Plath, S., [1965] 1999. *Ariel*. Faber, London.

Powell, D. A., 2009. *Chronic*. Graywolf Press, Saint Paul, MN.

Preston, C., 2006. *Bee*. Reaktion Books, London.

Ratnieks, F. L. W. and Carreck, N. L., 2010. "Clarity on honey bee collapse?" *Science* 327 (5962), 152–3.

Sandilands, C., 2014. "Pro/polis: Three forays into the political lives of bees" in Serenella Iovino and Serpil Oppermann eds., *Material ecocriticism*. Indiana University Press, Bloomington, 157–71.

Shakespeare, W., [1600] 1995. *King Henry V*, ed. T. W. Craik. Arden Shakespeare–Methuen Drama, London.

Shapcott, J., 2011. "Six bee poems." *Poetry Review*. https://poetrysociety.org.uk/poems/six-bee-poems/ (last accessed 1 October 2017).

Steele, L., 2007. "Buzz off: Gay, Mandeville, Eutopia." *Intercapillary Space*. http://intercapillaryspace.blogspot.co.uk/2007/11/buzz-off-gay-mandeville-eutopia.html (last accessed 22 October 2017).

Stein, G., 1953. *Bee time vine and other pieces [1913–1927]* with preface and notes by Virgil Thomson. Yale University Press, New Haven; Oxford University Press, London.

Virgil, [1940] 1983. *The eclogues, the georgics*, trans. C. D. Lewis, with introduction and notes by R. O. A. M. Lyne. Oxford University Press, Oxford.

Watanabe, M. E., 2008. "Colony collapse disorder: Many suspects, no smoking gun." *BioScience* 58.5, 384–8.

Whittier, J. G., [1868] 1871. "The Hive at Gettysburg." *Miriam and Other Poems*. Fields, Osgood & Co., Boston.

Williams, R., 1973. *The country and the city*. Oxford University Press, New York.

10 Salvaging the fragments

Metaphors for collapse in Virginia Woolf and *Station Eleven*

Alexandra Peat

In her 1927 essay "The narrow bridge of art," Virginia Woolf invites the critic to "turn around and, shading his eyes in the manner of Robinson Crusoe on the desert island, look into the future and trace on its mist the faint lines of the land which some day perhaps we may reach" (1958a, p. 11). Woolf's essay, originally titled "Poetry, fiction, and the future," is an artistic manifesto for a radically new kind of fiction to suit the needs of the modern age. Woolf asks how writers and critics can acknowledge the past while responding to the changing needs of the time. It is curious and striking that Woolf should build her vision for the future of literature on images of collapse: an island, a castaway, and art among the wreckage. Woolf imagines literary history as a shipwreck and the critic as a castaway caretaker of literary tradition as she asks: what books do we rescue from the wreckage? What do we need? What do we carry with us? What do we leave behind? She is clear that "some renunciation is inevitable," extending the shipwreck metaphor as she notes, "You cannot cross the narrow bridge of art carrying all its tools in your hands. Some you must leave behind, or you will drop them in midstream or, what is worse, overbalance and be drowned yourself" (p. 22).

This chapter extends Woolf's inquiry by asking what "tools" we can carry across the "narrow bridge of art" to articulate our contemporary age of environmental collapse, and what new "tools" we might need to express a phenomenon which seems to elude traditional narrative modes. A recent spate of self-consciously literary novels takes up this challenge, including Colson Whitehead's *Zone One* (2011), Cormac McCarthy's *The Road* (2009), and works by Margaret Atwood. Literary fiction's encroachment into science fiction and thriller territory suggests changes in the book market and readerly appetites, but it also intimates that collapse is being taken seriously as an urgent problem for humanity and thus for art.[1] This chapter focuses particularly on Emily St. John Mandel's 2014 novel *Station Eleven*, a critical and popular success at the vanguard of a contemporary poetics of collapse. Mandel both uses experimental forms to tell a story of collapse and, in an imaginative move reminiscent of Woolf, self-consciously interrogates inherited and experimental modes of storytelling. She crafts a dual timeline that switches between the outbreak of the Georgian Flu that wipes out much of humanity and events twenty years later in a tentatively hopeful post-collapse society. Punctuated by unresolved narrative gaps, *Station Eleven* becomes both a lament for what has been lost and a meditation on how to tell the story of this loss in order to move forward. Set around the borders of what were Canada and the United States, the novel loosely follows the itinerant journey of the Travelling Symphony as it performs Shakespeare for the disparate communities of the post-collapse world. Shakespeare, chosen because he represents "what was best about the world" (Mandel 2015, p. 38), becomes an emblem of a lost literary past that leads to a larger consideration of the role of art in a ruined world and the possibilities of stories as solace, keepsake, and sources of reinvention.

In its depiction of a collapsed world, Mandel's *Station Eleven* engages with the same questions about literary value, tradition, and renewal that animate Woolf's "The narrow bridge of art." Such commonalities are not coincidental: Woolf's early twentieth century was, like our own turbulent times, an age when, "we [were] not fast anchored where we are" (1958a, p. 11). Earlier in this volume, Michael Egan astutely links our current understandings of collapse to the world-changing events of the first half of the twentieth century, and the thinkers and writers such as Walter Benjamin who offered models of response or at least modes of articulation. In Woolf's lifetime, two world wars, various revolutions, and the fall of an empire led to a sense that the world was being forcibly undone: "all the old hedges were being rooted up; all the towers were being thrown to the ground" (1958b, p. 114). While we should not overplay the early twentieth century as the birthplace of radically different understandings of collapse, it was characterized by an increased anxiety about rupture on a global scale and a co-commensurate representative crisis.[2] Julie Taylor notes that "the understanding of modernism as a radical break or rupture with the immediate past was promulgated by the moderns themselves" who were seemingly obsessed with dates of rupture (2012, p. 25).[3] Such a preoccupation fueled imaginative attempts to find new ways to figure and write the catastrophes of the time, which seemed, in scale, degree, and type, to defy traditional representational models.

The historical tendency is to imagine collapse as a totalizing, annihilating event, but, as Guy Middleton notes elsewhere in this volume, it might, in the end, not be apocalyptic. We might muddle through; we might not be wiped out, but transformed. The proliferation of dates of rupture in modernism noted previously marks an emerging sense of plural collapses, and Woolf offers an alternative to the traditional model of collapse as a singular catastrophic event with work that instead depicts multiple "past and imminent traumas" that seep into everyday life (Saint-Amour 2015, p. 103). She also provocatively raises the possibility that collapse can be liberating as well as traumatizing if it undoes outdated certainties, useless hypocrisies, or dangerous structures; in any case, she affirms that rather than wiping out the world, collapses inevitably leave traces of what was before. Salvage from the wreckage is thus possible, but it is neither easily won nor without cost, for, she reminds us, "some renunciation is inevitable" (1958a, p. 22). Woolf thereby encourages us to consider what we can craft from the fragments we find in the wreckage of a post-collapse world. In "Character in fiction," she notes that "we must reconcile ourselves to a season of failures and fragments," celebrating the "vigorous and stimulating sound" of the axes that are tearing apart a stale literary tradition (2009a, p. 53). As Matthew Griffiths argues in his work on climate change, modernism offers "disjunctive, ambiguous and associative writing" which both resembles and reflects the ways in which environmental collapse "disrupt[s] previously cherished conceptions of the word" (2017, pp. 5, 10). Stories must fit their times and fluent, tidy tales are no good for an age of catastrophes. Modernist metaphors and figurations of crisis, collapse, fragmentation, and reconstruction thus give us a language and a series of analogies that can apply to our own moment. Translated to the crises of our age, modernist metaphors of collapse remain representatively useful. Furthermore, even if we reject them, they suggest how the figurative language we carry or leave behind shapes our understanding of the past and prepares us for possible futures.

Coming to terms with collapse is a representative challenge that emerges from what Seamus O'Malley calls an "aporia of necessity and impossibility" – the simultaneous impossibility of representing catastrophic events and the imperative not to leave such events outside representation (2015, p. ix). In these times of collapse, words can fail us, but they are also necessary. According to Hayden White, figurative language "*gives directions* for finding the set of images that are intended to be associated with that thing" and "*tells us* what images to look for in our culturally encoded experience in order to determine how we *should feel* about the thing represented" (2002, p. 201). He thus suggests that metaphors not only describe but also enable sensations and experiences. Sarah Copland similarly reminds us that literary representations have both linguistic and cognitive effects when she argues, with specific reference to modernist fiction, that innovative depictions of metaphor, metonymy, and analogy, "do not, in and of themselves, change the world, but they create new conceptual structures that can lead to real-world transformative action" (2008, p. 156). The literary figurations available to denote collapse thus impact the kinds of collapse we recognize as well as our capacity to understand and act upon them. More broadly, fictional narratives of catastrophe offer what Ursula Heise describes as, "one of the most influential forms of risk communication," allowing us to imagine dark possible futures and thus guard against them (2008, p. 122). Furthermore, Heise equates risk analysis and communication with "typically high modernist patterns of narrative" that emphasize "indeterminacy, uncertainty, and the possibility of a variety of different outcomes" (p. 142). Heise echoes Woolf's call for innovative fiction to suit the new age when she articulates the need for a narrative form "commensurate with the complexities and heterogeneities of cultures joined in global crisis" (p. 208). Heise suggests that finding words for the experience and sensation of collapse can become a way to contend with it. Perhaps it is the only way we have.

The shipwreck

The shipwreck is the metaphor to which Woolf turns most frequently in her writing. According to Laura Doyle, "no other English-language novelist's work is as completely flooded with waves, water, wrecks, and drowning as Virginia Woolf's" (2008, p. 413). In her first novel, *The voyage out*, the heroine Rachel Vinrace looks for "the black ribs of wrecked ships" floating beneath the *Euphrosyne* as she sails from England to South America (2000b, p. 24). When Septimus Smith returns from war in *Mrs. Dalloway*, he feels like "a drowned sailor, on the shore of the world" (2000a, p. 79) And, as John Brannigan notes, "thoughts of shipwreck haunt" *To the lighthouse*, including "a drowned sailor," "images of a 'silent apparition of an ashen-coloured ship,'" and "Cam's dark contemplations as she looks down into the depths of the sea" (2014, p. 115). What, then, are the implications of this persistent metaphor? As a shipwreck reveals the fragility of man-made vessels in an unpredictable natural world, it suggests the precariousness of civilization despite the technological trappings of progress. The ship has long been a symbol of human adventure and advancement, a metonym for human civilization. Thus, Angeliki Spiropoulou argues, Woolf's use of the trope critiques modernity's "false equation of progress with destructive exploitation of nature and technological advancement" (2010, p. 16).

The shipwreck is a complexly resonant metaphor that evokes both strange riches and disaster. Those things lost under the waves never disappear, even when they remain inaccessible to us. There is always the possibility that they will one day be washed up or that we could dive down deep enough to find them. To return to the site of the wreckage (imaginatively or literally) is to perform an act of salvage. While the word salvage has become almost a dead metaphor in the general meanings it has accrued (everything from cakes to trips to the beach on rainy days have been "salvaged"), it is worth remembering that word's roots in the verb "to save." Salvage is originally a nautical term used to describe the aftermath of a shipwreck. The metaphorical interdependence of shipwreck and salvage, catastrophe and salvation, reveals a hopefulness that can be applied to the uncertain potential of the future after collapse. We may retrieve things from the wreckage, but what they are and what we can do with them remains unclear. Shipwreck and salvage make us think too of treasures: unexpected items of untold value may wash up among the objects that we choose to carry with us. Salvage, then, does not simply reaffirm human agency and design in the aftermath of a shipwreck but rather implies a symbiosis between humanity and the environment, where human endeavor can only work within the rhythms and caprices of the natural world.

Wreckage also implies fragmentation, but fragments are, Woolf shows, "the stuff that life is made on" (Kopley 2011). In her work on the "aesthetics of the fragment," Paige DuBois invites us not to dwell on what is lost but to find joy in what remains. She notes that fragments ask us to confront our "desires for wholeness, for more, for coherence, for linear, narrative familiarity" (1995, p. 53). The fragment, with its fractured edges, reminds us of a lost totality, but, DuBois asserts:

> Perhaps if we accept the necessity of fragmentation, . . . we can contemplate a new relationship between ourselves and the archaic past, one that focuses not only on its irretrievability, but also on what pleasures it offers, what identifications or estrangements it allows, how it can be used, . . . what kinds of empowerment or utopianism or imagination of the future it enables.
>
> (pp. 53–54)

The fragments returned from the sea suggest the power of transformation. They can be imaginatively combined in new orders to create new worlds or new ways of seeing the world. The shipwreck is thus an associational metaphor of collapse that, rather than privileging apocalyptic destruction, imagines the possibility that "nothing . . . doth fade" but transforms into "something rich and strange" (*The tempest* I.ii).

As a metaphor for human history, the shipwreck intimates that history does not remain in the past but is rather always present beneath the surface. The persistent presence of wreckage provokes the question of whether we can ever make an entirely new world, even if that's what we want or need. The shipwreck thus becomes an apt metaphor for literature's relationship to its own history, particularly the way in which words are, as Woolf says in "Craftsmanship," "full of echoes, of memories, of associations" (2009b, p. 88). It is no coincidence that the character Woolf alludes to in "The narrow bridge of art" – Robinson Crusoe, perhaps the most famous castaway of all – is also the hero of what is commonly recognized as the first example of the novel. It would seem that fiction and shipwrecks have been entwined from the very start. The metaphor of the shipwreck encourages us to consider what it might mean to salvage the fragments after collapse, both literally as human agents in an age of catastrophe, and imaginatively as the chroniclers of collapse who ask, "how can we combine the old words in new orders so that they survive, so that they create beauty, so that they tell the truth?" (Woolf 2009b, p. 89).

Station Eleven

Like Woolf's works, Emily St. John Mandel's *Station Eleven* is replete with recurring images of ships and wreckage. This whole fictional world is shipwrecked. The novel opens with the arrival of the Georgian Flu seen through the eyes of Jeevan Chaudhary, who hides with his brother in a Toronto tower-block looking out on Lake Ontario. When Jeevan finally ventures back into the decimated outside world, he traces the shore of the lake where there is, we read, "only Jeevan, only the water, only whatever frightened souls still remained" (p. 191). Like a modern-day Robinson Crusoe, Jeevan builds a shelter from driftwood and, feeling himself "a small, insignificant thing, drifting down the shore," is both fearful of and hopeful to meet other survivors who could destroy or save him (p. 193). Another fragmentary scene set in the same period depicts Miranda Carroll (a character whose name most overtly recalls that famous Shakespearean survivor of shipwreck but also evokes Lewis Carroll and his "looking glass" world) standing "on a beach on the coast of Malaysia looking out at the sea" (p. 218). She thinks of "how casually everyone had once thrown the word *collapse* around, before anyone understood what the word truly meant," as she watches the lights from a stranded shipping fleet on the horizon (p. 218). At a moment when Miranda knows that the world is no longer secure ground, the lights in the boats are like a lighthouse promising safety. In this shipwrecked world, she is the stranded one; the people out on the boats are those who have found safe harbor. As Miranda starts to feel ill with the flu that will soon kill her, she sketches "a rocky island with a small house on it, lights on the horizon" (p. 226). The literary allusions accumulating around Miranda multiply as here she resembles Woolf's Lily Briscoe who also paints a lighthouse and feels "on a narrow plank, perfectly alone, over the sea" (2006, p. 141). The lights on the sea's horizon both represent the promise of solace and foreground a yearning sense of loss.

Miranda is the creator of the graphic novel called "Station Eleven" that becomes a shadow text to Mandel's *Station Eleven*. As a synecdoche for Mandel's post-collapse world, this text also relies upon the metaphor of shipwreck. Station Eleven is a satellite colony that consists of "a series of islands that once were mountaintops" dotted among the oceans and, in the Undersea, "an interlinked network of vast fallout shelters" (p. 83). The unpublished generically liminal text – her "graphic novel, her comic-book series, her whatever-it-is" (p. 82) – tells the story of events a thousand years in the future, when the hero-physicist Dr. Eleven and a band of colleagues flee a colonized Earth for an artificial planet called "Station Eleven." Station Eleven's refugees are divided between those who "after fifteen years of perpetual twilight, long only to go home" and those who, like Dr. Eleven, seek to find a way to live in an inhospitable new world (p. 83). This question of whether to look toward a lost past or try to make sense of an uncertain future haunts many of *Station Eleven*'s characters. In one memorable scene, Miranda sketches Dr. Eleven "as he stands on the outcropping of rock, the little dog by his boots," thinking, "*I stood looking over my damaged home and tried to forget the sweetness of life on Earth*" (p. 105). For Mandel, an ocean divides pre- and post-collapse worlds, but her various fictional worlds remain connected by a shared sense of homesickness. *Station Eleven* thus suggests that homesickness for a lost past is not simply a product of collapse but an essential human condition; the castaway is not created by collapse but is rather a transcendent metaphor for humanity.

The wreckage

Miranda's graphic novel is an elegy for a lost world that also becomes a guide-book for survival when it washes up on the shores of the post-collapse world; it is both a memento of the past and a fitting narrative for the times. While Jeevan declares that there is "drawn through his life," a "divide between *before* and *after*" (p. 20), Mandel suggests that the pre- and post-collapse worlds are both ineluctably divided and constantly seeping into one another. Throughout the novel objects, people, and stories recur unexpectedly. The Symphony actress Kristen carries a treasured copy of "Station Eleven," a text that is also important to the ominous prophet who threatens to destroy the Travelling Symphony. A remembered magazine is found in an abandoned house. A character who the reader presumes dead reappears toward the end of the novel. The survivors of the Georgian Flu flee around North America but come together again, unknowingly connected by their ties to a Canadian actor, Arthur Leander, who died of a heart attack the night the flu arrived in Toronto. The coincidences multiply but they are not mere narrative expediency; rather, they suggest the ways in which, for better or worse, the old world is not gone but instead seeps into the new world. There are always traces.

The very structure of *Station Eleven* rejects historical or narrative progression. Philip Smith describes the novel as cyclical, noting that the plot "continues to circle the moment of collapse with increasingly large revolutions" (2016, p. 290). However, the smooth model of the circle does not capture the haphazard route that *Station Eleven* steers through an accumulation of disjointed, fragmented details. Jeevan, Miranda, and Kristen tentatively attain the status of central characters, but their stories are told in scraps and interspersed among other stories about a whole cast of characters who float in and out of the narrative, becoming more or less central at different moments. On the surface, there is one plot: a rather mundane, quasi-detective story concerning what's happened to the missing friends of the Travelling Symphony, who the mysterious prophet might be, and what risk he might pose to the Symphony. The surface plot never gains urgency, though, and is resolved almost in an aside near the end of the novel; it is, moreover, constantly disturbed by stories from the pre-collapse world or philosophical ruminations on the very nature of collapse that erupt throughout the novel like frozen moments out of time. These scenes from the past become blockades to straightforward narrative progression.

As the past accumulates like debris in a Benjaminian sense, the reader risks feeling overwhelmed by the task of making sense of it all or at least figuring out who or what is important. Page DuBois asks if the "contemplation of ruins remind[s] us of our own mortality, but also comfort[s] us with the recognition of survival of some ruins" (p. 36). As "clues" from a "lost world," the wreckage in *Station Eleven* provides a tentative line of continuity between the present and the submerged past (Mandel p. 130). For example, we partly understand what kind of man the prophet is when we learn that he is Arthur Leander's lost son and another fan of "Station Eleven", and Kristen's identity as an actor is rooted in her experiences as a very young girl performing in *King Lear*. At other times, however, the fragments refuse to add up to a coherent whole. Some of the stories that emerge do not connect to any coherent narrative thread. Other stories stubbornly remain submerged. Kristen, for example, cannot remember anything from her "first year on the road," including "what had caused the scar on her face, or where she'd lost more than two teeth" (p. 202). The collapse itself is presaged by moments of forgetfulness: a "forgotten scarf draped over the back of a seat" in the abandoned theatre (p. 9) and more significantly, Leander forgetting the lines from *King Lear*, and stuttering in time, "skip[ping] back twelve lines" (p. 3). Throughout the novel, time does not stay in its place. Ultimately, Mandel evokes a sense of synchronous time. For the reader of *Station Eleven*, and perhaps for the characters too, the pre- and post-collapse world unfold simultaneously; we cannot read of the pre-collapse world without the knowledge that the collapse has, somewhere, somehow, already happened and we cannot read of the post-collapse world without being reminded of the past that created it. The collapse instigated by the Georgian Flu is simultaneously waiting to happen and already in the past, only half remembered.

Mandel's novel tentatively balances nostalgia and hope. At times, *Station Eleven* shows reverence toward the banal treasures of the lost world, as Mandel writes with a sense of wonder:

> No more diving into pools of chlorinated water lit green from below. No more ball games played out under floodlights. No more porch lights with moths fluttering on summer nights. No more trains running under the surface of cities on the dazzling power of the electric third rail. No more cities. . . . No more flight. No more towns glimpsed from the sky through airplane windows, points of glimmering light; no more looking down from thirty thousand feet and imagining the lives lit up by those lights at that moment. No more airplanes . . .
>
> (p. 31)

Mandel uses the rhetorical technique of paralipsis, mentioning things by describing them as no longer there. The lost porch lights, moths, trains, and airplanes are resurrected and preserved by language. The accumulating "no mores," rather than providing emphasis, fade through repetition and what we are left with are the concrete images. After the collapse, all we have of the lost world are images and stories, but, on the other hand, these can make up a world. Mandel has described the novel as "a love letter written in the form of a requiem" to "this extraordinary world in which we live" (Michel 2014). Mandel looks forward to look back, thus making a kind of nostalgic future. Such nostalgia, however, also risks allowing us to recreate a past where we ignore the mistakes and problems that brought about collapse. Susan Stewart explains nostalgia as a "narrative process" by means of which "the present is denied and the past takes on an authenticity of being, an authenticity which, ironically, it can achieve only through narrative." Nostalgia, she continues, "is always ideological: the past it seeks has never existed except as narrative, and hence, always absent that past continually threatens to reproduce itself as a felt lack" (1992, p. 23). Mandel makes us nostalgic for a world in which we already live by imaginatively relocating it in the narrative past. If nostalgia is, in Stewart's words, "the desire for desire" then the book inspires an undirected sense of longing for a world that, for the reader, has neither been lost nor fully exists. One task of the novel, then, might be, in Ursula Heise's terms a kind of "risk communication" that urges us to value what is beautiful and to reconnect imaginatively with the world that is before us before it is too late (2008). Yet, the very things that the novel seems to revere are the same things that make civilization so vulnerable. The airplanes that become a quasi-sacred reminder of the pre-collapse society are the same airplanes that allowed the Georgian Flu to be carried so quickly from place to place. The novel laments isolation but also recognizes the dangers of hyper-connectivity.

The collapse depicted in *Station Eleven* is initially positioned as something beyond human agency: it is, significantly, a plague, not an environmental catastrophe or a war. The collapse comes apparently out of nowhere. One moment there are dinner parties and plays, streetcars and airplanes, smart urban offices and television stations, and the next moment, a decimation of the human population and the end of civilization. On closer look, however, there are signs that the epidemic is arriving while people are paying attention to other things. The flu becomes an apt metaphor for the perils of human distraction and connection. It is a trope of collapse that provokes questions about how close we can get to other people without getting hurt and how we can protect ourselves as we live in an increasingly interconnected world. Isolation is both the only prophylactic against and an unfortunate symptom of the disease. The Georgian Flu first appears in the form of rumors from far places: Jeevan remembers "a story . . . about an alarming new flu in the Republic of Georgia. . . . Details had been sketchy" (p. 17) and social media networks are "filled with rumours" (p. 223). Then, we read, the "local news became more and more local" until the flu is literally at the door (p. 176). We may not notice the arrival of collapse, Mandel suggests, until it is too late. That the flu comes from, and is named for Georgia, a country straddling East and West, is also significant in a novel that is ambivalent about globalization and depicts a return to a smaller, more local world. The collapse comes from outside the West and the novel singles out for salvation Shakespeare, whose work, Philip Smith argues, "inevitably brings with it a colonial agenda . . . [and] has historically been mobilized as affirmation of British cultural and moral superiority in the wake of English imperial expansion" (p. 298). Thus the Georgian Flu must ultimately be understood not as an act of the gods, but as a geographically and culturally situated phenomenon.

Salvage

Mandel asserted in an interview that "constant mayhem isn't a particularly sustainable way of life" (McCarry 2014). While she admits the fragility of civilization, noting, "what we take for granted could fail quite easily," she also suggests that our natural tendency will be to rebuild, to find structures to make sense of and to allow us to live in a post-collapse world. For the characters in the Travelling Symphony, Shakespeare is what "made it bearable" (Mandel p. 47). Shakespeare is defended not only as "what was best about the world" (p. 38), but also as an appropriate guide for the post-collapse age because he too "lived in a plague-ridden society with no electricity" (p. 288). The Symphony thus recognizes the importance of preserving past stories and the need to translate these to the changing needs of the age. Shakespearean drama achieves an urgency and a relevance in the post-collapse world that it seemed to have lost in the preceding era. The book opens with Arthur Leander performing *King Lear* on the stage of the Elgin theatre in Toronto. To prepare for the role, he studies with a "Shakespeare expert, . . . a scholar" (p. 209). This is the version of Shakespeare about which Virginia Woolf complains, "[H]is fame intimidates and bores" (2009d, p. 108). Indeed, the audience at the Elgin are so detached from the performance that they scarcely notice when Leander messes up his lines and are not sure whether he is still "acting" when he begins to stumble (Mandel p. 3). This stage is cut off from the outside world; a million miles away from the Georgian Flu that is arriving outside the theatre doors, it is an island in an aesthetically pure "pool of blue light, unmoored" (p. 3). Shakespeare, however, moves from an example of stale metaphors and art that is out of touch with humanity to a touchstone in a brave new world. While he sometimes is a sacred figure in the world of *Station Eleven*, he also goes back to being commonly appreciated and consumed. This salvaged version of Shakespeare emerges demythologized from the wreckage and is made into something both newly vibrant and practical for surviving in the world. The way in which Shakespeare is simultaneously salvaged and transformed in *Station Eleven* is signaled by Leander's name – this is Lear with an "and" inserted in the middle or, if you move the letters around a little, a Lear that incorporates an "end."

We might expect the Shakespearean play most prominent in *Station Eleven* to be *The tempest*. The story of a shipwreck, an island, and castaways searching for survival in a "brave new world" seems particularly relevant to Mandel's novel and is certainly evoked, most overtly through Miranda's name. Yet, the plays that attain most significance are *King Lear* and *A midsummer night's dream*. Lear not only serves as a foil for Arthur Leander, the flawed hero at the heart of the novel, but is also a fitting tragedy for the eve of the end of the world. *King Lear* is, after all, a play about the frailties of the older generation, the fragility of civilization, and the loss of a kingdom. It would be a mistake, however, to map *King Lear* too neatly onto *Station Eleven*; as Mandel surely warns us with Arthur's name and when he mixes up his lines, this tragedy is unfolding to a different rhythm, in another order. *King Lear* is juxtaposed with *A midsummer night's dream*, the comedy that the Travelling Symphony performs "in a parking lot in the mysteriously named town of St. Deborah by the Water" (p. 57). As Philip Smith notes, "If *King Lear* heralds the apocalypse, then *A midsummer night's dream* heralds the possibility of rebirth" (p. 294). This play is about transformation, different possible versions of reality, and the role of theater itself. The play-within-a-play-within-the-novel (that has a comic within it) invites questions about both the craft of invention, and the privileges and demands of being in the audience. Smith reminds us of "the ways in which Shakespeare's works grapple not only with the fragility of civilization but also with the fragility of text and performance," as texts are, of course, also "vulnerable to loss and destruction" (p. 295). Mandel's overt and busy textuality recalls again Virginia Woolf who in *Between the acts* (her own novel about a play, also set in a time of catastrophe) similarly piles up intertextual references, including to Shakespeare, to show how inherited stories seep into the present as well as how they can be reshaped according to the needs of the age and the responsibility of the audience. *Between the acts* explores both the impulse to metaphors and rhyme and the inadequacy of these to give voice to experience and sensation: Woolf's pageant play ends by urging us to "*break the rhythm and forget the rhyme*" (1992, p. 111).

Mandel's characters salvage Shakespeare to remember the past and make sense of the present, thus revealing the value of vibrant and kinetic art in the post-collapse world. Mandel reminds us both of the ways in which Shakespeare's time resembles the world of her novel and of the many ways in which it was different: a character called the clarinet (who finds Shakespeare "insufferable") notes that "the difference was that they'd seen electricity, they'd seen everything, they'd watched a civilization collapse, and Shakespeare hadn't. In Shakespeare's time the wonders of technology were still ahead, not behind them, and far less had been lost" (p. 288). Shakespeare, then, is a reminder of the transcendence of art but also its impermanence and fragility. He is, at best, an imperfect guide who must be followed with care and who must be adapted according to the new world's needs. As the clarinet notes, Shakespeare looked to the future and thus looking back at his works through a nostalgic lens risks ironically missing the spirit of the plays. The clarinet attempts to write her own play, weighing words "like coins or pebbles turned over and over in her pocket" (p. 289). She comes up with a fragment of a monologue (a broken rhyme), incomplete and misinterpreted by her friends, but still the beginning of new art salvaged from the wreckage of the collapse.

Ultimately, the Travelling Symphony does not salvage Shakespeare alone. His plays wash up alongside the clarinet's fragmented monologue, an old copy of *Dear V: An unauthorized portrait of Arthur Leander* (the trashy tell-all that the young Kristen packs in her bag when she leaves Toronto), Miranda's "Station Eleven," song lyrics, scenes from old movies, lines from TV shows, and stacks of gossip magazines that Kristen collects from abandoned houses.

Written on the side of the caravan and serving as a kind of artistic manifesto is a quotation from *Star trek: Voyager:* "survival is insufficient" (p. 119). Kristen has the same words "tattooed on her left forearm" and declares it her "favourite line of text in the world" (p. 119). This mix of literatures suggests that in the post-collapse world the old distinctions between "high" and "low" art no longer hold true. With so little left, everything becomes precious. It also suggests that while some stories might be kept because they are unique or valued, other things survive by happenstance. Mandel thus insists on the accidental nature of history: what endures is not always predestined or pre-planned, but, while it does not always make sense and may not seem helpful, the unexpected wreckage of the past can be merged in surprising combinations and used in productive ways.

The characters of *Station Eleven* use salvaged stories, from Shakespeare to "Station Eleven" to *Star trek: Voyager*, as guidebooks to help them navigate the post-collapse world, but these works can only ever be partially useful. They can be put to some purpose, but they alone cannot save us. For example, when the Georgian Flu arrives, Jeevan's response is rooted in pop cultural references: he has R.E.M.'s "It's the end of the world" stuck in his head and he knows how to react because he's watched the right kind of films. His "understanding of disaster preparedness was based entirely on action movies," we read, "but on the other hand, he'd seen a lot of action movies" (p. 21). Hiding in his brother's apartment, watching on TV as the Georgian Flu demolishes civilization, it all seems "like a horror movie that wouldn't end" (p. 176). Nonetheless, Jeevan's "cinematic daydreams" all end with "everything back to normal again," and when his brother challenges him that this may not happen, Jeevan must admit that "words failed him" (p. 179). There is no existing story sufficient for this experience of collapse, no metaphors that make sense of these emotions. He needs a new plot and a new form with which to understand the end of the world.

The question of what to do with the salvaged wreckage of the old world is brought to the fore in Mandel's depiction of the "Museum of Civilization." This museum, curated by Arthur Leander's old friend Clark in the Sky-miles Lounge in the Severn City airport, begins by accident with a discarded iPhone, an abandoned Amex card, and a left-behind driver's license (p. 254). In some ways, it is a poor example of a museum, a random accumulation of what washes up rather than a purposeful collection, but, nonetheless, Clark, believes that "all objects were beautiful" and is "moved by every object, . . . by the human enterprise each object had required" (p. 254). Each object connects, for Clark, back to a larger story. Looking at a snow globe, for example, he considers everything from "the white gloves on the hands of the woman who inserted the snow globes into boxes" to "the card games played belowdecks in the evenings on the ship carrying the containers across the ocean" (p. 254). The museum is a Noah's Ark full of useless items that serve as souvenirs of pre-collapse society. In some cases, these are transportive objects of alternative reality, like the gossip magazines that

Kristen reads to imagine a "shadow life" where the "collapse didn't happen" (p. 201). However, the museum also reminds us of the various purposes such stories from the past can serve. To remember the past is not always a purely nostalgic act. Indeed, remembering is a vital part of the mourning process for, to begin to mourn, we must be able to name what has been lost. The Museum of Civilization is, like the novel, a compendium and a requiem, but it is also a space that allows Clark to imagine a different future. Sitting in the museum he envisages the possibility that "somewhere there are ships setting out" and finds that "he likes the thought of ships moving over the water, towards another world just out of sight" (p. 332).

Let me end this chapter by returning to Virginia Woolf who, in the short essay, "The Elizabethan lumber room," imagines her own version of a Museum of Civilization, similarly random, precious, and corrupt, spilling out from the pages of the sixteenth-century travel writer Hakluyt's *Trafficks and discoveries*. Woolf calls Hakluyt, "not so much a book as a great bundle of commodities loosely tied together, an emporium, a lumber room strewn with ancient sacks, obsolete nautical instruments, huge bales of wool, and little bags of rubies and elements," that the reader immerses herself in "while outside tumble the huge waves of the uncharted Elizabethan sea" (2003, p. 39). The treasures of a prior age have their dark side. For Mandel's Clark, they are the totems of a globalized, capitalistic society; for Woolf, the plunder of Empire. Hakluyt's accumulation of things represents an age of possibility where "the fabled land of uncounted riches" might lie "only a little farther up the coast," and where "pebbles . . . might be emeralds or sand . . . might be gold" (p. 40). Woolf's essay is also about language itself, particularly what Ann Fernald describes as "the transformation of the English language from the humble, pragmatic language of ordinary people into the language of Shakespeare" (2009, p. 51). The "new words, the new ideas, the waves, the savages, the adventures," Woolf states, "found their way naturally into the plays which were being acted on the banks of the Thames" (2003, p. 42) and "helped to inspire the greatest age of English poetry" (p. 43). Like Mandel's characters, Woolf is drawn to the Elizabethans; Hakluyt is particularly appealing because of his works' lack of organization, completeness, or conclusion and, moreover, because of their mixture of practicality and fancy. She writes:

> Now we are in the presence of sublime imagination; now rambling through one of the finest lumber rooms in the world – a chamber stuffed from floor to ceiling with ivory, old iron, broken pots, urns, unicorns' horns, and magic glasses full of emerald lights and blue mystery.
>
> (p. 47)

For Woolf, to open Hakluyt and to read words from the Elizabethan era is both an act of recovery and an experience of mutually transformative words and worlds. She looks back to the past to open potential futures, and the value of Hakluyt lies in its very muddle, transience, and uncertainty. Woolf, nonetheless, tempers the sense of wonder with a word of caution about the dangers of "fine stories" that can lead lives to vanish "beneath the waves" (p. 41, p. 40).

Mandel's characters are also searching for a "fabled land," but in the final lines of *Station Eleven* it remains "just out of sight" beyond an ocean. *Station Eleven* does not go so far as to imagine a new world after collapse. It can only dare to hope that a new world might someday be imagined. Perhaps, in the end, it does not even find the new metaphors, forms, or plots that its characters crave. As a narrative of collapse it is fragmentary and flawed, but this might, after all, be the only way to get close to imagining the collapse. The characters of *Station Eleven* must, as Woolf warns, "tolerate the spasmodic, the obscure, the fragmentary, the failure" (2009a, p. 54). Finding a way forward after the collapse entails salvaging the fragments from the wreckage of history and, by putting them together in new combinations and rhythms for perhaps unanticipated purposes, transforming them. As a form of "risk communication" (Heise 2008, p. 122), *Station Eleven* ultimately asks us to consider the kind of world in which we want to live and how we might make such a world from words, which, for all their ambiguous power, might be, in the end, all that we can pass on and all that we have left with which to build.

Notes

1 For example Ursula Le Guin condemned Atwood's self-definition of her work as "speculative fiction" as exploiting an "arbitrarily restrictive definition" to "protect her novels from being relegated to a genre still shunned by hidebound readers, reviewers and prize-awarders" (*The Guardian* 2009). Laura Miller's article in *Slate* offers an analysis of this phenomenon in the popular sphere, declaring, with regards to Mandel, "the line between literary fiction and science fiction has become harder and harder to draw" (2017).
2 See, for example, Lecia Rosenthal, who notes: "It has become commonplace to acknowledge that at some point in the last century the speed and scale of human history not only changed, but changed in unprecedented ways" (2011, p. 26). We might ask if there is something fundamentally different in either nature or scale about the events of the modern era in comparison to, for example, the plague of the fourteenth century or the collapse of Maya civilization in the ninth (see Guy Middleton in this volume for a discussion of the latter event as "collapse"). We also continue to see iterations of old Judeo-Christian apocalyptic models in modern configurations, with Derrida's famous piece of nuclear criticism describing possible nuclear war as "the End and the Revelation of the name itself, the Apocalypse of the Name" (Derrida, Porter, and Lewis 1984, p. 31).
3 In "Mr. Bennett and Mrs. Brown" Woolf famously writes that human character changed in 1910. This was the date of the post-impressionist exhibition at the Grafton Gallery in London, but, for Woolf, also the moment of a class shift. For Ford Madox Ford and others, 1914, which saw the outbreak of the First World War, was a significant date. Willa Cather declared that "the world broke in two in 1922 or thereabouts" (1992, p. 25). Janis P. Sproutt (2006) notes that 1922 was the year that Eliot's *The wasteland* was published but that Cather's statement can also be linked to the publication of *One of Ours,* which received negative reviews.

References

Brannigan, J. (2014). *Archipelagic modernism*. Edinburgh University Press, Edinburgh.

Cather, W. (1992). *Willa Cather: Stories, poems, and other writings*. The Library of America, New York.

Copland, S. (2008). Reading in the blend: Collaborative conceptual blending in the *Silent travel* narratives. *Narrative 16.2*, 140–162.

Derrida, J., C. Porter, and P. Lewis. (1984). No apocalypse, not now (full speed ahead, seven missiles, seven missives). *Diacritics 14.2*, 20–31.

Doyle, L. (2008). *Freedom's empire: Race and the rise of the novel in Atlantic Modernity, 1640–1940*. Duke University Press, Durham and London.

DuBois, P. (1995). *Sappho is burning*. University of Chicago Press, Chicago and London.

Fernald, W. (2009). *Virginia Woolf: Feminism and the reader*. Palgrave, London.

Griffiths, M. (2017). *The new poetics of climate change: Modernist aesthetics for a warming world*. Bloomsbury Academic, London.

Heise, U. K. (2008). *Sense of place and sense of planet: The environmental imagination of the global*. Oxford University Press, Oxford and New York.

Kopley, E. (2011). 'Scraps, orts and fragments': Collecting Virginia Woolf. http://web.stanford.edu/dept/libcommdev/wredenprize/wreden2011/KopleyEssay.pdf

Le Guin, U. K. (2009). The year of the flood by Margaret Atwood. *The Guardian*. www.theguardian.com/books/2009/aug/29/margaret-atwood-year-of-flood (Accessed 29 August 2009).

McCarry, S. (2014). 'I want it all': A conversation with Emily St. John Mandel. *TOR* (www.tor.com/2014/09/12/a-conversation-with-emily-st-john-mandel/) Accessed 12 September 2014.

McCarthy, C. (2009). *The road*. Picador, London.

Michel, L. (2014). Interview with Emily St. John Mandel. *National Book Foundation* (www.nationalbook.org/nba2014_f_mandel_interv.html#.WX9QXcbMyCQ).

Miller, L. (2017). Dark futures: What happens when literary novelists experiment with science fiction. *Slate*. www.slate.com/articles/arts/books/2017/05/literary_fiction_is_borrowing_the_tools_of_the_science_fiction_genre.html (Accessed 27 May 2017).

O'Malley, S. (2015). *Making history new: Modernism and historical narrative*. Oxford University Press, Oxford and New York.

Rosenthal, L. (2011). *Mourning modernism: Literature, catastrophe, and the politics of consolation*. Fordham University Press, New York.

Saint-Amour, P. K. (2015). *Tense future: Modernism, total war, encyclopedic form*. Oxford University Press, Oxford and New York.

Shakespeare, W. (2014). *The Tempest*. Alden Vaughan and Virginia Vaughan eds. Bloomsbury Arden, London.

Smith, P. (2016). Shakespeare, survival, and the seeds of civilization in Emily SJM's *Station Eleven*. *Extrapolation 57.3*, 290–203.

Spiropoulou, A. (2010). Woolf on nature, history and the modern artwork: *Virginia Woolf miscellany*. *Woolf and Nature 78.16*, 15–17.

Sproutt, J. P. (2006). Between two wars in a breaking world: Willa Cather and the persistence of war consciousness. *Cather Studies 6*, 70–91.

Stewart, S. (1992). *On longing: Narratives of the miniature, the gigantic, the souvenir, the collection*. Duke University Press, Durham and London.

St Mandel, E. J. (2015). *Station eleven*. Picador, London and New York.

Taylor, J. (2012). *Djuana barnes and affective modernism*. Edinburgh University Press, Edinburgh.

White, H. (2002). The historical text as literary artifact, in Brian Richardson ed., *Narrative dynamics: Essays on time, plot, closure, and frames*. Ohio State University Press, Columbus, 191–210.

Whitehead, C. (2011). *Zone one*. Doubleday, New York.

Woolf, V. (1958a). The narrow bridge of art, in *Granite and rainbow*. Hogarth, London, 11–23.

———. (1958b) (1947). The leaning tower, in *The moment and other essays*. Hogarth, London, 105–125.

———. (1992). *Between the acts*. Penguin, London and New York.

———. (2000a). *Mrs. Dalloway*. Oxford University Press, Oxford and New York.

———. (2000b). *The voyage out*. Oxford University Press, Oxford and New York.

———. (2003). The Elizabethan lumber room, in *The common reader*, Vol. 1. Vintage, London, 39–47.

———. (2006). *To the lighthouse*. Oxford University Press, Oxford and New York.

———. (2009a). Character in fiction, in David Bradshaw ed., *Virginia Woolf: Selected essays*. Oxford University Press, Oxford, 37–54.

———. (2009b). Craftsmanship, in David Bradshaw ed., *Virginia Woolf: Selected essays*, 85–91.

———. (2009c). Mr. Bennett and Mrs. Brown, in David Bradshaw ed., *Virginia Woolf: Selected essays*, 32–36.

———. (2009d). On Being Ill, in David Bradshaw ed., *Virginia Woolf: Selected essays*, 101–110.

Index

Page numbers in italics indicate figures on the corresponding pages.

Benjamin, W. 15–16, 18, 23, 179;
on barbarism 19; on the enemy as
victorious 29; on the historian's task 25
Berger, P. 117
Between the Acts 188
Bible, the 27, 95–96, 145–146
binary perspective on nature of collapse
and catastrophe 20–21
Biosphere 2 132–134
Blanchard, O. 118
Borodale, S. 169–170, 172
Boulding, K. 129
Bowlby, R. 4
BP Deepwater Horizon spill 120
Braasch, G. 59
Bradley, R. 103
Brannigan, J. 181
Brautigan, R. 70
Brexit 18–19
Bringhurst, R. 155
Brown, L. 92
Buchs, A. 118
Buell, F. 4
Bulfin, A. 92
Bulletin of Atomic Scientists 57
Burgin, V. 8
Burke, E. 57
Burnside, J. 171–172, 174
Burtynsky, Edward 143–144, 150–153
Butler, J. 82

Caldwell, P. 73
Cameron, A. 96, 97
Camus, A. 147–148
Carreck, N. L. 162
Carroll, L. 183
Carson, R. 130
Cartier-Bresson, H. 8
Castoriadis, C. 67
catastrophic history 15–17;
Anthropocene as pivotal vantage
point for 21–22; binary perspective
on nature of collapse and catastrophe
20–21; chronic conditions and acute
events in 17; crisis of man and 17;
historian's task in 25–26; human
culpability for 27–28; Judeo-Christian
psyche and 27; Marxism in 24; moral
catastrophes in 23; new panoply
of analytic vocabulary in 19–20;
normalization of 28–29; as a series
of episodes 23; slow disaster in 18;
theories of collapse in 18–19; utopian
and dystopian thought in 26–27

Cavalcanti, S. 117
China project 151
Chirac, J. 74
chronic conditions 17
Chute, H. 68, 76
Clark, T. 176n9
climate change: in comics (*see Saison
brune*); photojournalism and (*see
photojournalism*)
*Climate Changed: A Personal Journey
Through the Science* 66
Climate Outreach 58
climate reductionism 54–55
Cline, E. 94, 105–106
Club of Rome 3, 131
Coleman, V. 154
collapse *see* environmental collapse
Collapse (National Geographic) 93
*Collapse: How Societies Choose to Fail
or Succeed* 1, 101, 104, 160–161
colony collapse disorder 160; analogy
to humans 171–173; bee-human
relations and 170–172; bees in
literature and 163–166, 171, 175n6;
bees in poetry of Duffy and 166–168;
continuity of 173–175; research on
162–163, 169–170
comics: as belonging to textual or visual
world 83n12; definition of 82n2; use
in teaching and learning 82n6; *see
also Saison brune*
Conley, D. 41, 44n6
Contagion 100
Copland, S. 180
Cottle, S. 56, 59
Country and the City, The 167
"cowboy economics" 129
crisis of man 17
Critias and Timaeus 96
Crookes, W. 98
Crowe, R. 96
cultural heritage, apocalyptic collapse
as 95–100
Cumming, G. 4, 5
*Cyclopedia of Everything Pertaining to
the Care Of the Honey-Bee, The* 169

Daily Mail Online, The 101
D'Annunzio, G. 26
Davis, H. 8
Davis, M. A. 129
Dawkins, R. 4, 5
Day After Tomorrow 57, 100
Day of the Triffids, The 92

196   *Index*

CPSIA information can be obtained
at www.ICGtesting.com
Printed in the USA
BVHW052007190323
660605BV00020B/170

9 780367 507640